WOMEN WORKERS AND GLOBAL RESTRUCTURING

BOOKS IN THE INTERNATIONAL SERIES

Cornell International Industrial and Labor Relations Report Number 17

WOMEN WORKERS AND GLOBAL RESTRUCTURING

Edited by Kathryn Ward

ILR Press
School of Industrial and Labor Relations
Cornell University

HD
6073
.O33
W66
1990
153738
Sept. 1991

Cover design by Kat Dalton

Library of Congress Cataloging-in-Publication Data will be found at the end of this book.

Portions of the chapter "Disguised Industrial Proletarians in Rural Latin America: Women's Informal-Sector Factory Work and the Social Reproduction of Coffee Farm Labor in Colombia" are from Cynthia Truelove, "The Informal Sector Revisited: The Case of the Colombian Mini-Maquilas," in Richard Tardanico, ed., *Crises in the Caribbean Basin: Past and Present,* pp. 95–110, copyright 1987 by Sage Publications. Reprinted by permission of Sage Publications, Inc.

Copies may be ordered through bookstores or directly from
ILR Press
School of Industrial and Labor Relations
Cornell University
Ithaca, NY 14851–0952

Printed on acid-free paper in the United States of America
5   4   3   2   1

CONTENTS

For Rachel and Rose

ACKNOWLEDGMENTS

This book had its origins in a session in 1986 on women and international development that Cynthia Truelove and I organized for the Political Economy of the World-System Section of the American Sociological Association. Many events, or what Bettina Aptheker (1989) has called women's tapestries of life, have occurred between that session and the publication of this book. The original participants have updated and extended their research, and some authors have been added. We have worked on this book via mail, phone, and international electronic communications. During this time, we traveled abroad, began and ended relationships, nursed sick friends and family members, moved across the United States, started new jobs, finished dissertations, and sent daughters off to college and other distant places. And we survived.

I would like to thank Gunseli Berik, Patricia Fernandez-Kelly, and an anonymous reviewer for their perceptive and helpful comments. Laura Whistler Cates did much of the word processing on the individual chapters and on the references. I acknowledge the patience of my friends and colleagues who have heard about this book for several years, in particular, Melanie P. Baise. The women at ILR Press have made publishing a pleasant experience. Erica Fox did a tasteful and thorough job of copyediting; Andrea Fleck Clardy provided crucial conceptual clarity over several meals. Last but not least, Frances Benson had the patience, wit, and wisdom to guide and shape an initial interest in women and transnational corporations into this book.

1

INTRODUCTION AND OVERVIEW

Kathryn Ward

Recent theoretical and research developments have inspired innovative scholarship on women, work, and the restructuring of the global economy. This volume presents some of the most recent research.

Global restructuring refers to the emergence of the global assembly line in which research and management are controlled by the core or developed countries while assembly line work is relegated to semiperiphery or periphery nations that occupy less privileged positions in the global economy. The global assembly line approach to production is attractive to transnational corporations (TNCs) and to employers seeking greater access to markets, diffusion of political and economic costs, improved competitive abilities, and product diversity. Within developing countries, restructuring is marked by growth of the service sector and specialization in export industries such as electronics, garments, and pharmaceuticals as a development

I gratefully acknowledge the comments of Rita Gallin, Linda Grant, Rachel Rosenfeld, Patricia Fernandez-Kelly, Anna Elfenbein, Patricia Searle Ward, Beth Hartung, and Marcia Bedard on this chapter and the long phone conversations with Cynthia Truelove. I also received valuable feedback when I presented parts of this chapter at California State University at Fresno, the University of California at Santa Cruz, and the University of Texas at Dallas. Nevertheless, the contents of this chapter remain my responsibility.

strategy. Restructuring is also marked by increasing use of female industrial workers in the informal sector.

The growth in the number of informal-sector and women workers is the centerpiece of global restructuring. Gita Sen and Caren Grown (1987:36–37) note that women informal-sector workers in developing countries engage in "such activities [as] declining handicrafts, home-based production, small-scale retail trade, petty food production, and other services catering to urban workers, and domestic service." In contrast to the formal sector, the pay and working conditions in the informal sector are unregulated by labor legislation.[1] Capitalists and TNCs thus use informal-sector workers, particularly women, instead of formal wage workers to avoid labor legislation and to keep labor costs low (Portes and Sassen-Koob 1987). Most important, by subcontracting industrial production to informal factories or home-based workers, employers can minimize competitive risks, wages, and the threat of unionization, while maximizing their flexibility in hiring, their overhead costs, and their production processes.

Recent research has examined the links between global restructuring and housework, informal-sector work, and formal labor (see Roldan 1985; Schmink 1986; Beneria and Roldan 1987; Wolf 1988b; Truelove 1988). In many parts of the world, including the United States, many women now work triple shifts (Hossfeld 1988a), so that each day they labor at some combination of housework, home work, and/or peddling *and* at formal work in factories or in agriculture or services.

Development planners once touted women's employment by transnational corporations as a panacea for women's exclusion from industrial jobs in the formal sector in developing countries (Lim 1985). As the contributors to this volume demonstrate, researchers are now exploring some of the contradictory effects on the empowerment of

---

1. Alejandro Portes and Saskia Sassen-Koob (1987:31) define the informal sector as "all work situations characterized by the absence of (1) a clear separation between capital and labor; (2) a contractual relationship between both; and (3) a labor force that is paid wages and whose conditions of work and pay are legally regulated ... the informal sector is structurally heterogenous and comprises such activities as direct subsistence, small-scale production and trade, and subcontracting to semiclandestine enterprises and homeworkers."

women of such employment and the ways in which the state or government can intervene to encourage or discourage women's participation as workers for transnational corporations (see chapters 4, 5, 8, 9; Ward 1988a; Elson and Pearson 1981a, b; Nash and Fernandez-Kelly 1983).

Some researchers in the past viewed women workers in developing countries as passive targets of patriarchal control. Today, many studies reveal examples of resistance to control by men and employers and to global restructuring (see chapter 8; Andreas 1985; Aptheker 1989; Bookman and Morgen 1988; Desai 1989; Dill 1986, 1988; Mies 1988b; Nash 1988; Ong 1987; Westwood 1985; Westwood and Bhachu 1988). This resistance takes many forms: working even though it is against cultural norms; manipulating racist and sexist managers into giving women privileges; participating in engagement parties and worker weekends; and unionizing.

Finally, whereas researchers once focused only on the additive dimensions of class, gender, or race in women's lives, they are now examining the interrelated effects of gender, race, and class. Class and race mediate the processes of global restructuring as capitalists seek women of color and working-class women to meet their needs for a flexible labor supply (Joseph 1980; Sassen-Koob 1983, 1984; Lamphere 1987; Baca Zinn 1988; Fernandez-Kelly and Garcia 1988; Hossfeld 1988a; Zavella 1987, 1988). Studies indicate that women workers' struggles with global restructuring affect both their autonomy and their control over their lives.

Using some of the most recent studies on women and work, the contributors to this volume examine how capital's demand for the economic participation of women has generated contradictions and tensions at the intersections of home, the informal sector, and the formal sector and the patriarchal institutions and ideologies that define women's work and family roles (for background, see Bernard 1987; Hartmann 1976; Tiano 1987a; Ward 1984, 1988a; Westwood 1985). What is the importance of informal and subcontracted work in women's lives in the global economy? Does their work enhance or marginalize their socioeconomic position vis-à-vis the men in their households? How do women manage the time pressures and tensions resulting from their heavy work loads, their relationships as wives and mothers, and their sense of self? How have women resisted oppressive forces and acquired more control over their lives? What is the role of the state or government in these processes? These are among the questions this book addresses.

The rest of this chapter examines some of the recent theories and research (from both developed and developing countries) that have redefined women's work while linking their formal, informal, and housework activities; reexamined the effects of TNCs on women's work and empowerment; and redefined women's resistance.

NEW DEFINITIONS OF WOMEN AND WORK

The latest research seeks to remove the artificial boundaries between the various facets of women's work and the larger global economy. In so doing, the concept of work has been redefined to include housework and informal-sector work (as previously explored by Kuhn and Wolpe 1978; Young et al. 1981). Earlier research showed that development displaced or marginalized women from paid agricultural and industrial work to the service sector, the informal sector, and/or unpaid work within the home (Boserup 1970; Papanek 1979; Tinker 1976).

Much of this research was based on an underlying capitalist model of development that assumed that the economic status of women within a country would improve if only they could be incorporated into the paid labor force (Beneria and Sen 1981; Redclift 1985; Scott 1986). Little attention was given to the direct links between the larger global economy and women's position relative to men's (Ward 1984, 1985b, 1987). Additionally, although researchers recognized the links between women's roles as mothers and workers, this aspect of their lives was not tied theoretically to changes in the larger global economy (see chapter 2; Ward 1988a; Wolf 1988b).

The increasing employment of women by transnational corporations has permitted researchers to analyze women's direct links to the global assembly line. It has also provided an opportunity to evaluate how work—formal work, informal work, and housework—affects the socioeconomic empowerment of women. As Lisa Leghorn and Katherine Parker (1981:226) have said, work leads to empowerment when it "makes survival easier for women, increases women's access to resources, or gives women more tools to fight with, more respect, or opportunities to get together and build networks" (see also Bunch 1974).

Although much of the research on women and TNCs has contributed to an understanding of the formal work of some women in the world economy, it has focused on only a small portion of the global female work force. Women formal workers in TNCs comprise only a small proportion—28 percent—of all women formal workers (although a higher proportion in Asia, Central America, and the Caribbean) (Lim 1985:7). Many more women work in agricultural and service-sector formal work or in unprotected informal work, which can encompass industrial assembly work within the home, sweatshops, or factories, and/or housework. Further, by examining only women's formal work, researchers have perpetuated the artificial divisions between the so-called public (male) and private (female) spheres. In so doing, they have failed to analyze the permeable or overlapping boundaries between women's formal and informal work and housework relative to the distinct boundaries between men's formal work and their contribution to housework, or lack thereof. As a consequence, theoretical integration of all facets of women's work has suffered.

Recently, several researchers have begun to address the connections between formal labor, housework, and informal-sector production (Sokoloff 1980; Aguiar 1986; Acker 1988; J. Smith 1984, 1987; Beneria and Roldan 1987; Mies 1986; Mies et al. 1988; Fernandez-Kelly and Garcia 1988; Hossfeld 1988a, b; Truelove 1988). Their research redefines our traditional definitions of work, employment, and production to encompass all facets of women's work roles instead of only labor that is exchanged for wages in production.

In two thought-provoking books, Maria Mies (1986, 1988a) redefines production to incorporate women's everyday work: production for life and for subsistence. Women's work is thus contrasted with men's and capitalists' productive activities, which consist of the exploitation of women's formal and unwaged work and other persons' labor and the sale of male formal labor. The subordination of women is part of the same process that has generated the exploitation of colonies, peripheral nations, and people of color in the world economy. Mies demonstrates how patriarchal ideologies and economies have defined the work that women do as merely "housewifization" or an extension of their roles in the home. As she explains, this ideology is interwoven in the capitalist economy to justify women's subordination on the global assembly line, in the home, and in the informal sector. Thus, although the nature of women's work may vary by class, race, and geographic location, the sum of their work ensures the reproduction and growth of the global economy.

Finally, in further redefining the concept of work, Claudia von Werlhof (1985) notes that waged laborers are scarce relative to the numbers of laborers in the informal sector and in housework. Most production and subsistence around the world is being provided by informal labor and unwaged labor, such as housework. Von Werlhof questions past ties between work and exchange production and argues that theories of production and work should be reformulated to include integral patterns of production based on the informal sector and housework. These redefinitions further point to the need for a reconstruction of the links between the types of work women do.

LINKING WOMEN'S WORK

For a long time, feminist researchers have written about women's double shifts as housewives and formal laborers. More recently, researchers have documented how more and more women are engaged in some combination of housework and formal *and* informal labor. The third shift has been added because of economic necessity and for survival.

Scholars have scrutinized the continued presence of the informal sector in light of predictions that this supposedly precapitalist or subsistence sector would disappear. Alejandro Portes and Saskia Sassen-Koob (1987), for example, argue that the informal sector now constitutes disguised waged labor that capitalists are employing so as to compete in the global economy, to circumvent labor legislation, and to control unionization. By emphasizing the similarities between informal and formal work, however, such researchers ignore the important links between informal work and housework that shape the nature of the informal sector and its role in global restructuring.

Informal-sector work should be distinguished from formal labor, particularly in analyses of women's work. Informal-sector work provides the intermediate link between formal waged labor and unpaid housework in that it contains characteristics of both. As defined, informal work is unprotected waged labor. As performed by women, informal work, like housework (which is also unpaid and not covered by Social Security), contributes to the reproduction and survival of the household. The boundaries between the informal sector and housework often depend on whether or not the women receive wages for their cleaning, assembly, ironing, or cooking. As discussed below, women and men have different experiences in informal-sector work relative to matters of control, autonomy, activities, and earnings (Redclift 1985; Saffiotti 1978; Simms and Dumor 1976–77; J. Smith 1984; von Werlhof 1980, 1984, 1985, 1988; Arizipe 1977; Jelin 1977, 1980; Moser 1978; Chaney and Schmink 1980; Bunster et al. 1985; Portes et al. 1989; and more recently Truelove [chapter 3]; Hadji-costandi [chapter 4]; and Hossfeld [chapter 7]). Unfortunately, many researchers exclude housework from their definitions of the informal sector that pays wages, albeit low wages.[2]

Questions remain: What are the roles of women's housework and biological and social reproduction in the generation of value under capitalism? How are these roles linked to informal-sector work? How are the processes of such reproduction gendered? Nanneke Redclift (1985:120) argues, for example, that "production and reproduction are a unity, but of an often contradictory rather than functional kind." The exclusion of housework and women's reproductive labor hinders the formulation of a comprehensive look at gender-based tensions or contradictions between women's and men's work and family lives. These tensions emerge most clearly in the reasons women and men seek informal-sector work. It appears that, over time, most women engage in informal-sector work for survival and maintenance of their families, while most men do for mobility (Schmink 1986).

Some recent research on the informal sector ignores these gender differences, however. Portes (1985) and Portes and Sassen-Koob

2. For a debate on this question see J. Smith 1984 and von Werlhof 1984. Joan Smith argues that women's housework enhances or transforms the value of commodities bought by wages, while informal-sector work creates something of value that eventually can be exchanged. Von Werlhof argues that the two forms of labor are similar because they underwrite the capitalist economy.

(1987) discuss how some informal workers make more money than formal workers, while other informal workers make less than both more privileged informal workers and the formal group. They ignore gender stratification in the informal sector (Truelove 1987). They also fail to acknowledge that, in general, middle- and/or upper-class men organize the subcontracting networks while most of the women work as informal subcontracted workers and receive less money than the supervisory men. And, although the authors note how both industrial and informal employment have grown, they ignore data indicating a relationship between declines in women's formal work in industries (Chaney and Schmink 1980) and the growth of informal assembly work in the home or factories (Hossfeld 1988a; Truelove 1988; Beneria and Roldan 1987). Increasingly, women take work home from factories or work only at home at the bottom of a subcontracting pyramid controlled by men. In Greece and Italy, for example, home-based assembly work by women is a government-approved development strategy (see chapter 4; Mingione 1985). Sallie Westwood (1985) describes yet another variation in which women sell cosmetics, clothing, and so on to their co-workers during breaks at factories.

Cynthia Truelove (personal communication) notes that men quite often enter the informal sector for mobility, while almost all women enter for survival. In her research in Colombia, she found that when male factory managers retired, their employers often provided them with discarded equipment that the retirees used to start their own businesses and sweatshops. Women were only workers in these sweat-shops (Truelove 1987).

This omission of women from past theoretical analyses of the informal sector is regrettable, especially when one considers that in Latin America and Asia the informal sector consists mostly of women (International Center for Research on Women [ICRW] 1980a). Further, the informal sector is critical to the operation of the global economy and the survival of households. Informal work subsidizes workers' wages, lowers the risks of capitalists, and together with housework stabilizes or maintains the class positions of households (see, for example, Merrick and Graham 1979; Schmink 1986; Sharma 1986). The ICRW (1980a) estimates that the wages from informal and household labor performed by women (and their children) are used to meet more than half the subsistence needs of households. Joan Smith (1987) estimates, for example, that most of the economic growth in the United States is the result of formal work and housework performed by working-class women. Coping with the demands of their work loads can consume much of the daily existence of women, especially if they do informal work in the home (see chapter 4; Mingione 1985; Roldan 1985). In her study of Silicon Valley electronics workers, Karen Hossfeld (1988a) found that many women worked up to nineteen hours in a combination of formal, informal, and household labor. Meanwhile, many of their husbands were unemployed or refused to participate in home production.

Many women undertake informal-sector work in addition to their previous work out of economic necessity and to survive conflicts with their husbands regarding divergent economic interests. Lourdes Beneria and Marta Roldan (1987) have described how gender and class are intertwined in working-class households in Mexico City. Working-class wives rarely know their husbands' salaries, and women often are reduced to begging and pleading with their husbands for money, which frequently leads to quarreling and domestic violence against them. Thus many women undertake subcontracted home work in the informal sector as well as occasional formal work to make ends meet. Similar situations can be found in Asia and Africa (Simms and Dumor 1976–77) and in Britain (Westwood 1985) and in both rural and urban areas (Spalter-Roth 1988).

Some researchers might argue that women's participation in the informal sector as domestic or home workers empowers them. From this perspective, such work provides women with the autonomy to acquire resources, to work in their homes and care for children, and to retain control over the profits of their labors. Roldan (1985) found women home workers experience some such improvements in self-respect, and Judith Rollins (1986) and Bonnie Thornton Dill (1988) have documented how some women have sought domestic work so as to have a sense of autonomy over their work.

But as several of the contributors to this volume demonstrate, informal-sector and subcontracted work often constrain women's options. The women often have to provide much of the infrastructure costs, such as machines and electricity (see chapter 4; Redclift and Mingione 1985), and the work isolates them (particularly home workers) from other women workers and adds yet another shift to their crowded schedules (Hossfeld 1988a). At the same time, employers rationalize paying both female and male workers low wages because they assume that the women can make up any difference between wages and subsistence costs by performing informal work and housework. Other women seek vending or informal-sector work as a means of escaping the oppressive control of male managers in factories, only to encounter sexual harassment on the street (Spalter-Roth 1980).

As research also shows, subcontracting often provides only limited entrepreneurial opportunities. Maria Patricia Fernandez-Kelly and Anna Garcia (1988), for example, have found that Hispanic women in California use their subcontracting work as a way to cope with work and family pressures. At the same time, their subcontracting activities are tied to production for former employers or brokers. These women have the smallest shops, are the least able to compete, and are subject to more government inspections than the men. In sum, they operate the most economically vulnerable businesses in the entire garment industry.

Income-generation projects assembling garments, making handicrafts, working in cooperatives, and so forth, which are basically informal-sector work, are a related problem. Cornelia Butler Flora (1987) notes that such projects become popular during downturns in industrial activity. She also notes that it is hard for such projects to compete with both formal organizations and exploitative sweatshops. Consequently, planners' goals of empowering women are rarely realized.

Additionally, as Hossfeld (1988a) points out, combining formal and informal work with housework depends on the labor of other females who look after the workers' children and help distribute the products (e.g., tamales). These activities add another shift to other women's labor. Victoria Byerly (1986) found that white women who worked in southern textile mills in the United States hired African-Americans as domestic workers. The labors of these domestics enabled the white women to engage in formal work. Judith Rollins (1986) has documented this pattern for other white women workers. Likewise, Vickie Ruiz (1988) describes how Mexi-

can-American women factory workers in Texas have eased their
housework burdens by hiring Mexican domestic workers. When
these women used other women's labor in the household, they
avoided confronting a major contradiction in their own and men's
work and family lives: who does the housework (Rollins 1986)?
Once again, this research demonstrates that class and race can affect the boundaries between and what is defined as informal work
and housework.

Nor does informal-sector work provide women with increased
economic power relative to men in that men often view the work as
an extension of the women's housework and as less important than
their own economic activities (for an example in Colombia, see Deere
and Leon de Leal 1981). Hossfeld (1988a) found that in California
unemployed minority men refused to participate in their wives' informal work because they felt they could be called away at any time
for a waged job. When the men did find work, it was more lucrative
than the women's informal-sector work, thereby reinforcing gender
disparities in income (Roldan 1985).

Obviously the processes that determine women's work activities
are complex. Recent research by Joan Acker suggests that one should
look at both the relations of production and the relations of distribution, that is, at the "sequences of linked actions through which
people share the necessities of survival" (1988:478). One should
examine women's participation in formal work and informal-sector
work *and* their access to resources in the relations of distribution vis-
à-vis their husbands, families, race and ethnic groups, and communities (see Dill 1986; Bookman 1988; Westwood 1985). The resulting gender and class (and race) structure is "a process in which
women and men, in determinant relations of production and distribution, identify their antagonistic interests, and come to struggle,
to think, and to value in gender/class [and race] ways" (Acker
1988:497). This structure provides a more realistic view of the interrelationships between women's and men's work and family lives
than earlier formulations, which assumed a unity of interests and
strategies between women and men in households (Wong 1984;
Ward 1987, 1988a; Wolf 1988b), and explains some of the contradictory effects of employment in TNCs on the empowerment of
women.

WORK IN TNCS: ECONOMIC LIBERATION
OR SUBJUGATION?

Some researchers have argued that TNC employment provides economic opportunities for women and leads to liberation from economic marginalization and local patriarchal constraints (Lim 1983a,
b, 1985; Tinker 1976). Linda Lim (1983a, 1985) argues, for example,
that women TNC workers enjoy better wages and working conditions
than women who work in local factories and other jobs (see also Sen
and Grown 1987; chapter 9). These wages enable the women to
acquire life experience, possessions, and status outside the family
and to delay marriage and childbearing. Further, women who work
outside the home after marriage may have greater decision-making
power within their families than women who do not work outside
the home (Lim 1985).

Other researchers have argued that, instead of liberating women,
such employment only intensifies and reinforces their subordinate
position in their society (Elson and Pearson 1981a; Fuentes and
Ehrenreich 1983; Ward 1986, 1988b; Young 1984, 1988). Governments and TNC factories may selectively manipulate women's family
and work roles to satisfy the demand for women workers (see chapters 6 and 8; Walby 1986; Fernandez-Kelly 1983). In Puerto Rico,
for example, TNCs have encouraged increased investments in ster-
ilization and birth-control programs to ensure a supply of women
workers (Enloe 1984). And when the Irish government feared that
women's industrial work would threaten the family, the government
selectively recruited foreign investment that provided men with jobs
while using state policies to limit women's employment (see chapter
5). Finally, Japan has orchestrated women's entry in and out of the
labor force based on educational and marital status (see chapter 6).

Patriarchal Control

Men, families, and TNCs also manipulate women's work lives. Young
women move from the control of their fathers and families to industrial plants that have male managers and limited managerial opportunities for women (Fernandez-Kelly 1983; Grossman 1980;
Pena 1985). The TNCs try to create passive female workers through

such means as sponsoring beauty pageants that foster Western feminine behaviors. Meanwhile, the men work in positions as supervisors and technicians, where they earn more money and can ascend managerial ladders (see Fernandez-Kelly 1983; chapter 7).

Wages

Many women receive wages barely at the subsistence level even by their own country's standards and up to 50 percent less than local men (Grossman 1979; Elson and Pearson 1981a). TNCs have paid women electronics workers hourly wages as low as 17 cents in Indonesia and $1.20 in Singapore (Grossman 1979). Wages for women workers in garment industries "can run to 16 cents an hour for China, 57 cents an hour in Taiwan and over $1 an hour in Hong Kong" (Serrin 1984:5). Many women also must remit most of their earnings to their families, and, as Diane Wolf discusses (chapter 2), sometimes families subsidize the female workers (see also Wolf 1988b).

Unionization

Organizing women workers in TNCs is difficult but not impossible (Grossman 1979; Gloster et al. 1983; Ehrenreich and Fuentes 1981). When women workers have organized into unions for better wages, some TNCs have responded by closing their plants or violently harassing the organizers (Fuentes and Ehrenreich 1983; Grossman 1979). In some cases, governments have suppressed unionization by using military and security equipment supplied by the United States (Enloe 1983; Siegel 1979).

Turnover

Women's work becomes tied to global restructuring when women's jobs are vulnerable to industrial downturns. This is particularly true in electronics. With the end of export processing zone incentives in Jamaica and Puerto Rico (e.g., the return of taxes and tariffs), many TNCs departed and women lost their jobs (Bolles 1983; Fuentes and Ehrenreich 1983). As a consequence, these unemployed workers, who had depended on the TNC work for household survival (see chapter 9), had to find new jobs in economies with high unemployment. Given the unemployment in many countries (and in certain depressed areas in the United States) and the earlier exclusion of women from formal work, many women had to seek work in services, the informal sector, and/or prostitution (Barry 1979; Neumann 1979; Sassen-Koob 1984).

Thus, in the short run, it appears that global restructuring and the global assembly line have made some work opportunities available to some women. In the long run, however, women workers are confronted with job turnover, lack of mobility, hazardous working conditions, and low wages (Ward 1988b). Additionally, with continuing automation in areas such as microchip fabrication, there will be fewer jobs available for women workers in TNCs (O'Connor 1987). Many TNCs move their plants to the countries with the lowest operating costs and minimal economic and political risks. Women workers experience decreased bargaining power and earnings as a result of these decisions. Likewise, informal-sector subcontracting for TNCs or other informal-sector activities (sales of food, clothing, cosmetics, and so on) provide few options for the long-term economic empowerment of women.

At the same time, employment in TNCs provides some women with opportunities to defy traditional familial constraints, gives many women some economic independence, and gives all women a chance to come together in a gender-segregated setting where they can recognize their joint interests as women workers. As I discuss in the next section, women rarely have been passive participants in global restructuring.

REDEFINING RESISTANCE

Researchers and organizers have often misinterpreted and misunderstood the diverse forms of resistance employed by women workers. Women have often appeared as passive pawns of men, their families, religion, underdevelopment, modernization, and global restructuring. Further, labor organizers have defined women as difficult to unionize. More recent research, however, has noted many acts of resistance that escaped notice because the scholars typically had defined women as passive beings and resistance only as unionization (see Chafetz and Dworkin 1986; Bernard 1987; Bookman and Morgen 1988; Westwood and Bhachu 1988; Asian Women United of California 1989; Collins 1989). Resistance takes a variety of forms, such as going to work and organizing in defiance of men and cultural traditions, achieving autonomy as planters and traders in subsaharan Africa and the Caribbean (Mintz 1971; Kandiyoti 1988), as well as more overt and passive actions. At the same time, women's resistance is intertwined with contradictory elements that reinforce their traditional roles as wives and mothers.

Bettina Aptheker (1989) suggests that women engage in diverse acts of resistance every day in their work and family lives. Dill (1986) has argued that survival is one form of resistance, particularly for women of color in the United States, who have used their families and meager resources to thwart cultural cooptation and to ensure the survival of the next generation (see also Asian Women United of California 1989; Collins 1989). Many women worldwide have resisted class, cultural, and religious traditions by working in some combination of formal and informal work and housework as a survival strategy for their households. When the debt crisis generated an economic crisis in Bolivia, Nash (1988) found that the class struggle moved from formal labor to issues of family and community survival, as voiced by mobilized housewives who had formed coalitions with labor unions. In Chile, the intrusion of government violence into the home via the disappearances, tortures, and deaths of family members resulted in the mobilization of numerous women against the Pinochet dictatorship (Ximena Bunster, personal communication). And Igbo women in Nigeria went to war against the British in 1929 because the women's socioeconomic autonomy as traders and farmers was threatened by colonial taxes (van Allen 1976; Tilly 1986; Ward 1988c).

Women in factories and sweatshops have also adopted innovative forms of resistance by laughing at time-and-motion researchers (Bookman 1988), telling male managers that women workers require unique rest periods (chapter 7), having bridal and baby showers on the shop floor (Westwood 1985), and forming unions and striking (Bookman 1988). Such behavior builds solidarity despite language barriers. In some cases resistance begins among women

co-workers in a sex-segregated workplace, which, given family constraints on women's time, may be a better site for organizing women
than union meetings after work.

In other cases, the resistance begins at home. Women delay marriage and insist on recognition of their work roles (see chapter 2).
Others leave violent households (Aptheker 1989). Still others form
gender- and race- and ethnic-specific groups in the workplace and
the community (Andreas 1985; Giddings 1984; Byerly 1986; Dill
1986, 1988; Bookman 1988; Zavella 1987, 1988; Mies 1988b; Westwood and Bhachu 1988; Asian Women United of California 1989;
Collins 1989). Dill (1988) has found that domestic women workers
also use the support of other women they meet riding or waiting
for the bus. Finally, Aihwa Ong (1987) has found that some Malay-
sian women workers in TNCs indirectly resist their employers by
claiming to be possessed by religious spirits.

Women's lives are balancing acts in which women seek to juggle
the demands of household survival with cultural or religious traditions that define work as a male domain (see Westwood and Bhachu
1988; Aptheker 1989; chapter 8). Research by Ann Bookman and
Sandra Morgen (1988:vii) points to examples of "consent and resistance," whereby women act in seemingly contradictory ways in an
effort to deal with multiple demands. Dill (1986) notes that with the
end of slavery in the United States, African-American women insisted that, like white women, they had an equal right *not* to work
outside the home. These assertions occurred in defiance of racist
expectations that African-American women would labor outside the
home and despite the women's desperate need for household income. When economic discrimination against African-Americans resulted in most African-American women working outside the home,
the women developed a variety of strategies to retain their self-
respect relative to their employers. Westwood (1985) describes another example of consent and resistance in a British factory which
manifested as elaborate prewedding parties for both Anglo and Indian women that glorified women's roles as wives and mothers. And
Hossfeld (chapter 7) notes that despite their position as sole wage
earners, many women perceive their wages as secondary to that of
men, even if their husbands are unemployed or they are divorced
or widowed. In turn, factories use ambivalence regarding gender

and race as a rationalization for treating women as "special workers" and for paying them lower wages than the men. Louise Lamphere (1987) describes coping and consent strategies of women workers who keep track of their own production records while tacitly consenting to conditions over which they have little control, such as sexual harassment by supervisors. Finally, Deniz Kandiyoti (1988) compares bargaining strategies women use in societies where they have some power (subsaharan Africa) with those used in classical patriarchal societies (the Middle East, China, and India), where women's survival depends on manipulating men so that they can fulfill their traditional male obligations. As studies by Westwood, Hossfeld, Lamphere, and Aptheker indicate, women actively resist day-to-day as well as long-term control at work, whether it be in factories or other settings.

SCOPE OF THE BOOK

The contributors to this book elaborate on and provide insights into the themes touched on above of redefining work, juggling formal and informal labor and housework, the costs and benefits of TNC employment, resistance versus consent, and the intersection between race, gender, and class.

They use a variety of research methods, including fieldwork, survey research, and analysis of government policies and data. They focus on nations at the core (Japan and the United States), the semi-periphery (Greece, Ireland, and Taiwan), and the periphery (Colombia, Indonesia, and Mexico) of the global economy; on different industries—electronics, garment manufacturing, and others in the service and informal sectors; and on plants with different markets—domestic and export—and in different settings—urban and rural.

Part I explores the impact of TNCs and factory work on the informal sector in rural regions of peripheral and semiperipheral countries. Diane Wolf explores the interdependence of women workers, families, and factories and the intersection of what Joan Acker (1988) has termed the relations of production and distribution. From her fieldwork in Indonesia, Wolf found that, contrary to public statements by TNC managers, women's wages meet only part of their subsistence needs. Families subsidize the women's employment,

thereby keeping down the factories' labor costs and stabilizing household income. TNC employment means that the women can gain
some degree of independence and at least partly support themselves,
but Wolf questions whether, over time, women are actually empow-
ered by such work.

Cynthia Truelove explores the interrelationships between TNCs,
agribusinesses, and women's informal-sector participation in Colombia's coffee-growing region. She argues that the disguised proletarianization of women in the informal sector reproduces the
coffee export sector via the maintenance of male laborers. The coffee
industries have formed mini-*maquilas* in garment construction and
shoe assembly for export. These cooperatives use female labor and
provide wages at 70 percent of subsistence costs. Workers make up
the difference by increasing their production and competing for
bonuses. Managers hire women on the basis of their attitudes and
cooperative appearance (e.g., appropriate female behaviors), and
their employment ensures a cash flow to households throughout the
year and when men are unemployed. Thus women's factory work
subsidizes and reproduces agricultural labor. Further, the cooperatives form the lowest point of subcontracting pyramids in that the
women workers constitute disguised wage workers for TNCs and
national industries that subcontract piecework to rural factories
sponsored by the coffee sector.

Joanna Hadjicostandi examines the semiperipheral country of
Greece, where women are engaged in the production of garments
for export. She finds many similarities between the positions of
women factory workers and women home or piece workers, although
the latter work many more hours (twelve to sixteen hours a day). As
in other countries, the women's wages are considered supplemental
to the men's, resulting in no change in the household division of
labor. She finds that, because of these cultural norms, women are
reluctant to organize.

Part II focuses on how governments simultaneously promote development and reinforce social and legal ideologies about women's
primary roles as wives and mothers. Jean Pyle describes how the
Irish government actively pursued foreign corporations that employed predominantly male workers to concur with constitutional
mandates that ensure women's primary roles as wives and mothers.

Industries that did invest have higher proportions of male workers than comparable industries in other countries. Thus Pyle shows how greater foreign investment in so-called women's industries can have a negligible effect on women's labor force participation rates and can result in maintaining women's traditional socioeconomic roles.

Larry Carney and Charlotte O'Kelly have studied the history of working women in Japan, particularly since 1945. When Japanese political and economic elites formulated Japan's strategy for successfully competing in the world economy, they emphasized patriarchal ideologies that stressed the centrality of the family and obedience to authority. Women's work outside the home was defined as subservient to their family roles, and this cheap and flexible labor force provided a basis for Japan's position as a core nation in the global economy. These strategies resulted in women's work lives including early retirement, limited education and training, no access to the lifelong employment system, part-time status, and the shaping of their work relative to their roles as wives and mothers. White-collar women workers are hired for their decorative appeal in the workplace. As a result of all of these working conditions, Japanese women experience the contradiction of being sought as part-time laborers but do not acquire economic autonomy. Japanese economic growth is increasingly dependent on female workers, however, and Japanese women are beginning to organize around such contradictions.

Part III examines the gender- and race-specific tactics used by employers to control women workers in factories and how women resist such strategies. A shorter version of Hossfeld's chapter won the 1988 Dissertation Award from the Sex and Gender Section of the American Sociological Association. Hossfeld's study of women production workers in Silicon Valley, California, points to how managers (most of whom are white males) use tactics based on gender and race to hire and control women workers, particularly minority and immigrant women. Hossfeld also notes how the women resist control by the managers by manipulating their sexist and racist assumptions through individual and small-group activities. For example, given their sexist assumptions about women's fraility and menstrual "problems," some managers give their women workers several "hormone breaks" per day. Likewise, women play on managers' racist stereotypes by insisting that ethnic workers should train members of their own group, by arguing, for example, that new Chinese workers must be chaperoned by other Chinese women. Contradictions remain, since managers define women as secondary wage earners even when they are hired for their so-called special skills and even though many women are primary wage earners. The women also express ambivalence about earning more money than men and maintaining their femininity while working. Hossfeld argues that, although women's individual acts of resistance may alleviate oppressive working conditions in the short run, collective *and* organized resistance is more effective in the long run in empowering women workers.

Rita Gallin focuses on Taiwanese women, who have been incorporated into the labor force during Taiwan's economic growth but have been unable to form active women's unions or organizations. She finds that patriarchal norms of hard work, subordination to men's and family interests, and compliance support ideologies favoring women's economic participation before they are married but discourage women from working outside the home after they are married. As a consequence, these ideologies about women workers inhibit a commitment by married women to work outside the home and their potential solidarity.

Susan Tiano divides theories about the determinants of *maquiladora* (factory) employment into two categories: those that focus on the effects of male unemployment and those that focus on women as a new category of worker. In her study of women garment, electronics, and service workers in Mexicali, she found that *maquiladora* employment has failed to improve the unemployment problem for either women or men. Further, many women are primary breadwinners or support others in their households, and although many are drawn into the labor force via export processing, many have extensive work histories, especially the garment workers. Yet they earn less than subsistence wages. Most of the women express ambivalence about their need and desire to work and about social norms concerning their femininity if they work.

These studies collectively suggest a need to redefine dramatically our understanding of women's work and resistance to gender- and race-based oppression. First, although development and industrial production may have meant economic advancement for women in core countries in the past, the incorporation of women into the global assembly line via formal labor, informal work, and housework has often meant the continued control of women by capitalist men. At the same time, global restructuring has generated diverse forms of empowerment and resistance for women.

Second, the effects of gender, race, and class in combination have shaped specific survival strategies. As Wolf points out, the subsidization of female labor by peasant families is an example of one such strategy that is ultimately exploited by TNCs. Race, gender, and class are powerful social constructs that govern the allocation of immigrant women workers in assembly work and/or informal-sector work while their male partners are given jobs as technicians.

Third, the state plays important direct and indirect roles in women's work lives; the state is not gender-neutral in its policies (Walby 1986). Because many immigrant and working-class women lack education and resources, often as the result of state policies, many are limited from participating in some forms of remunerative labor. Thus women are channeled into the informal sector, into sweatshops, home work, or domestic work, are forbidden from working in factories (see chapter 5), or are encouraged to retire from formal employment upon marriage (see Afshar 1987; chapter 6).

Fourth, the global assembly line has added a new shift to women's work: home work or informal-sector work. This work enables women and men to resolve temporarily the contradictions between women's patriarchically defined roles as wives and mothers and the demand for cheap female labor that subsidizes male labor and factories. Capitalist/patriarchal institutions remain relatively intact, and women experience limited empowerment from such activities.

Fifth, and finally, women workers engage in forms of resistance that might not be apparent to those who define resistance as only strikes, demonstrations, and union activities. As Hossfeld (chapter 7), Bookman and Morgen (1988), and Aptheker (1989) suggest, work that defies cultural norms about female employment is a form of resistance. Patriarchal practices engaged in by capitalists limit women's empowerment, especially when women insist on continuing to perform traditional female roles and resist through reliance on gender stereotypes. Obviously the new definitions of work generated by global restructuring will require that we look for and develop new survival strategies and tactics for empowerment for those women workers who are divided by race, class, and geographic location. As Hossfeld proposes (page 177), ethnic and immigrant women workers can offer "their numeric strength . . . [and] also a wealth of insight, creativity, and experience that could be a shot in the arm to the stagnating national labor movement."

PART I

INTERCONNECTIONS BETWEEN FORMAL AND INFORMAL WORK

2

LINKING WOMEN'S LABOR WITH THE GLOBAL ECONOMY: FACTORY WORKERS AND THEIR FAMILIES IN RURAL JAVA

Diane L. Wolf

THIRD WORLD WOMEN AND INDUSTRIALIZATION

The success of export-oriented industrialization in the cities and free trade zones of Asia continues to draw research attention (Martin 1987; Deyo 1987), but what is often overlooked is that much of this industrial growth has occurred at the expense of young, poorly paid female workers. Influenced by world systems theory, researchers have analyzed the interplay between traditional gender hierarchies and the growth of global capitalism as they intersect in the selection and employment of docile Third World women in multinationals oriented toward the world market (Grossman 1979; UNIDO 1980; Fernandez-Kelly 1983; Lim 1983a; Safa 1983; Ward 1984). Al-

A major portion of the research (1981–83) on which this chapter was based was funded by a Title XII grant administered through the Program in International Agriculture, Cornell University. A follow-up study conducted in 1986 was funded by the Graduate School Research Fund, University of Washington. I am indebted to the Lembaga Pengatahun Ilmu Indonesia (LIPI) and the Population Studies Center, Gadjah Mada University, Yogyakarta, for sponsoring my research. This chapter was originally presented as a paper at the 1986 Annual Meetings of the American Sociological Association in New York. I am grateful to Kathryn Ward and two anonymous reviewers for comments.

though such studies have contributed to an understanding of the social effects of global economic change, in much of this research a micro level of analysis, focusing on individual workers, is linked directly with macro-level theory without addressing the intermediary forces operating between these levels.[1] Few researchers have studied workers within the context of their domestic unit or the community that affects their individual behavior and decisions (Fernandez-Kelly 1983; Kung 1983; Salaff 1981), and even fewer have contextualized this research within the urban-rural economic dynamic (Ong 1983).[2]

My research contributes to this growing body of literature with a case study in which I present a detailed analysis of the complex economic relationships between factories, female workers, and their rural families in Java, Indonesia. Analyzing the connections between workers, their families, and their roles in the agricultural-industrial nexus extends our understanding of the relationship between gender, labor, and the global economy.

My study suggests that five different economic relationships are occurring simultaneously. First, Indonesian factories are not paying female workers even a subsistence-level wage. As a result, poor rural families are subsidizing the factories by providing for some of their daughters' needs. In this way, the "superexploitation hypothesis"— that women are paid less than what is necessary "to cover the reproduction of labor-power expended . . . and minimum physical subsistence" (Lim 1983a:77)—is verified. That alone is not sufficient, however, to understand women's factory work in the Third World. Second, daughters who work in factories contribute little, if anything, from their weekly wages to the family economy, challenging the assumption that a female worker's wages from factory work are

---

1. These gaps in empirical research reflect major problems in using the global economy as a unit of analysis or the world systems approach (Wallerstein 1974). A global economy approach obscures the issues of class formation and interclass relationships within a specific country. A recent attempt has been made to link households with the global economy (Smith et al. 1984). Although this effort constitutes an important theoretical advance, there is little discussion of households and the local class system. Rather, households are discussed in relation to the global economy, disengaged from their daily context.

2. In part this omission may be logistical, in that most workers in urban areas are migrants.

automatically part of the family's financial portfolio. Instead, and third, the daughters' wages stabilize the economy of rural, semiproletarian households, preventing further deterioration of their already low socioeconomic status. Fourth, while the economic rationale of factory employment has become more obvious to parents over time, my research shows no evidence of a concerted, developed household strategy. Rather, the women appear to act relatively autonomously in making socioeconomic and behavioral decisions. This study thus argues against automatically equating a worker-daughter's actions with her household's collective needs or interests.

Fifth, and finally, this study and others in this volume should dispel any assumptions that the new international division of labor affects Third World women workers similarly and equally. Third World women experience global economic change differently from one another, depending on their class position, ethnic background, culture, and country's position within the world market. Women are not simply passive sexual victims of capitalist "penetration" but social actors in their own right. Because economic structures are both "constraining and enabling" (Giddens 1984:169), women workers in different settings react to and reshape such structures differently (Ong 1987).

Conceptual Approach

Carmen Diana Deere and Alain de Janvry (1978) provide an analytical framework for studying the integration of peasant households into a capitalist economy. Their framework integrates key variables for analysis at the micro level—age, gender hierarchies, class differentiation, life cycle stage, and labor allocation—with macro-level structural change. I applied their model so as to analyze class differentiation, household employment, the determinants of factory employment, and the relationship between factory wages and the reproduction of the household.

The framework was applied in two stages. First, I tested the proposition that an inverse relationship exists between a household's access to the means of production and its integration into the labor market. In other words, members of poorer households are more likely to participate in waged labor to ensure household survival. I

expected and found that factory workers came from poorer households compared with their "nonfactory" peers.[3] I also expected that
contributions from their wages to the household economy would be
substantial since, according to the model, those who seek waged
employment do so for the purpose of household survival.

CASE STUDY OF JAVA

Research Site

The research site is a rural subdistrict (*kecematan*) in Central Java
that has a population of 83,500. The site is approximately sixteen
miles south of Semarang, a large port city, and has easy access to a
highway that connects Semarang to several cities in Central Java. In
the early 1970s, provincial and district-level government officials
began to encourage foreign and domestic urban investment in the
area. According to my informants, factories were built here beginning in 1972 and as of 1988 continued to be built here. The area
may eventually develop into a periurban site, but in that the majority
of the population is engaged in agricultural production, it is still
basically rural. The factories are located in two villages, and many
are in the middle of ricefields.[4]

---

3. I compared thirty-nine village females (and their households) who worked in
factories with ninety village females who had never worked in a factory. The factory
workers came from poorer households at a later stage in the life cycle (as indicated
by the consumer-worker ratio and the dependency ratio) so that their parents could
forgo the daily returns on an adult member's labor. Households with land and labor
shortages could not afford to release a daughter for factory employment. Results
from a logistic regression model demonstrated that the most significant factors in
affecting the probability of a female seeking factory employment were children ever-
born (p < .01), followed by class status (p < .05) and two life cycle measures, the
consumer-worker ratio (p < .10) and the presence of other able-bodied females (p
< .10) in the household (see Wolf 1986a, chapter 7).

4. In 1983, there were nine large-scale factories and three medium-sized factories,
and three large-scale firms were under construction. The largest factories produced
textiles, followed by garments, food processing (bread, cookies, bottling), furniture,
and buses. The two largest firms were foreign-owned (textiles and spinning), and the
four largest (textiles, spinning, garments, and glassware) were export-oriented. The
four export-oriented firms employed 76 percent of the work force in manufacturing
in the subdistrict. These twelve factories employed almost six thousand workers.
Three-fourths of the labor force consisted of village females between the ages of
fifteen and twenty-four, most of whom were unmarried (Wolf 1984). Migrant workers
constituted less than 10 percent of the work force.

Unlike the research sites for most of the studies mentioned earlier, this one is not a free trade zone. Firms in free trade zones tend to be dominated by multinational corporations and to be exclusively export-oriented, whereas some of the firms at this site are nationally owned, and most have primarily domestic markets. More important, at most other sites the majority of the work force are migrants. At this site 90 percent of the work force consisted of local residents who lived at home. The rural location and the familial ties added an important and unusual dimension rarely found at other Third World industrial sites.

I lived in an agricultural village located several miles from the factories. It had easy access to public transportation, enabling me to study both workers who commuted to the factories and their peers in the village who worked in agriculture or the household. After establishing the class position of the factory workers' households within their villages, I sought to determine the extent of the workers' contributions to their families.[5] My theoretical expectation that they contributed a high proportion of their wages to the family economy was bolstered by empirical findings across time and cultures (Hareven 1982; Salaff 1981; Tilly and Scott 1978).

Factory Wages

At the time of my study, female factory workers earned an average salary of $24 per month for a forty-eight-hour workweek.[6] Workers often had access to a few dollars more than their wages, however, because of cash transfers from parents, repayments for debts, sav-

---

5. A household was defined as a co-residential group sharing the kitchen and food. In two agricultural villages studied (250 households), almost all households consisted of nuclear or extended families. In this chapter, I use "family" and "household" interchangeably, although no assumptions are made about family structure (see Wolf 1986 for further discussion).

6. In such a rural site, workers are less educated than their urban counterparts, which allows factories to pay below the minimum wage without confronting protests. As of late 1982, the minimum wage in Central Java was 625 rupiahs daily (about $.96) for these permanent daily workers (*harian tetan*). Many factories paid below the minimum wage, however, averaging 500 rupiahs daily. It is not surprising, therefore, that the owners and managers interviewed were attracted to this area compared with urban sites because of the cheaper labor, land, and utilities. During my follow-up research, I found that wage levels had increased but were almost the same in dollar terms.

ings, and loans. Table 2.1 contrasts the buying power of the women
workers in Central Java with women workers in other Asian countries. Wages in Indonesian manufacturing are among the lowest in
the world (Frobel et al. 1980:35; *Financial Times of London,* June 29,
1981), and their wages buy much less. Women at the research site
had to work for almost three hours at minimum wage to buy a bar
of soap, and only rarely were minimum wages paid. Furthermore,
the national union (FSBI) calculated that a single worker in Central
Java needed about 24,250 rupiahs (Rps.) a month for subsistence—
almost 50 percent more than these workers earned. These calculations and data demonstrate that factory wages for female workers
in Central Java are not even subsistence-level.

Gender, Agrarian Households, and Subsidization

Several interrelated reasons create the justification for the low wages
paid to female factory workers: the traditional gender hierarchies,
the presence of the family, and the rural-agrarian location of the
factories.

A young woman in Java is considered the dependent of her father
or husband even if her financial contribution to the family economy
is crucial. Celia Mather (1982) found that such income is viewed as
secondary or supplemental, which actually inverts her strong economic role and puts it under patriarchal control. From the perspective of the industrialists at the research site, such gender norms
are used to justify the wage structure. The same ideological reasons
are given to justify paying male factory workers an average of 22,000
rupiahs, or 40 percent more than the average wage earned by the
females. Two of the five male factory workers surveyed received the
amount a Department of Labor official thought would be subsistence-level, and two others were quite close to that level.[7] The managers and owners of the factories claimed that males were paid more

----

7. On average, these male workers contributed 15 percent of their wages to their
families, in cash or in kind. Of those who contributed (excluding one migrant), their
contribution averaged 19 percent. A higher contribution to the household may be
correlated with a higher wage. The female dorm residents in the textile mill had
higher wages and also reported remitting large proportions to their families; this was
not verifiable, however.

TABLE 2.1. The Comparative Buying Power of Asian Females

				Time Worked[a]			
Item Purchased	Sri Lanka	Malaysia	Thailand	Philippines	Hong Kong	Indonesia[b]
1 kg rice	2 hrs. 41 min.	1 hr. 15 min.	55 min.	1 hr. 10 min.	55 min.	4 hrs.
1 egg	29 min.	14 min.	10 min.	20 min.	5 min.	45 min.
1 Coke	1 hr. 24 min.	45 min.	23 min.	27 min.	11 min.	4 hrs.
Cheapest meal out	2 hrs. 14 min.	1 hr. 58 min.	55 min.	2 hrs. 3 min.	56 min.	1 hr. 15 min.
Average Daily Wage (U.S. $)	$2.40	$2.60	$3.40	$2.40	$6.90	$0.96

Sources: Balai, Asian Journal 2 (December 1981), market survey in Central Java, and fieldwork 1981–83.
[a]Except for Indonesia, wages and prices are from 1981.
[b]Prices are from the research site only and are based on a situation in which the minimum wage was paid. Not all factories pay the minimum wage.

because they had to support families. Most male factory workers were unmarried, however, and their factory wages were not used to meet their daily subsistence needs.

This ideology, that females are economic dependents of males, working mainly to supplement family income, is further strengthened by the presence of the families at the site. While low wages force the women to remain economically dependent on their parents, the presence of their families, who quite naturally provide the women with food, a home, and other goods, benefits the factories by keeping the women's cost of living low and thereby helps justify the low wages. Deere and de Janvry (1978) assert that such subsidization is common in situations in which waged workers have access to their families and constitutes indirect exploitation of the peasantry under capitalism (see also Wolpe 1972). Wages can fall below subsistence level in such situations because "some of [their] needs are provided by the family in the home production process" for free (Deere and de Janvry 1978:12). Thus the labor of semiproletarian peasants (or, in this case, factory workers) remains cheap. In urban factories, where typically a high proportion of the workers are migrants, owners cannot use the argument that workers are economically supported by their families to justify paying lower wages.

The rural, agrarian setting provides industrialists with yet another rationale for paying females low wages. Most of the industrialists are well-off, urban Chinese-Indonesian residents who look down on the rural Javanese villagers. The Javanese managers, who are also urban dwellers, expressed the same scorn for the villagers. Further, the managers believe that villagers obtain sufficient livelihoods from agriculture, a serious misconception in rural Java today. One manager stated, for example, "Working doesn't affect their lives because they are from rural families and don't need the income to live. They don't consider income and the family. They don't know how to save. They just live for each day and spend what they have." His rationale, that surplus income (that beyond basic subsistence) is unnecessary income, is one managers apply to the income of others but not to themselves.

Java's rural environment also has a less educated, more docile female work force than periurban or urban sites, where factories do not dare pay below-minimum wages because there is greater awareness among workers and more potential for protest (Mather 1982;

Sutoro n.d.; INDOC 1981). Although factory owners in all parts of Java capitalize on traditional Javanese female traits of shyness and fear as a way to prevent protests about wages, the problem is compounded in this particular area because the workers have limited education. From her research in the 1950s, Anne Ruth Willner unwittingly summarized the advantages of rural-based industrialization in Java:

> The additional costs involved in the supply, transport, technological, and distributive aspects of setting up factories in economically less desirable locations may well be offset in some instances by the *savings implicit in the lack of necessity to provide benefits and services that are provided by the community. The indirect costs of industrialization in the form of labor protests partially derived from the strains, tensions and dislocations of urban life and the need to overcome them by welfare expenditures might be saved at the source.* (1961:341, emphasis added)

Design of Income-Expenditures Surveys

Results from a one-month daily survey of the income and expenditures of twelve single women workers had demonstrated that almost all went into debt and borrowed money from their parents to cover expenses (Wolf 1984). I then conducted a more extensive survey that included questions about access to other income (other economic activities, money borrowed, loans repaid, and the like), debts, and savings. The sample for this survey included three groups of single workers: commuters, migrants, and residents. The commuters (N = 10) lived with their parents in an agricultural village and were the only group that had been included in the initial survey. The migrants (N = 15) boarded in an industrialized village, and the residents (N = 7) lived with their families in the same village.[8] Literate workers kept daily records on forms they were provided and

---

8. There were almost two hundred migrant workers in the industrialized village, of which I sampled fifteen. It was difficult, however, to find young women from the industrialized village who lived with their families and worked in the factories. Most women in the industrialized village preferred to sell goods and services such as food, clothing, and haircuts to the migrant boarders. These women did not like the time and discipline within the factories and preferred the slower pace of the informal economy.

Table 2.2.   Net Contribution to the Family Economy[a]

	Commuters	Migrants	Residents[b]
Number	10	15	7
Average net contribution (2,011 Rps.)[c]	300 Rps.[b]	900 Rps.	−400 Rps.
Net contribution as proportion of salary	−9% (3.6)[c]	5.5% (13.6%)[c]	−8.6%

[a] Net contribution for commuters and residents was calculated as money to family plus goods and food bought for family minus money from family. For migrants, it was calculated as money to family minus money from family. Many migrants brought rice and other foodstuffs from home, but it was not possible to calculate this for the month of the survey.

[b] At the time of research, 650 Rps. = $1.00.

[c] Excluding one outlier.

were interviewed every three days. Illiterate workers were interviewed every two days.

Contribution to Family Economy

How much did workers contribute to their family economies? Tables 2.2 and 2.3 present the net contribution, which reflects money given to the family plus food and goods bought for the family, such as kerosene and durables, minus money the family gave the worker. With the exclusion of two outliers, the net contribution was only 3.6 percent, 5.5 percent, and 13.6 percent for commuters, migrants, and residents respectively.

Thirty percent of the commuters gave their families nothing or took money from them; the remaining 70 percent contributed small amounts. Commuters contributed an average of 300 rupiahs a month, less than $0.50. More than half the migrants gave nothing to their families during the month surveyed, but among those who contributed, the average was 900 rupiahs ($1.50). Many migrants said that they were ashamed (*malu*) to return home unless they could bring their families money. With the exception of one resident whose family gave her 15,000 rupiahs, the residents, on average, made a higher net contribution to their families than the commuters did. In all cases, the contributions were surprisingly small.

TABLE 2.3.   Range of Contributions, by Worker Status

	Percentage of Workers		
Negative[a]	10%	6.7%	28.6%
Zero	20	46.7	0
1–1,000 Rps.	50	13	0
1,001–3,000 Rps.	20	13	28.6
+ 3,000 Rps.	0	19	42.8
	100	100	100

[a]Range was from − 15,000 to − 4,000 Rps.

In both surveys, the commuters responded that they remitted meager amounts, or nothing, to their families. In the second survey, most of the commuters replied that their contribution was even lower—20 percent versus 8 percent of their wages. The two surveys were taken in different months. If monthly differences are to be expected, then parents subsidize their daughters more in some months than in others. Likewise, workers may contribute more in some months, particularly if there is more strain on the household's finances because of the agricultural cycle. To understand more fully the economic relationship between female factory workers and their family's economy, other expenditures must be examined.

Expenditures

Table 2.4 illustrates several striking patterns. All the workers spent a substantial proportion of their wages on food, and commuters and residents spent most of this money on lunch. Two basics—transportation and lunch—consumed more than 40 percent of the commuters' salaries. Maria Patricia Fernandez-Kelly found, by comparison, that workers in maquiladoras spent 14 percent of their wages on these items (1983:57).

The cost of commuting increased during the research period by 50 to 75 rupiahs daily. Because wages are so low, this increase, while small (equivalent to 7 to 12 cents), had a major impact on a worker's net income. Commuters bought very little food or other goods for

36   *Wolf*

TABLE 2.4.   Selected Expenditures as Percentage of Salary

Expenditure	Commuters	Migrants	Residents
Clothing[a]	14.0	11.0	16.0
Food[b]	20.0	29.0	20.0
Transportation	25.0	9.0	10.0
Household goods	0.1	2.0	0.6
Toiletries	3.0	5.0	9.0
To family	2.5	6.3	17.7
Haircuts, jewelry, entertainment	6.1	2.6	10.0
Savings	26.0	40.0	30.0
Average monthly salary (in Rps.)	15,383	16,211	15,324

[a]Clothing includes clothes bought outright and debts paid for clothing.
[b]Food includes lunch, snacks, and food bought for the household. In general, commuters and residents bought little food for their households; most of their expenditures on food were for lunch and snacks.

their families, but they did take care of most of their clothing needs. Indeed, the juxtaposition of the unexpectedly small amounts they contributed to their families with what they spent on luxury items is perhaps the most striking insight from this table. Residents gave their families a higher proportion of their wages than did commuters, but they also received a substantial amount of money from their families. The consumption patterns of residents also shows that they spent more on luxury goods and leisure than did other workers.

Migrants tended to lead the most frugal lifestyles of all three categories of workers, perhaps because they were more on their own financially. Rent is not included in the table because boarders paid rent in two to three annual installments, and none paid rent during the time surveyed. The average monthly rate for rent was 1,180 rupiahs, however, or 7.3 percent of their average monthly salaries. Migrants spent 11 percent of their wages on clothing, while the other two groups spent about 15 percent.

Finally, because their wages could not possibly meet their daily and monthly subsistence needs—food, rent, transportation, clothing, toiletries, and the like—workers in all three categories received free goods from their parents. Commuters and residents received free housing, at least two meals a day, and other goods. If home production were given a monetary value, these workers would probably spend 60 to 80 percent of their wages on food alone. This economic dependence on family underlies the response of one commuter to a question about whether she would ever consider boarding closer to the factory to save money on transportation: "No, I'd lose money; my money would be spent on food alone. If I'm at home, I can eat with my parents." Although migrants did not eat with their parents, they returned from visits with rice, other foodstuffs, and household goods, so that their food expenditures do not represent all their food needs. In addition, twenty-two of the workers surveyed (69 percent) overspent their wages in the month surveyed, and parents made up some of the difference with cash.

Parents' Responses

When asked whether their daughters' wages contributed to the family economy, most respondents felt that their daughters contributed either directly or indirectly, by taking care of their own cash needs. Others were not so sure, and a few were openly displeased with what they perceived as their daughters' selfish behavior. There was a range not only of contributions but of responses.

Comments such as the following illustrate the gamut of responses to the question of whether their daughters contributed to the family economy: "Yes, a little, for example, she often leaves money underneath the tablecloth for daily [food] shopping. But if she doesn't leave it, I don't ask for it. I've never looked for money in her room." Or, "If she's asked, yes, she gives us money. But if we don't ask, she doesn't. Sometimes we ask, but she says she doesn't have any." Another parent was very pleased that her daughter, who had formerly been a servant to another family in the village, was now earning money, because she could "buy anything. . . . I'm happy she can work, and I don't want to ask her to contribute to the family."

A few parents were openly dissatisfied with their daughters' behavior. "Every day she just has fun from morning till evening. Her money is spent just for play. She never helped us; in fact, she often asks us for transportation money." Or, "No, she doesn't contribute to the family. Her money is spent just for her own pleasure" (*untuk senang senang sendiri*). These voices reflect the inevitable tension that develops between generations when economics are involved.

Although their daughters' wages did not necessarily contribute directly to the family economy, the parents generally felt that the wages fulfilled a role they could not play. "At home we can't fulfill her needs, so it's better she's working in the factory. We're happy she's working because we can't buy her anything, we can only feed her." Another parent said, "At home, what kind of work can she find? Anyway, we can't fulfill her needs (*mencukupi kebutuhanya*). If it was only food she needed, we could. But I can't buy other things. Anyway, girls need a lot of things. She has three kinds of face powder, shoes, and sandals." Another parent felt ambivalence and embarrassment about her daughter's economic position: "A girl working in a factory isn't right; it shames us. But at home, we don't have money for her needs."

The parents felt they had little control over their daughters' wages. Half the parents in the agricultural village said that their daughters spent their wages as they pleased, without asking advice, whereas several complained that they never received any cash from their daughters. The other 50 percent said that their daughters asked their advice before purchasing an expensive consumer item.

Although factory wages were not sufficient to relieve the parents fully of providing for their daughters' consumption needs, their daughters' wages were used to fulfill some of these needs. By purchasing their clothing and one meal each day, their daughters contributed indirectly to the family economy by lessening the demands for cash and other consumer items. The crucial link between the women's wages and their family's economy was neither food, clothing, nor cash remittances, however. Rather, all the workers put away approximately one-third of their wages in savings.

Savings

Three-fourths of the workers surveyed participated in a rotating savings association (*arisan*). Each payday, members of the *arisan* meet and contribute a certain amount of cash, which is pooled. The names of one or two members are then drawn from a bottle to receive the cash. It is a "fixed lottery" in that each person receives the cash once before someone receives it twice. Depending on the size of the group, workers can win the *arisan* once to several times a year. It is a safe way to save money because there is no danger of loss or corruption, and it serves a social function.

Several workers participated in more than one *arisan*. During the month of the survey, eight workers in a sample of thirty-nine received 5,000 to 100,000 rupiahs from the *arisan*, or an average of 39,000 rupiahs ($60).

The *arisan* is a temporary "anti-household" strategy in some sense since it makes part of the women's wages inaccessible to members of their household. Many workers said that without the mechanism of the *arisan*, they would not have been able to save money because family members would have requested it. As one commuter said, "If you don't participate in an *arisan*, there's nothing left over to show for your work."

Not all parents could forgo the wages the women brought in, and the women in these families saved little. One-third of all the single factory workers sampled did not participate in the *arisan* at all during the time studied. Among the commuters, four of these women came from families in the poorest socioeconomic class. This suggests that only daughters in slightly better-off families who do not have to help meet the pressing daily needs of their families can afford to save.

Workers used their savings to pay off debts, to buy gold jewelry or livestock (both of which are considered savings), and to purchase goods for the family. One very poor commuter from a landless family lived in a tiny two-room house made of bamboo walls. There was no furniture—not even a chair—and all interviews were conducted outside. After receiving an *arisan* of 100,000 rupiahs, she had the inner walls of the house rebuilt with wood and bought living-room furniture. The *arisan* enabled her to buy goods she and her mother could not have otherwise afforded.[9]

---

9. Unfortunately, her story did not end happily. When I returned in 1986, she had two children with a man she had not married. He lived in a nearby town and was not contributing financially to his children's upkeep. She was still working in the

This is perhaps a dramatic example, but parents in other families were quick to point out the much-appreciated consumer goods their daughters had bought with their savings—cupboards, radios, beds, clocks, dishes, pressure lamps, and so on. Further, workers used savings from the *arisan* not only to pay off debts but also as collateral to obtain advance credit (Willner 1961:258).

Another aspect of factory employment that is attractive both to the workers and their families is the annual Lebaran bonus workers receive right before Idul Fitri, the end of the fasting month of Ramadan. This is a very consumption-oriented time of year when people buy new clothes, fix up their homes for guests, and cook special food.

The average bonus among commuters in 1981 was 22,000 rupiahs ($33.85). Bonuses ranged from 8,000 to 35,000 rupiahs, depending on the worker's diligence and seniority. Because of the increased demand for cookies during the holiday, the biscuit factory worked overtime during the entire month of Ramadan. Workers there received higher-than-usual wages because of the overtime, as well as the bonus, which could total as much as $100. The comparatively low daily wages at the biscuit factory were quickly (and temporarily) forgotten as people gossiped about the size of the bonuses. Most workers used them to buy gold jewelry and new clothes for themselves and their family members, and some bought new furniture. Villagers were clearly envious of these workers' access to cash and buying power at this time of year.

Savings, and to some extent the bonus, were used in part to obtain consumer goods and to start accumulating a dowry. The gold or livestock belonged to the women, and most said that they would take these goods with them if they married and moved elsewhere. While the capital from the *arisan* could be used to start a dowry, which might make the worker more marriageable, the money was often spent before the woman married or for her marriage. One worker,

---

factory to support her family but could not afford to spend $1.00 (U.S.) a week to buy dried milk for her thin and hungry children. Nor could she afford to participate in the *arisan*. After a few years, the furniture had broken, and she had thrown it out. Once again, her tiny living room consisted of one wooden box on which to sit.

for example, sold her ten ducks at a loss at the end of Ramadan because her family needed cash. Several workers lost part or all of their gold savings to family loans, which were never going to be repaid. In one family in which two daughters worked in factories, one daughter's gold and her sister's goat were sold to pay for a wedding for one of the daughters.

It is important to distinguish between the commodities the workers purchased and productive investments. In this case, the capital accumulated was not used for productive investments such as fertilizer or land, which would have affected and improved the family's economic condition in the long run. There is, however, another type of "productive investment"—that of marriage. If factory employment improves a woman's chances of vertical mobility by enabling her to acquire a better spouse—either by working hard and earning a reputation for diligence or by acquiring consumer goods and savings—it can be considered a productive investment in her future and that of her family of origin. Seven parents out of sixteen who were interviewed felt that factory work improved their daughters' chances of attracting better husbands. Six did not know what the effect would be, and three thought there would be no effect. Several former factory workers were asked if factory employment actually did improve their marriageability, and they were divided evenly on the subject.[10]

I returned to Java in 1986, and by then another advantage of factory employment had become apparent. Rat infestation had ruined the rice crops, and many families had neither food nor income. Families in which daughters had worked in the factories were able to keep afloat during this difficult period by selling off the gold jewelry or livestock the women had bought with their savings. The only other options would have been to seek work far from the village or to sell off the family's possessions, including their already small landholdings. Savings from factory work staved off disaster for these poor, semiproletarian families and prevented further deterioration

---

10. My 1986 research on marriage indicates that female factory workers tend to marry men whose family economy is higher than their own. The proportions marrying up were similar, however, among nonfactory females (Wolf 1988a).

of their socioeconomic position. Factory work had become a crucial form of disaster insurance and emergency aid.

Women's Perspectives on Factory Employment

Despite their exploitative wages and need for subsidization, female factory workers in Central Java derive both economic and social benefits from factory employment. These benefits have little to do, however, with their household's collective good or reproduction. The young women said that they wanted money of their own to buy their own soap. They stated that they wanted to work in factories just like their friends. They perceived their status as enhanced by their factory work because the labor was nonagricultural and steady and the environment was clean and cool. Their skin stayed lighter than that of agricultural workers, reflecting their nonmanual and therefore higher-status work. Factory work allowed them to leave their parents' homes, to travel, and to meet young men and women from other villages. Several romances and marriages had resulted between male and female workers or between female workers and drivers of local transportation.

Factory workers in one village I studied exhibited an air of assertiveness compared with their peers who had never worked in a factory. Their makeup, nail polish, and in a few cases long pants were statements of modernity—that which is outside the village. Many stated defiantly that they, not their parents, would choose their future mate.[11]

Employment opportunities for rural Javanese women have become increasingly limited over the years because of the commercialization of agriculture. Young women are usually involved in household and farm production, agricultural waged labor, trade, or domestic service. Agricultural work is seasonal, and wages therefore fluctuate. Many of the young women who became factory workers had been domestic servants in the village or nearby city. They de-

---

11. More than twenty years ago, Willner observed similar patterns; female factory workers were similarly thought to have a reputation for independence, extravagance, and moral laxity (1961:234).

tested the job, which required long hours but paid little. They found domestic service too arduous and controlled since they had to be on duty from early in the morning until late at night.

Factory workers continually stressed that they had no other options; without their factory jobs, they felt they would be unemployed: "If I'm at home, what kind of work will I do? I can't just plant rice." A parent of one factory worker summarized the choices and contradictions in this situation: "No, she can't save from her salary; it's used up for transportation, fun, and contributions for friends' weddings (*nyumbang*).... But at home there's no work, just playing around. If she was at home, she could help gather fodder (*rumput*), but at the most, she'd only receive a little money."

Indeed, initially I confronted a seemingly contradictory situation. Workers receiving below subsistence-level wages perceived themselves to be privileged. Rather than dismiss their voices as "false consciousness," the task was to understand, in light of their exploitation, what had given rise to that sense of privilege. Given the concrete socioeconomic reality of rural Java and women's low opportunity costs, these women were in a somewhat privileged situation having steady, remunerated jobs. Given that factory jobs increased their access to cash and status, it was not difficult to understand why young village women sought factory employment.

Parents' Perspectives on Factory Employment

One might ask why the parents allowed their daughters to work if they were still a drain on the family economy. While there are several rationales, it is important to understand that the parents did not and could not control their daughters' employment. Many of the women had sought their jobs without or against their parents' wishes (Wolf 1988b). Unlike the situations in North America, Europe, or East Asia, parents did not direct and control their daughters' labor.

Nonetheless, the parents provided several reasons and rationales, most financial, for their daughters' employment. Some parents felt that any job was better than sitting idly at home. Some felt that their daughters demanded less cash from them, since they used their wages for items such as clothing. As mentioned earlier, some hoped that their daughters' jobs would enable them to marry a man from a better-off family. Finally, over time, the function of the *arisan* proved crucial in the parents' attitudes toward factory employment.

During the early 1980s, when I did the first part of my research, some of the parents expressed pleasure over the goods their daughters had bought with their savings. As described earlier, the importance of such savings became obvious during the crop failure. It is well recognized that peasants do not replicate the capitalist motive of profit maximization. A primary goal of a peasant family is to ensure survival, which may entail accepting lower but steady returns on labor. The risk in this situation is extremely high for those living close to the borderline of survival, and factory employment provides insurance and emergency aid when families are endangered. It stabilizes semiproletarian families.

When I returned to Java in 1986, I found that some of the young women—now wives and mothers—were still working in factories but not so much for the weekly wage as to amass savings with which to build their own houses. The capital they had accumulated was facilitating their moves from extended families into their own nuclear families. These moves were occurring years earlier than they would have had they not worked in factories or had savings. Over time, as events such as crop failures and marriages occurred, the savings had proved more and more useful, and their parents had become more convinced of the benefits of factory employment. Indeed, factory employment has now become a normal part of the female life cycle for almost all younger women in the village.

Summary and Theoretical Discussion

This case study has demonstrated that although female workers are undeniably contributing to their families' economies, parents are subsidizing their daughters' factory wages, which do not begin to meet the subsistence needs of one person. At the very least, most workers live and eat at home. Parents must remain at least partly responsible for their daughters' economic welfare. Factories rationalize paying women below the minimum wage, which is also below subsistence-level, by calling upon existing gender ideology, which is reinforced by the presence of the family and the illusion that the agricultural economy is equitable. Clearly, although the "superexploitation hypothesis" is borne out here, it does not adequately explain other important economic relationships.

The data on the family economy presented here contrast with findings from both historical and contemporary research on female factory workers. The direct weekly or monthly cash remittances the women make to their families are not substantial, and in some cases they are negligible. Factory wages do contribute to the family economy indirectly, however, by providing the workers with cash to meet some of their consumer needs. Likewise, those workers who can afford to participate in savings associations contribute to their families in the long run by providing them with consumer goods, gifts, cash, and, as became apparent over time, insurance against disasters.

While workers and families have benefited economically from the development of an industrial capitalist economy, the factories have benefited from the free goods and services provided by the rural, subsistence-level family economy, resulting in an interdependent intersectoral relationship. Given the minimal employment opportunities available to young rural women, parents may not view partial subsidization as an unusual drain. And given low opportunity costs, the women's access to cash and goods should not be downplayed. The level of exploitation industrial capitalism has imposed on these women is intensified, however, by a combination of factors, particularly their gender, the rural locale, and the presence of the workers' families. The two factors that made the research site unique—the familial context and the rural locale—contributed significantly to the higher level of worker exploitation.

One important theoretical implication stemming from this study is that participating in factory employment may be an indication that proletarianization of the peasantry is increasing or is part of the transition to a capitalist mode of production. Participating in factory work may offset that tendency, however, by allowing rural, semi-proletarian families to reproduce themselves without a loss of goods or status. Thus this research suggests that factory employment is useful for poor families less because it provides daily subsistence than because it ensures their existence in the long run and, at the very least, maintains the status quo. This process appears to reflect "peasantization of wage employment" (Ong 1983:436) as much as the proletarianization of the peasantry.

Propositions drawn from Deere and de Janvry's framework were only partially applicable to this study. The inverse relationship found between class status and labor market integration fits their prediction. In addition, the particular dynamic, that of capitalist firms paying semiproletarian labor wages that are below subsistence-level and that are subsidized for free by the peasant family's labor, also fits their model. Assumptions about how households operate were much less applicable. In their model, "the household" is asserted to function as a unified entity, with one voice and one interest—reproduction. Their assertions concerning the direct contribution of household members' wage income toward household reproduction assumes a high level of control and perhaps altruism not evident in the Javanese household. Although parents enjoyed the consumer goods their daughters bought with their savings and had access to the savings in times of need, parents tended to exert little control over their daughters' wages. While these young women relinquished their savings to parents during times of need, they acted fairly autonomously and somewhat individualistically with respect to their weekly wages.

This situation does not reflect the tightly controlled household discussed in the peasant economy literature (de Janvry 1987), the industrialization and family history literature (Hareven 1982; Tilly and Scott 1978), or studies of rural Java (Hart 1986; White 1976). Some of the differences between Java and other parts of the world could be attributed to the bilateral Javanese kinship system, which traditionally accords women a relatively high degree of economic autonomy. In addition, Javanese parents have little control over the economic decisions of young women pioneering the new life cycle stage of prolonged adolescence, for which there are few traditional norms (Wolf 1988c). This contrasts with the highly patriarchal and patrilineal kinship systems found in East Asia, where parents almost completely control their daughters' decisions, behavior, labor, and income (Salaff 1981; Kung 1983; Greenhalgh 1985).

Another explanation for this difference is that studies of peasants in Java and elsewhere have assumed that households are composed of undifferentiated individuals whose actions are taken for the household's good, as a survival strategy, or to meet collective interests (Folbre 1986; Hart 1988; Watts 1988; Wolf 1988b). In such studies, women are "equated with households" (Ward 1988a:1). Researchers have assumed that any income earned by household members will automatically be pooled within the household (Smith et al. 1984). Indeed, Deere and de Janvry's supposition that any wages received automatically count toward household reproduction is faulty. As a result of this assumption and others like it, the model does not fully account for daughters' behavior or for any other intrahousehold power relationships between genders and generations. Clearly, academic views concerning households in the global economy need to be returned to the drawing board for some serious remodeling.

3

DISGUISED INDUSTRIAL PROLETARIANS IN RURAL LATIN AMERICA: WOMEN'S INFORMAL-SECTOR FACTORY WORK AND THE SOCIAL REPRODUCTION OF COFFEE FARM LABOR IN COLOMBIA

Cynthia Truelove

As industrial capitalism has extended its tentacles further into the rural periphery, scholarly analyses of capitalist social relations have become overly general and at times obsolete. Evidence garnered from social science research during the last thirty years has clarified the unfolding process of the expansion of capitalism to the rural periphery. These analyses resoundingly confirm that the location of waged workers in semi-proletarian rather than in proletarian households has been the statistical norm (Wallerstein 1984). Impressive case studies of regions and households throughout the rural periphery unveil the multifarious ways in which subsistence production interfaces with waged labor to reproduce rural households both socially and physically. Earlier studies demonstrate the

I am grateful to Stephen Bunker, Maria Patricia Fernandez-Kelly, Alejandro Portes, and Kathryn Ward, who each read earlier versions of this chapter and offered their insights as my research progressed. Portions of this chapter appear in my article "The Informal Proletariat Revisited: The Case of the Colombian Mini-Maquilas," in *Crises in the Caribbean: Past and Present*, Richard Tardanico, ed. (Beverly Hills, Calif.: Sage, 1987). The field research on which this chapter is based was funded by the Central American and Caribbean Studies Program of the Johns Hopkins University School for Advanced International Studies, the Fulbright-Hayes Commission's Dissertation Grants Program, and the Inter-American Foundation Doctoral Research Fellowship Program.

increased participation of female members of rural households in subsistence production, accompanied by the partial, or complete, entry of male members of the household into waged labor (Deere 1979). More recent evidence, however, seems to indicate that access to the means of subsistence production is declining among rural female subsistence producers. As a result, these women are entering the ranks of the semiproletariat and, as the following Colombian case reveals, are at times functioning as disguised waged laborers whose wages contribute to the reproduction of less proletarianized male household members. This process constitutes a reversal of the earlier arrangement and raises new questions about gender relations under the expansion of industrial capitalism.

The decline in subsistence production comes at a time when both core and peripheral industrialists are seeking new sources of cheap labor for incorporation into production hierarchies in locations from rural Malaysia to the Silicon Valley in California. To keep production costs down in the face of highly competitive markets, and to squelch the demands of organized labor, these industrialists continue to search for unprotected, or informal, laborers. They thus avoid having to pay social security benefits and taxes and are not subject to labor legislation.

This chapter focuses on informal-sector women who are employed as piece-rate workers in rural factories of southwestern Colombia. It provides evidence that the unprotected employment of these women, whose labor is subcontracted by both multinational and national industries, makes possible the social reproduction of male seasonal coffee laborers and small-scale coffee producers. A critical finding of this case study is that outsourcing arrangements have expanded to include rural, subcontracted laborers who are directly linked to commercial agricultural production. Specifically, this case explores the structural arrangements through which commercial agriculture in the Valle Department of Colombia collaborates with multinational and national industries to reduce migration while providing a source of unprotected labor.

DISGUISED INDUSTRIAL WORKERS: THE CASE OF THE COLOMBIAN MINI-MAQUILA

The assembly factories of the Talleres Rurales del Valle (TRV) Precooperative, located in the coffee-producing zone immediately north of Cali in southwestern Colombia, were established jointly by the Valle Departmental Committee of Coffee Growers and the committee's social assistance agency, the Central de Cooperativas Agrarias de Occidente, Ltds (CENCOA), on September 15, 1974, with the following stated objectives:[1]

> a) to lend dignity to the peasant woman; b) to diminish rural to urban migration; c) to diversify the income of rural families; d) to provide educational experiences to rural women; e) to integrate women into the national economy; f) to unleash the productive processes which can come through the applied use of cooperative methods; and g) to establish a sound foundation for the development of a legally recognized cooperative at a later data. (CENCOA 1978:4)

The first two factories were located in the small rural towns of Venecia and San Antonio in the Valle Department. They produced commercial clothing and stitched the uppers for the cloth shoe industry. Since the level of production remained fairly low for the first two years of operation, representatives of the Valle Departmental Committee of Coffee Growers pursued more formal ties with national and multinational industries. By late 1975, arrangements were completed with Croydon/UniRoyal of Colombia to subcontract work from Croydon to the TRV program.

According to the present executive director of the TRV program, Croydon was eager to link its operations with the program as part of a larger campaign to dismantle its formal-sector plant operations in nearby Cali. Representatives of Croydon argued that the costs of social benefits for the factory workers had risen to the point of making Croydon's athletic shoes less competitive with similar shoes

---

1. The TRV program was initially established as a "precooperative" under Colombian legal statutes governing cooperative enterprises. The law states that during the first ten years of operation an established patron organization shall retain legal guardianship of the newer cooperative. Legal guardianship entails that the patron organization retain the majority of the voting members on the cooperative executive committee and oversee the cooperative's accounting, expenditures, and general revenues. In 1986, the TRV precooperative was legally upgraded to a fully autonomous cooperative, although extra-legal mechanisms remain in place that reinforce the control of the Valle Departmental Coffee Growers Committee, the initial patron organization. For example, the cooperative's executive director is still selected, managed, and partially paid by the committee, although the membership of the cooperative officially retains the right to fire and hire this person.

legally imported to Colombia or sold on the black market. Having established subcontracting agreements with the TRV program, Croydon closed its formal operations in southern Colombia. The company gave part of its machinery to the TRV program and the remaining portion to retired Croydon employees, who themselves became labor contractors who employed an informal-sector labor force.

Throughout the 1970s, Croydon remained one of the TRV program's chief clients, and the number of rural mini-maquilas grew to meet the demands of contracts to stitch athletic shoes, jute sandals, and other products. By 1976, the first two factories legally annulled their individual status as separate nonprofit enterprises and were incorporated, along with six newer *talleres*, or workshops, into the Talleres Rurales del Valle Precooperative, Limited.

The legal documents creating the TRV program state that the Valle Departmental Committee of Coffee Growers and CENCOA were to be the legal advisers and the entities to which the TRV program was to be subject for a term of ten years. This arrangement, which is standard for Colombian cooperative enterprises, supposedly favors newly constituted groups, which may not possess the administrative training necessary to accept the legal responsibilities associated with producer cooperatives. While the latter is certainly the case for a number of newly organized agricultural producers' cooperatives, the consequences of the precooperative arrangement for the women who work in the TRV program's rural assembly factories merit particular attention.

Under the initial arrangement with the Valle Departmental Committee of Coffee Growers, the TRV program, and particularly the individual mini-maquilas, ceded their rights to participate in the negotiation of contracts for the piece-rate wages for which they worked. The TRV program retained less that half ownership of the program's assets and had only limited representation in the direction of the enterprise. Management of the program rested in the hands of an executive director who was appointed by the committee and who reported directly to its members regarding the daily management of the program.

As one publication about the TRV program states, the Committee of Coffee Growers is in charge of planning and financing the groups according to proposals presented by local municipalities regarding the installation of a new factory based on socioeconomic studies of each region. The committee determines the most viable locations for erecting factories based on criteria related to coffee production and local social conditions. The committee is also involved in planning production in the factories, arranging contracts pertaining to the sale of manual labor, and diversification of lines of production (CENCOA 1978:8).

The legacy of this arrangement has been the centralization of managerial power in the hands of the committee, insofar as it is ultimately responsible for negotiating contracts with national and international industries. In turn, this arrangement is advantageous to industrial firms since they are able to get contracts with rates favorable to their cost-saving interests without having to negotiate directly with cooperative members, who as piece-rate workers are more likely to push for higher pay for each unit produced. Thus both the committee and the industrial firms limit the participation of cooperative members in the preparation of contracts for the sale of their labor.

When the TRV program reached full cooperative status under the law, in 1986, the mechanisms for self-management were put in place. But the legacy of dependence on the Committee of Coffee Growers for daily management and for the negotiation of contracts left a rigid hierarchy in place, and the workers remained at the bottom of the power pyramid. While legal responsibility for managing the cooperative actually rests with an executive council, composed principally of cooperative members, day-to-day operations of the enterprise rely on the extra-legal role of the Committee of Coffee Growers. Investment of working assets for health, education, and insurance, for example, is managed by the president of the Coffee Bank (Banco Cafetero), who also serves on the executive council. Though the worker representatives on the council can legally demand control of these funds, this responsibility remains under the control of the president of the Coffee Bank because of his expertise in financial management. No attempts have been made to assist the workers in acquiring similar skills.

The women who participate in the TRV program have general membership assemblies, elect representatives to an executive council, and theoretically may be appointed to submanagerial positions at the level of the workshop; they have been unable, however, to alter the policies that most affect their lives as piece-rate workers. The women are officially classified as "*socias*," or members of a worker-managed cooperative, but this status is primarily a legal convenience for industry and the executive branch of the TRV. As will be discussed later, the women in the rural cooperative factories function as piece-rate laborers for an intermediary that is responsible for managing them, for administering finances for the cooperative, and for negotiating contracts. Neither industry nor the social service agency is responsible for indirect wages, such as social welfare payments or retirement. Moreover, the cooperative status of the TRV program permits the process by which the piece-rate workers must provide for their own reproduction since the services they receive (i.e., health, education, and retirement) are paid for through a general assets fund built from the forced contributions of a percentage of each worker's monthly wage. Thus the companies subcontracting to the rural factories avoid paying the benefits that are guaranteed to legally protected workers while members of the cooperatives provide their own insurance and health care based on what they earn through piece work.

SUBCONTRACTING AND THE COLOMBIAN MINI-MAQUILAS

During the years of its operation, the TRV program has retained subcontracting arrangements with a variety of national and international firms. Under Colombian legislation entitled the Plan Vallejo, partially processed industrial goods, such as those assembled in the TRV mini-maquilas, may be brought into the country duty-free and are protected under article 806.7.3 so that they may reimported into the United States. Under the provisions of article 806.7.3, U.S. firms pay duties based only on the value added abroad (Nash and Fernandez-Kelly 1983).

According to estimates provided by an official of the Colombian Agency for Export Promotion (PROEXPO) for 1984, the TRV program was among the top five Colombian firms involved in off-shore assembly arrangements with U.S. industry. Subcontracting agreements have been made with London Fog, Bobbie Brooks, College Town, and Levi-Strauss. Though the TRV program discontinued its participation in the Plan Vallejo for 1985 and 1986 because of problems associated with the late delivery of assembled goods, plans are under way for major expansion into two new areas where it is expected that two new plants will employ approximately three hundred cooperative members to do assembly work for the U.S. company K-Mart.

The mini-maquilas are also a key source of disguised wage labor for the ailing Colombian textile industry, located in the Antioquia Department. Since the decline of the Colombian textile industry in both the national and international markets, Colombian textile producers have strategically pursued segmented production arrangements. Thus simple garments are cut in the formal factories and sent to the mini-maquilas for stitching. The TRV program retains contracts with Fabricato, Linea Senorial, MultiHogar, Manizol, Lindo Hogar, and Everfit of Colombia, among others.

Simple comparisons of working conditions and labor relations in the TRV program's mini-maquilas with those of other off-shore assembly operations is difficult. The TRV program functions, at least legally, as a workers' cooperative. Thus there is access to limited benefits, including medical services, family educational loans, rotating loans for domestic crises, limited life insurance, and dormitory facilities for women who live too far away to commute. Nevertheless, the women are by no means "given" these services, which are considered overhead in the initial calculation of the piece-rate wage. The women receive 70 percent of the piece-rate wage as base pay. The workers may earn more than the base pay through a production incentive system. The women themselves are responsible for generating the 30 percent margin necessary to receive the social services and other benefits; industry *does not* provide this indirect wage.

The TRV program claims to function as a cooperative social education program for rural women. Yet, like other maquilas, it clearly discriminates against certain women through selective entry policies. In the past, potential candidates had to be fifteen to forty years old. Furthermore, they were subjected to a "test" period to ensure they could "adapt" to the work and accommodate to the "spirit" of cooperativism. As an ideology, cooperativism promotes a sense of teamwork among TRV laborers and helps reduce tensions between the workshops, which operate at differing levels of profitability and efficiency. Tense relations have developed in some instances, for example, when less successful workshops have contributed substantially less to the TRV program than other workshops during plant stoppages or while they waited for a long time to receive new contracts.

Beginning in 1984, the TRV program began to administer manual dexterity tests to potential cooperative members. The women I interviewed did not have any specific reaction to the test. Nonetheless, the chief social worker for the TRV program admitted that she had heard complaints from women whose daughters, sisters, and other relatives had been denied entry into the program. The social workers responsible for reviewing applications for entry into the program explained that they are coached by management to judge the physical attributes of the women they interview. For example, they are told to "look for good hands" since management assumes that women whose hands are calloused and cracked are less adept at fine and intricate sewing. The social workers also note whether applicants exhibit eye strain or have unusually thick glasses and their general attitude.

Labor relations in the TRV program have begun to show signs of worker-management tension in the last few years. Perhaps the keenest example of this tension took place in the Venecia workshop in 1982 when management reportedly would not provide the Christmas vacation benefits the members felt they deserved. Summoning the executive director for consultation, the women called a workshop meeting at which they proceeded to surround the executive director and lock him in the workshop for an entire day and part of an evening.

Work stoppages have occurred in some workshops because the women felt they were being forced to work too many shifts and the negotiated piece rate represented less time than it took to produce a product. A prime example is the piece rate negotiated with Catalina for the production of bathing suits. Sewing bathing suits requires precise manipulation of miniscule stitches, tiny straps, and small pieces of elastic. According to the women in the workshop, this process takes much more time than the production engineers who calculate the piece rate estimated. The women have asked to be included in the time and motion studies used to calculate piece rates since they claim to have a more realistic view of efficiency, timing, and the like. They have been told that "production engineers have to go to college to learn to do these studies" and that conducting these studies requires skills that the women do not possess.

To the outside observer, it is clear that worker-management relations in the TRV program are more characteristic of profit-making industry than of worker-operated or worker-owned production. While the surplus value generated through this labor arrangement is directly manifested in the profit generated for industry through the employ of cheaper labor, the larger goals of the Valle Departmental Committee of Coffee Growers are directly related to its own survival needs in the face of an increasingly unstable international coffee market.

THE CONJUNCTURE OF THE COFFEE MARKET
AND THE MINI-MAQUILAS

Since the mid-1880s, coffee has constituted one of the key sources of foreign exchange for the Colombian national economy. Consequently, the interests of coffee growers and producers have been among the most articulated private-sector interests in Colombia. The Federacion Nacional de Cafeteros Colombianos (Colombian Federation of Coffee Growers—FNCC) is by far the key private-sector organization in Colombia because of the international, national, and regional resources it commands. Many interest groups merely articulate desired political and economic outcomes in the countries where they operate. The FNCC, however, is particularly powerful at regional and local levels in that its decisions regarding exports clearly affect coffee cultivation.

The FNCC is composed of departmental committees through which all coffee in Colombia is officially required to pass before it may be sold internally or exported. Each departmental committee contributes a specified amount of coffee to the FNCC. Based on a formula that gives preference to the departments in order of the amount of coffee they produce annually, the FNCC apportions departmental contributions to the national exports. Based on this system of differential contributions, departmental committees receive different budgets for their production and political activities (Palacios 1980).

Of particular relevance here is the decline in the total coffee exports attributable to the Valle Department of Colombia. Since the mid-1970s, the Valle Department has dropped from second to fourth place in its contribution to coffee exports. The reasons for this drop are the diminished output by small-scale coffee producers and the increased rates of rural-to-urban migration by seasonal manual laborers who harvest coffee on farms in the department's highland communities. In the mid-1970s, as the introduction of Green Revolution varieties of coffee in surrounding departments increased the work opportunities in those areas, landless male coffee pickers from the North Valle began to migrate to these areas, creating a shortage of available labor for the Valle coffee farms. The Valle Departmental Committee of Coffee Growers responded by initiating a variety of social welfare programs to "improve the lives of small producers and those of the small towns and villages where they reside" (CENCOA 1978).

CENCOA, one of the first social assistance agencies organized by the Valle Departmental Committee of Coffee Growers, has worked to promote rural cooperatives of small-scale coffee producers and their families throughout the Valle Department. Its stated goal is the improvement of coffee production through cooperativism. As a recognized nonprofit organization, CENCOA has received grants from international development assistance agencies as well as from the Inter-American Development Bank. CENCOA has become the direct channel through which the Valle Departmental Committee of Coffee Growers has sought to ameliorate the social conditions that threaten the level of coffee production in the region. The primary return on this collaborative effort has been the survival of a relatively healthy and nourished rural labor force for seasonal work in coffee harvesting.

In the 1970s, the committee became particularly concerned with "dead time" between the harvesting seasons, as a result of the decline in the number of small plots held by individuals who cultivated subsistence crops during the off season and the outmigration of large numbers of persons in search of more steady and remunerative work. Thus the committee's director reportedly searched for programs that CENCOA might organize to bring additional sources of income to the families of small-scale coffee producers and seasonal laborers. In 1973, after consultation with managers of multinational and national industries, the Committee of Coffee Growers decided to assist CENCOA in organizing the TRV program.

As discussed above, the timing of this effort to stay migration coincided with that of the textile and shoe industries' need to reduce the number of formal employees. Thus the establishment of the TRV program enabled an integration of the interests of both agrarian and industrial sectors.

Surveys completed by the TRV social work staff have found that at least 60 percent of the fathers of the female TRV workers own plots of land with fewer than six plaza (one plaza is approximately three-quarters of an acre); that 60 to 70 percent of their fathers, husbands, and brothers work as day laborers; and that the women's wages represent one-half to three-fourths of their household's income, depending on which workshop is surveyed (CENCOA 1983). These findings further confirm that the households most affected by the TRV program are composed of small-scale coffee producers and coffee pickers. The relatively high percentage of their salaries that the women contribute to their households has direct consequences for the maintenance of the coffee-producing labor force in the area. According to personal interviews I conducted with some of the women, their work in the mini-maquilas generates far more than supplementary income for their families. In most families, the women's wages are the only steady source of income, and they are necessary to maintain the household unit throughout the year.

This case, and similar cases in the rural periphery, encapsulate the dynamics behind the expansion of piece-rate wage labor arrangements that specifically link female informal workers, multinational industry, and large-scale commercial agricultural production. As informal proletarians whose wages are the bedrock for the maintenance and reproduction of informal agricultural producers and workers, the women in the TRV program provide important insights into some of the components of the unequal exchange equation within the rural periphery itself and between core and peripheral economies. As informal workers in the employ of multinational industry, they are critical to the perpetuation of dependent forms of economic development wherein national firms are tied to multinationals for raw materials, technology, and markets (Evans 1979). At the same time, the informal employment of these rural women structurally underwrites the continuation of more classical forms of economic dependence tied to the exportation of primary products. Coffee continues to be an important source of foreign exchange and national capital in Colombia, and its position in the world market depends on the maintenance of competitive prices, which are directly associated with the maintenance of competitive labor costs vis-à-vis other peripheral labor markets where coffee is produced.

This new evidence of the more direct articulation of classical and dependent forms of development—primary product agricultural exports and core-dependent industrialization linked by the work of rural females employed as informal-sector proletarians—raises key questions about earlier approaches to the study of development in the rural periphery. First, the recent tendency to explain the wage differences between core and peripheral economies as a result of the expansion of urban informal labor to the exclusion of similar production arrangements in the rural periphery needs to be reconsidered.

Second, the classification and analysis of economic development strategies in the periphery as either classical (primary commodities are exported) or dependent (industrialization is core-centered) merit further attention. A refined analysis of exchange relations in the periphery may present new evidence of the continued articulation of forms of industrialization and primary commodity exchange in the world market. Finally, how and under what conditions rural women are incorporated into the global assembly line raises critical questions about the impact of dependent development strategies on the lives of rural women and on the households in which they live.

GENDER AND DEPENDENT DEVELOPMENT

The expanded participation of female workers in the global assembly line since the 1950s has provided critical data on the working conditions associated with multinational subcontracting industries in the periphery (see Safa 1981, 1984; Sassen-Koob 1984; Nash and Fernandez-Kelly 1983; Fernandez-Kelly 1983; Lim 1985; Ward 1986). This research, as well as more recent theoretical debates focusing on the physical and social reproduction of the labor force (Beneria 1979; Deere 1979; Leon de Leal 1980), are critical to an understanding of the ways in which labor is absorbed into the production hierarchies in the world economy (Portes and Benton 1984).

The effect of dependent development on women's incorporation into the labor force has recently become a point of debate among scholars discussing the role of women in the periphery. Most researchers agree that dependent development has negative consequences for female proletarians and for women engaged in subsistence production. In her work on dependent development in Puerto Rico since Operation Bootstrap in the 1950s, Helen Safa (1984) reveals that both absolute and relative rates of labor force participation among women in the manufacturing sector have increased substantially. Research conducted by Saskia Sassen-Koob (1984) and others demonstrates that the overall participation rate for women in the industrial labor force has also increased significantly in those nations where development strategies have explicitly focused on export processing. Yet studies that have attempted to predict the status of women in particular peripheral economies utilizing core-peripheral dependency as an indicator reveal that, on the whole, women are still relegated to the service sectors and that their overall participation rates in the manufacturing sector remain low (Ward 1984).

We must be concerned with these somewhat contrasting findings if we are to identify the determinants of the gender division of labor in the peripheral labor force and its relationship to core-peripheral exploitation in the world system. Ward's work (1986), which is based on data from the International Labor Organization, cannot account for the informal-sector participation of women in the industrial labor force and hence may severely underestimate women's role in manufacturing activities while inflating their role in the "service" sector. The data more than likely subsume production *as well as* service activities whose locus is the informal sector. At the same time, separate case studies of women's formal and informal production activities in the periphery may obscure more macro processes and thereby result in findings that are not generalizable to other peripheral contexts. Left unanswered is the question of what critical dynamics affect the nature of women's incorporation into the work force during capitalist expansion into the periphery.

Recent studies on the process of expansion of the informal sector and the restructuring of the labor process in the core and the periphery provide solid evidence of the feminization of the most exploited segments of the paid labor force (Nash and Fernandez-Kelly 1983; Sassen-Koob 1984; Fernandez-Kelly 1985; Beneria 1985; Roldan 1985; Beneria and Roldan 1987). Although these theories contribute invaluable insights into the unpredicted expansion of the segmented international labor force, they do not provide sufficient explanations for the feminization of the unprotected industrial labor force (Roldan 1985).

This study demonstrates that only one set of options is available to capital to increase relative surplus value when female unprotected laborers are incorporated into segmented production arrangements. The TRV case and similar studies enhance our understanding of the complex processes through which the sexual division of labor reproduces and transforms the world economy. Since a great deal of information regarding the explicit participation of women in the manufacturing sectors in the periphery has gone unrecorded or been misclassified, it is hard to study the effects of dependent forms of development on women and even more challenging to compare these effects within peripheral economies. The inclusion of "disguised" proletarians and the recognition of the critical role of the informal sector in data collection in peripheral economies will significantly advance the validity and reliability of empirical research on the status of women under conditions of dependent development. The studies included in this volume contribute substantial findings to this knowledge.

More data on the various modes of participation by women in the rural and urban periphery will further demystify unequal exchange processes. In the absence of more reliable aggregate data, we must depend on case studies to answer our questions about women's role in the world system.

Case studies, including several cited in volumes mentioned above, demonstrate strong evidence of the increased location of female laborers in the informal proletariat. In most cases, these workers are functioning as disguised proletarians who provide below-minimum-wage labor either to national or multinational industries in the periphery. What explains this propensity of capital increasingly to incorporate female waged labor into industrial production? While capital's search for wages that fall below the social average is clearly a means to increase surplus value, the question of how gender relations function to retain the actual value of women's labor below the social wage has no single answer in that this is a variable social process whose differences are manifested within peripheral economies and between the core and the periphery.

CONCLUSION

This chapter has attempted to reveal the nexus within which informal proletarian women in the rural periphery reproduce household units composed of themselves and semiproletarian agricultural laborers. The relationship between the segmented informal labor market in the rural periphery and the reproduction of both classical and dependent forms of development appears to depend on the nature of the incorporation of female laborers. The degree to which one is able to decipher the complexities of unequal exchange are probably related to one's capacity to understand the ways in which gender and labor relations interact under specific conditions within the world economy.

Recent research on the informal sector in the periphery demonstrates that mobility for female informal-sector workers differs significantly within the periphery. While empirical research demonstrates that women are more likely to hold the most exploitative and lowest-paying jobs in the unprotected labor force, variation does exist with regard to women's informal-sector work in the world economy.

The reasons for the differences in mobility appear to be related to the position of the specific peripheral nation in the world economy and to the effect that differing modes of incorporation into the world system may have on the peripheral labor market. The particular social relations with regard to cultural expressions of capitalist patriarchy also seem to account for the ways in which women are exploited as informal laborers.

As the case of the Colombian mini-maquilas demonstrates, significant numbers of laborers who exercise an important role in international production are unaccounted for when dualistic criteria are applied to the measurement of labor market participation rates in the periphery. Consequently, the industrial work of significant numbers of rural and urban women disappears from view and we lose sight of one of the most important ways in which the capitalist world system is reproduced.

4

"FAÇON": WOMEN'S FORMAL AND INFORMAL WORK IN THE GARMENT INDUSTRY IN KAVALA, GREECE

Joanna Hadjicostandi

This is a regular day for me: get up at 5:30 A.M to prepare breakfast, and sometimes the main meal so my husband can have lunch. Then I have to prepare my son for school and the baby for his grandmother's home. I am lucky that my Petros [her husband] drops them off, so I can be at work by seven. When I get home after work, I have to take care of the rest of the housework tasks, prepare for dinner, and help my son with his homework. I usually do not go to bed before 12 midnight. (Hadjicostandi 1987)

The 1985 Nairobi International Women's Conference, which marked the end of the United Nations Decade for Women and its World Plan of Action, underscored the need for a more careful assessment of changes in women's participation in world economic development. Despite the U.N.'s commitment to women's equality and the many proposals aimed at women in development, numerous reports have revealed that, although a few women have entered high-paying, high-status occupations, there has been little improvement for most women in the Third World or for lower-class women in the "developed" world. Given that women have indeed been integrated in some fashion in the economies of their countries, the problem is not the lack of integration into the development process but the manner in which they are being integrated in production (as well as politics and reproduction).

Since the mid-1960s, industrial production has been internationalized at an increasingly rapid pace. Through direct investment or subcontracting arrangements, corporations from the United States and other industrialized countries have shifted many of their labor-intensive operations to low-wage export processing zones (EPZs) in Third World countries.[1] The availability of cheap female labor has become the primary criterion for investment, especially in garment manufacturing, textiles, electronics, and food processing (Enloe 1983; Fernandez-Kelly 1983; Fuentes and Ehrenreich 1983; Lim 1983a; Nash 1983; Safa 1981; Elson and Pearson 1981a). The introduction of large-scale commodity production outside the home, as well as the establishment of waged labor as the main source of family income, accounts for the increasing availability of women's waged labor in the international division of labor and in changes in the gender division of labor within the family (Beneria and Sen 1981). On the local level, existing divisions of labor have been transformed unevenly. Nonetheless, despite the increase in women's participation in the waged labor force in both "developed" and Third World countries, women still hold a disproportionate number of jobs in low-status occupations, many of which are in the low-paid "informal" labor market. These jobs are usually underrecorded in official statistics (Rollins 1986; Arizipe 1977; Jelin 1977). Helen Safa (1981) notes that the wage levels, working conditions, stability, and possibilities for occupational mobility offered Third World women by industrial employment could simply amount to a new form of exploitation and subordination. The statement quoted at the beginning of the chapter is representative.

Gender has become central in refining theories of development in the past three decades and has been incorporated as a key variable in the examination of women's changing status and sociopolitical and economic roles in both industrialized and Third World countries. This examination has taken place within two distinct paradigms. On the one hand, modernization theories that derive from classical and neoclassical economics explain women's status chiefly

---

1. Export processing zones are areas that attract foreign capital investment because of the many benefits provided, including the low-wage labor, minimal tax requirements, and few or no trade union demands for safety and health standards.

in terms of the degree to which they participate in production roles outside the home. As a result, such modernization theorists stress individualist solutions such as increases in education or factory work as most important in changing women's roles and status (Inkeles 1983; Marshal 1978). On the other hand, theorists within a Marxist tradition emphasize the effects on women of changes brought about by capitalist relations of production and class antagonisms, especially in societies where precapitalist relations still exist.

Women's conditions are very specific to their national economies, and, although domestic activities are overwhelmingly performed by women across countries, the differences are quite clear. Also, female and male workers are absorbed into the international political economy at different rates and under different conditions. Thus the new relations, while influential, can transform neither existing techniques of production contained in the division of labor nor family relations into "modern" ones. The particular way in which capitalist production is articulated with precapitalist modes of production is an important determinant of the economic action necessary to sustain people.

Given the different nature of women's participation in both the labor market and the domestic sphere, we need to understand the complexity of articulation between the existing modes of production and between production and reproduction to explain the gender division of labor as well as changes in women's status (Hen 1988; Beneria and Sen 1981; Deere 1986; Safa 1981).[2]

Garment manufacturing for export, based on foreign capital investment, has expanded during the past twenty-five years in northern Greece, and the industry employs predominantly women. In this chapter the impact of industrial expansion on women's status in the northern Greek city of Kavala is evaluated. The data were obtained in 1986 from a sample of sixty women who worked in the garment manufacturing industry in Kavala. In-depth interviews with factory workers (formal economy) and with home piece workers ("informal" economy) and nonparticipant observation provided a wealth of in-

---

2. Women's work is largely assumed to be within the sphere of social reproduction. This includes reproduction of the labor power on a daily basis (domestic work or daily maintenance activity) and the reproduction of labor over time (biological and child rearing).

formation about the women's background, family position, economic participation in the family, and trade union participation, as well as other detailed economic, attitudinal, and behavioral information.[3] The selection of the samples from both the formal and "informal" economy had a twofold purpose: first, to make possible an evaluation of the differences and similarities between the two groups of women, using the home piece workers as a control group; and second, to shed light on the little researched area of home piece-work employment known in Greece as *"façon."*[4] In both cases the women did the same type of work, assembling garments, but their conditions and circumstances were distinctly different. The factory workers were restricted to a specific, closely supervised environment, whereas the piece workers worked at home or in a small workshop attached to the home and considered an extension of it.

This study analyzes women's integration into international development by addressing the interconnections between international capital accumulation, class formation, and gender relations within a theoretical framework based on the articulation between modes of production and between production and reproduction.

WOMEN IN THE GREEK LABOR MARKET AND FAMILY

The turn of the century found Greece economically stagnant and politically devastated. Feudalist relations of production still persisted despite the expansion of trade and the establishment of small-scale manufacturing. The majority of Greek women and men were peasants and strongly tied to the land. The state, first the Ottoman and then the Greek, supported feudalist production because it owned

---

3. The formal economy is defined as paid work that is state regulated and in which employees have access to Social Security and fringe benefits. The informal economy here refers to *paid* work done outside the arena of the formal, regulated economy. It usually escapes official record keeping and can be poorly paid, irregular, unprotected, nonunionized, and has no Social Security or other fringe benefits. There is an ongoing debate in the literature over the formal versus informal economy (see Portes and Sassen-Koob 1987; Redclift and Mingione 1985; Hadjicostandi 1983, 1987; Bromley 1978; Moser 1978).

4. *Façon* is the French word for *subcontracting*. It is used very commonly in Greece with reference to piece work.

the largest part of the land. The transition from feudalism to capitalism, which began in the late 1800s, was very slow. According to
Pandelis Agianoglou (1982:12), the beginning of the change was
generated by class contradictions that arose as a result of the redis-
tribution of about three-quarters of the arable land in 1871. Before
the 1922 war in Asia Minor, which displaced thousands of Greeks
both inside Greece and in Asia Minor, local and diaspora capital
were invested in trade, not manufacturing. Many historians, economists, and other social analysts see this as the main reason Greek
capitalist "development" was so delayed. Only after 1927 was investment capital poured into industrial development, and this was
linked more to changes in the objective structural conditions within
Greece itself than to the shift in capital investment from trade to
industry (Agianoglou 1982:13–14). Nicos Mouzelis (1978:3–29) argues that Greek capitalism did not really take off until the interwar
and postwar years.

Today Greece stands in the gray area between "developed" and
Third World countries. Its economy is usually classified as semiperipheral, meaning that it has many of the contradictions and social
characteristics of both advanced and Third World countries.
Women, who were at the forefront of the long war of independence
from the Ottoman empire, not only constituted the main agricultural
force in the beginning of the century but also held an important
role as a source of cheap labor during the early years of industrialization. During the mechanization and commercialization of
agriculture, however, increasingly more men were employed in agriculture, and peasant women were led to industrial employment.
By 1928, about 23 percent of the economically active population in
manufacturing was female. Women thus were on the front line of
capitalist expansion, especially in textile, tobacco, and soft-drink
manufacturing. The gender inequalities in the labor market had
already been clearly established (Mears 1928), for women were un-
derpaid and unprotected by the state.

Women's position in the labor force did not alter dramatically until
sharp changes occurred in the Greek economy during the period
following World War II.[6] But although postwar industrial devel-

---

6. See Papandreou 1981 for elaboration on multinational expansion in Greece.
See Mousourou 1985 for further information on women's position in Greece.

opment was impressive, it did not mean the end of small, low-productivity industrial (i.e., footwear, clothing, and leather products)
units, which usually employed women at very low wages. Meanwhile,
capitalist economic development failed to support agricultural development and allowed family-based, low-productivity units to continue to exist (Mouzelis 1978:122). Furthermore, postwar economic
growth was accompanied by heightened income inequalities, persistent unemployment, massive flight to the cities, foreign migration,
and increased dependence on the United States and western Europe.
Capitalist expansion did not destroy all preexisting forms of labor
organization. On the contrary, a coexistence of capitalist and non-
capitalist ways of production is observed. According to Nicos Mouzelis, those engaged in agriculture became progressively worse off as
agricultural per capita income dropped from 83.3 percent of the
average income to 51.1 percent from 1951 to 1970 (1978:122–23).
The mass exodus of the rural population to the cities and then to
the European countries in search of better living conditions is thus
understandable.[7] Has industrialization provided for the improvement of people's condition? How has it affected women's position
and status?

A limited number of empirical studies have been done on the
effect of industrialization on the status of women in Greece. Joanna
Lambiri-Dimaki (1965) pioneered this line of work in her research
on women factory workers in the town of Megara. She concluded
that, despite the economic benefits it offered, the new work environment had affected women's ideas and values more than it had
provided them with an independent way of life and position in the
patriarchal family. She further found that women still adhered to
the "traditional" values of obeying their families, marrying early,
and acquiring a dowry. Thus any changes that did occur were in
the women's ideas rather than in their social actions. A study by
Magda Nikolaidou (1975) of the same town and factory fifteen years
later confirmed many of Lambiri-Dimaki's findings. Nikolaidou argues that a "cultural lag" was created because it took so long for the
society to accept the change in women's occupational roles. Although

---

7. For elaboration on the migration movements in Greece, see Kassimati 1984 (in
Greek); Filias 1975; Kudat and Nikolinakos 1975; Lianos 1975; Nikolinakos 1974
(in Greek).

paid employment enabled women to shake some traditional roles, their roles within the family remained the same. Nikolaidou further noted that the way the dowry was accumulated had changed: originally, all of it was given by the father, whereas now women worked for it. Finally, she concluded that women worked out of economic necessity. Such conditions are not evidence of drastic changes in their status, however, since traditional values and roles were constantly being reproduced in the workplace. I examined several of the findings from these earlier studies in my study, which took place in Kavala.

WOMEN IN THE KAVALA GARMENT INDUSTRY

Kavala, in northern Greece, is one of the most rapidly industrializing cities in the country, although its people still hold preindustrial ("traditional") values. In the early 1960s, Kavala's industrial infrastructure was minimal. Production was based on the processing of tobacco products and to a lesser extent on small-scale fish processing based on local fishing, olive-oil refinement, and textile manufacturing. Most of the industries were small and employed women on a seasonal basis, while men were usually occupied in small commercial enterprises. A chemical fertilizer plant, established a few miles from the city in 1960, employed men from Kavala and the surrounding area as unskilled laborers, mostly in construction. This did not solve the unemployment and underemployment problem, however, and in the 1960s the town witnessed staggering exoduses of both men and women laborers to various parts of Europe (i.e., Switzerland, France, and especially Germany) and to other parts of the world. This trend culminated in the 1970s when German and Greek migration policies changed. Migrants thus returned to Greece, mostly to big cities close to their villages. Many invested in businesses that had subcontracting arrangements with firms in Europe, especially Germany.[8] The garment industry provided many such opportunities. Cloth, usually

---

8. Upon their return to Greece, the workers, of course, hurried to buy their own houses, comfortable furniture, and other consumer goods. This appeared to be the ultimate dream of many migrant workers. Not surprisingly, very few emigrants returned to their villages to assume agricultural pursuits.

precut, was imported to Greece for assembly only and then exported as finished or semifinished products. Frequently, accessories for the assembly of clothes, such as thread and buttons, accompanied the shipment. This increase in export manufacturing provided employment for local Kavala women.

Government policies concerning subcontract manufacturing (similar to those in most export processing zones) prevent the sale of the garments in the local market. Subcontractors are thus parasites of the Greek economy: as a whole, manufacturers utilize almost no goods produced in the national market, and the final product is exported immediately. Subcontractors have a secure and stable income as long as they can guarantee good and reliable service to their foreign partners. And because they do not have to supply the local market, they are free of its irregularities. Statistics obtained from the records of the Union of Garment Export Manufacturers of East Macedonia and Thrace indicate that in 1983, 40 percent of the export garment factories of Macedonia and Thrace were established in the county of Kavala (34 percent in Drama, 11 percent in each of the areas of Komotini and Xanthy, and 5 percent in Evros).

The first sample of 50 women for my study was randomly drawn from a population of 206 women employed in two garment factories in Kavala. The second sample of 10 home piece workers was selected from the population of Kavala through informants.

The informal nature of home work and the absence of any official records made selection of the home workers a herculean task. The population of home workers in the greater Kavala area was not explored nor were home workers outside the garment industry. Data were obtained through in-depth interviews and through nonparticipant observation.

Garment Workers and the Household Economy

My findings indicate that there were no great differences in marital status, age, family size, household composition, social conditions, or family background between the home workers and the factory workers. The majority of women in both samples were between twenty-five and forty years old and married.

Before obtaining their present jobs, the majority of women in both samples either had been at home taking care of housework and other family-related duties (about one-third were not old enough to work) or had occasional jobs in other factories. Four women, two from each sample, reported having worked in factories in Germany and had found the experience rewarding. They preferred the working conditions abroad but had found the work to be more intense and alienating.

Those factory and home workers who had worked on the land were all married and older than twenty-five. Very few still had any agricultural duties. Two of the factory workers had been involved in office work before securing their present jobs, and two had been attending high school. One home worker told of washing clothes for wealthy households, but since the families had purchased washing machines, this had become an increasingly unstable activity and she had sought alternative means of earning an income. The majority of women considered these earnings as "pocket" money, however. The length of employment (or lack thereof) before seeking work in the factory appeared to be of crucial significance when correlated with other demographic factors, such as age or marital status. Most of the women had unstable incomes before they took their present positions, and most had relied on their parents or husbands for pocket money.

When asked about their motives in seeking their present work, most of the women were surprised and considered the reasons to be quite obvious: women had to seek jobs outside the household out of economic necessity. The overwhelming majority of the women came from working-class families where one wage was not enough to sustain the family. A high percentage of the spouses of both the factory and home workers were involved in seasonal work (41 percent and 43 percent respectively) and thus had unstable incomes; 27 percent and 43 percent owned small businesses such as restaurants or retail stores; and 29 percent and 14 percent were white-collar workers. Only 3 percent of the factory and none of the home workers' husbands were full-time farmers. This is not surprising, however, considering migration from and to the city of Kavala.

Eighty percent of the respondents revealed that family economic support or the capacity to supplement the family income was the main motive for seeking employment. Only 6 percent of the factory workers and none of the home workers decided to work to escape family pressure. Fourteen percent of the factory workers and 20 percent of the home workers decided to seek work to achieve both economic and personal independence. One can thus conclude that economic instability rather than personal independence led the women to seek paid employment.

For the factory workers at least, the meager thirty thousand to forty thousand drachmas[9] a month the women earn represent a fairly steady monthly income. The home workers confront hardships because of the instability of their income, which is dependent on each woman's daily piece-work production and the needs of the supplying manufacturer. Popi, a forty-year-old home worker described the situation very vividly:

> When you work very fast the pay is good. A young woman who is just starting can earn 2,000 to 3,000 drachmas a day. Someone who works very fast may make even 5,000 a day. It depends on the hours she devotes and the productivity. When you spend sixteen hours working at home at least nine have to be pure work if you really want to break even. You see, one has a lot of expenses to take care of, like thread, electricity, machine maintenance, and sometimes rent. I personally spend 1,200 a day on expenses. If I earn 2,000 it is too little. A woman in the factory earns at least 2,000 to 2,500 a day, so I have to make at least that to be satisfied.

The possibility of not making enough money and the flexibility to pursue more work may explain why home workers on average earn more than factory workers. More research is needed on this question.

Two major points emerged, however, to explain why home workers did not seek employment in factories. The first related to their degree of control over their labor, and the second to their family situations. They said that they did not want any "bosses over their head" and extended that to not having to deal with other women. Most important, they liked the flexibility of working at home. "I have to take care of my seven-year-old daughter," one woman said. Her answer reflected that of most of the other married workers and is one that is common to most studies on home work.

---

9. In 1986, there were approximately 130 to 150 drachmas to the dollar.

In addition, the investment in one or more machines and their installation in the home worker's kitchen, back room, or adjacent basement made switching to other types of work difficult. Ninety percent of the home workers owned their machines; approximately 50 percent had bought them second-hand at factory sales or through friends or relatives. The other women claimed that buying a new machine was a better investment since one did not have to worry about repairs or costly maintenance. Only one woman did not have her own machine. She rented it for a minimal monthly fee from the manufacturer for whom she worked. What would become of her machine if the woman decided to stop this work? "You'll be lucky if you find someone who would want to buy it," one woman said. She added, "Today if you are to do this type of work, you are better off buying a new machine. Who would want my old machine? I am probably the only one who can handle it. We know each other."

One woman said that she could only start thinking about working outside her home in another seven years, when her son began school, and even then she would need to think seriously about it: "I really want to have him under my supervision when he is out of school; otherwise he'll play soccer all day long and not study."

The majority of women in both samples were not satisfied with the wages they received. They had minimal buying power and thus could hardly afford necessities, especially if they had children. In response to a question about her buying power, Mary, a factory worker, asked, "What buying power are you talking about? This money is nothing. To give you an idea, yesterday I went to buy shoes. These cost five thousand drachmas. I earn seven thousand a week. You can imagine the rest."

In conclusion, my findings corroborate those of previous studies of Greece that women are still dominated by economic instability. Pressured by need, they seek employment in industrial production, which hardly ever provides the channels for occupational mobility and improvement of status.

Contribution to the Family Budget

Economic independence has often been equated with social independence, but how much more independent do women become when they earn a wage? One way to examine this question is to look at the way women spend their earnings: how much they keep for their own expenses, and how much they contribute to the family budget. Consistent with other findings of my study, I found that the majority of the married women in both samples contributed all of their wages (thirty-two thousand to forty thousand drachmas a month) to their families' budgets. Of the women who said that they kept all of their money for themselves, only one was married. Four women were separated and lived alone, four were engaged, and three were single. Those who were single or engaged indicated that they were saving some of their money for the future (they did not say for a dowry).

The pattern of contribution became clearer when they discussed the way household decisions were made regarding spending. Fifty-six percent of the factory workers and 60 percent of the home workers, the majority of whom were married, stated that financial decisions were made with their husbands or fathers, based on the needs of the household. They confirmed that they were free to purchase anything they wanted at any time, yet they never failed to mention the difficulties they faced in making ends meet. Twenty-six percent of the factory and 20 percent of the home workers stated that they made decisions alone regarding how money was to be allocated. This contrasts with 18 percent of the factory and 20 percent of the home workers (the majority of whom were married or engaged) who indicated that their husbands or fathers made such decisions.

Recognizing their double burden, most of the women admitted that they would stop working if they had economic independence. Mary, a factory worker, for instance, stated, "I wouldn't mind stopping work if he [her husband] had quite a lot of money and we could live comfortably." Sofia replied firmly, "If he has an income that would support us comfortably, I would stop because I am very tired. I've been working for too many years." When I asked her if she would consider advancing her education she replied, "I am already forty years old. It is impossible to do anything like that now." Other married women said that it would be "easier to take care of their kids" without having to work or that they were tired and wanted to escape the double and often triple burdens. But Katie, a factory worker, disagreed: "I have a sense of fulfillment when I'm working.

I wouldn't stop for anything in the world. I do think that women should have a job and keep it. In this way they are more respected in the family, since they contribute economically." She voiced the position of another five women who saw their jobs as a form of security.

Gender Relations within the Family

Changes in gender relations within the family, although not dramatic, were more pronounced than earlier studies found. The gender division of labor was altered, especially in families where the wife worked either in a factory or at home. Working outside the home for eight hours a day, five (sometimes six) days a week, or spending between eight and fifteen hours at a sewing machine objectively limited the amount of time the women could devote to housework. Most families were nuclear, so although parental help with household chores and care of grandchildren was evident, it was limited. In many families the husbands did some of the housework. A high percentage of the women stated that their husbands "helped" with chores (62 percent of the factory workers and 86 percent of the home workers). Nonetheless, the range of men's activities was quite limited, and 90 percent of the women saw them as "help." Typically, the husband helped when the wife did not "feel well" or was "very tired" or had a heavy task to accomplish (i.e., airing the carpets). One factory worker, however, said,

> He really helps a lot. He washes clothes, airs clothes; in general, he helps with everything. I don't want him to wash the dishes. He doesn't know how. I wouldn't allow it anyway. However, since we are both working he has to help out.

A twenty-eight-year-old woman who had been divorced for a year and had two children (ages two and five) said,

> I didn't really mind doing more work. I always had to do everything for him anyway. I was actually cooking two dishes every day because he was very peculiar with his food and the children did not get enough nourishment. He beat me up. The last time he beat me was in front of the children.

My oldest son then assured me that when he grew up he'd take care of him!

Most of the men helped with the children by taking them out of the house. "He takes the child to the park so I can do my work without being interrupted," one woman said. Another added that "sometimes he takes the child for a walk, and other times he helps with the housework."

These accounts illustrate that, although they "helped out," the men as a group did not assume any real responsibility for what was still viewed as "women's work." As a result, the married women had to combine their paid labor with domestic work and child care. And, as the women noted, many had yet another set of responsibilities, a "triple" burden, such as taking care of elderly parents or close relatives.

When single women were asked if they would expect their husbands to "help" around the house, the majority (in a pattern similar to that of the married women) responded that they would expect the husband to "help" (81 percent of the factory workers and 67 percent of the home workers). They often couched their answers by saying they wanted the help "when it is needed." A twenty-four-year-old factory worker said, "I don't want to be sitting when he is working around the house, like some other women do. Yes, I'd like him to help, but when I really need it."

Only one woman, twenty-eight-year-old Katie, said that her marriage was completely egalitarian. She explained that not only did she and her husband both have jobs but that they were also active in political meetings of the Greek Communist party (KKE) and therefore had to use their time efficiently. She said, "He helps with everything. Sometimes when I come home after working late I find everything ready. He is involved in everything. He is particularly good with our daughter, even when she was a baby." Political affiliation needs to be studied carefully as a variable in determining changing gender roles within the family.

The finding that working-class Greek women bear a double and often triple burden does not come as a surprise, since patriarchal relations supporting gender inequalities predominate in most capitalist societies. "Domestic" functions are still maintained in the private sphere rather than in the public. Thus, despite attempts by the government or the entry of women into waged employment (accompanied by slight changes in gender relations within the family), women's positions as well as their attitudes and behavior have not changed to a great extent. Most of the women did not mention or discuss dowries, but they were concerned with saving money for their new households. Furthermore, the need for increased decision making, respect for their opinions, independence, and changes in the power relations in the family were not discussed at any length.

Work Problems and Control

The problems home workers faced were different from those facing the factory workers. Most of the home workers complained about the long hours they worked and the difficulties of adapting to this schedule. A forty-year-old woman who had started working in her early twenties said,

> Yes, I faced a lot of problems. When I first started I was working nineteen hours a day to be able to pay for the machines. You see, I did not have any capital when I started and had to pay the machine off quickly so that I could make some profit for myself.

This woman's response touches on two of the most important problems the home workers face: the long and irregular hours that comprise their workday and the need to acquire and maintain their means of production. On the average, the women reported working twelve hours a day and at any time (day or night) when they were free from housework. In most cases, other members of the family worked with them. The advantage of home work, they said, was that they had total control over their time. In contrast, the major problem facing the factory workers was child care. Their schedules made it difficult for them to attend to their children's needs.

Health problems caused by sitting for long periods, poor lighting, and the lint and fluff were common among both the home and factory workers. In the case of the home workers, the problem was extended to the whole family.

Lisa expressed the factory workers' concerns about supervision and control:

> I am really satisfied because I am able to work [whether I am alone or with others]. Of course, when you have so many people above you controlling you and treating you like a "thing," then you realize that the only loser is you. When I'm at work sometimes I am appalled by women screaming and swearing at each other, especially when it involves a fifty-year-old woman. I see the injustice and feel that I have to try to change things.

Lisa was referring to the supervisor, who did not hesitate to use foul language to keep the women "in line." According to the owner, the supervisor was the best example of a good worker, because she was efficient and had taken only one sick day in ten years. She appeared to be friendly, but her mood could change in seconds. Her presence, coupled with the tight production quota that the women had to meet to receive full wages, discouraged any lengthy discussions during worktime. Moreover, a bonus system offered the opportunity to earn extra money by exceeding the set production quota. The women thus made every effort not only to meet the tight quota but to surpass it by working during their breaks or staying after work to get their "prim."[10] The "prim" is usually set by the German manufacturers. Greek managers, however, often find it necessary to modify the time needed to perform a certain task because of differences in the German and local machines and in the level and experience of the women involved.

In conclusion, through discussions with factory workers, it became apparent that patriarchal relations predominated in the workplace and traditional values and roles were constantly reproduced. The majority of the workers indicated, for example, that the best way to solve their problems was to "discuss them with the boss," as opposed to union representatives. This led to yet another form of dependence on an authority figure.

---

10. Derived from the word *premium,* the "prim" is a bonus based on the time spent on each garment, in fractions of a minute.

SUMMARY AND CONCLUSIONS

Contrary to assumptions about "modernization," factory work is not really providing the bridge to "modernity" and development for working-class women in Greece, as evidenced by the lack of significant differences between the women working in the factory and the women working at home. The historical comparison did not indicate dramatic changes, either.

The overwhelming majority of the respondents indicated that their decision to obtain waged or home work was economically motivated. The women saw waged work as an "unavoidable" but "temporary" necessity that would benefit their family in the future or improve the family's current standard of living. Although the women's responses indicated that "traditional" roles in the family have been shaken, the division of labor in the household has not changed significantly. Women are still burdened with the major responsibility for household tasks and child care. One change since Lambiri-Dimaki's and Nikolaidou's reports is that there is a decreasing emphasis on dowry. Does this mean that women have become more independent? Any answer should be given with great caution, since there is much evidence that women's dependence is reproduced in several ways, not the least of which is, as my findings have shown, their almost total responsibility for social reproduction.

Although one would expect that working outside the household would increase women's interactions with other individuals, thus affecting their attitudes, I found that this held true for very few of the factory workers. The double burden of work and home responsibilities makes "leisure" a male right. Further, in many cases the double burden becomes a triple burden when women have to finish their work at home or have to maintain households for their elderly parents.

Tight control over the women in the workplace, as a technique for meeting production norms, allows for very little interaction among them. Discussions with factory workers about the union and their political participation indicated that, although they were not indifferent or unaware of their condition, they were not ready to engage in any form of practical resistance. They were more concerned with receiving their wages, suggesting at times, "Let others do the changing. I need my day's wages." The attitudes of the home workers did not differ much from those of the factory workers. They indicated on several occasions that they were dissatisfied with their conditions but were also thankful to have work.

The paternalistic attitude toward women and women's unequal position vis-à-vis men was carried onto the factory floor, so that relations of dependency and subordinate female roles were clearly reproduced. The women's wages were considered "supplementary" to the family budget, and hence their attitude was that they would resign when "things get better at home."

This study has opened the way for two very important larger-scale investigations. The first would address the relation of export processing, which usually utilizes women's labor, to Greece's overall economy and consequently to the changes in women's and men's conditions. Questions concerning economic development and its impact on individuals need to be asked on a large scale. Are export-processing factories catalysts for the development of indigenous industry through technology diffusion (Nikolinakos 1983)? Can they serve as substitutes for primitive accumulation? Development is time-based. To trace the consequences of any particular articulation of modes of production, longitudinal research is critical.

The second investigation that is needed is an exploration of a most prominent and ever-expanding phenomenon, informal economic activity and its consequences on employment. What is the role of informal activity for development in Greece? Do informal activities expand in response to domestic demand? Or are they state-supported efforts to overcome a chronic lack of good jobs? Under what conditions are the rewards of informal activity greater for women?

Questions related to improvements in women's status and position must be explored through macro and micro interchange. Women's equality presupposes changes in the socioeconomic structure concomitantly with changes in the social construction of that structure. These changes must necessarily be part of the ongoing struggle for political emancipation from all forms of exploitation and oppression, be it class, gender, race, age, handicap, or sexual preference.

PART II

THE ROLE OF THE STATE

5

EXPORT-LED DEVELOPMENT AND THE UNDEREMPLOYMENT OF WOMEN: THE IMPACT OF DISCRIMINATORY DEVELOPMENT POLICY IN THE REPUBLIC OF IRELAND

Jean L. Pyle

The utilization of an export-led development strategy, accompanied by an influx of multinational corporations into a country, has been widely characterized at both general and case study levels of analysis as involving extensive use of female labor, leading to increases in their labor force participation rates.

At the general level, it has been argued that in contrast to import-substitution development, which has a dampening effect on women's share of industrial employment, export-led development is largely based on female labor (Sen 1981; Ward 1986). Employment under the latter strategy is largely in labor-intensive assembly operations in electronics or clothing, and employers in these industries benefit from the reduction in labor costs that use of female labor allows. Women's wages are kept lower than men's because of sex discrimination, the labeling of women's work as less skilled and therefore less valuable, and high turnover rates.

The use of female labor in export industries has been discussed generally and with respect to the Border Industrialization Program

This chapter is based on my book *The State and Women in the Economy: Lessons from Sex Discrimination in the Republic of Ireland* (Albany, N.Y.: SUNY Press, 1990).

in Mexico by Maria Patricia Fernandez-Kelly (1983). The phenomenon has been documented in a variety of national studies (for example, of Singapore, the Philippines, and Malaysia) and in industry analyses (electronics and clothing).[1]

In contrast to this trend elsewhere, however, increases in measures of women's participation in the labor force did not occur during the first two decades of the export-led development process in the Republic of Ireland (1961–81).[2]

As my research shows, the employment of women by multinational corporations can be constrained by the state. Irish state personnel designed policy not only to promote economic growth and development but also to reproduce traditional familial relations. As a result, the increases in female participation in the labor force expected by a reading of the literature on export-led development and female employment were precluded by policies designed to promote these dual goals.

The addition of the state and its dual purposes into an analysis of the effect of export-led growth on the sex composition of the labor force is complicated because the state's dual goals are contradictory and trade-offs are involved. By employing high proportions of women, for example, export-led development erodes traditional economic and social roles.

The first section of this chapter describes the export-led development process in Ireland and presents the virtually unchanging aggregate labor force participation data for Irish women during this period. The second section focuses on the two major goals of state policy, the contradiction inherent between them, and the problems this contradiction presents for policy makers. The third section examines the effect of policies designed to promote export-led development on the sex composition of the labor force. It analyzes the extent to which this particular component of state policy incorpo-

---

1. For example, see Wong 1981, Chapkis and Enloe 1983, Grossman 1980, Grunwald and Flamm 1985, and a number of references cited in Lim 1983a.

2. The Republic of Ireland consists of the twenty-six southern counties of the island of Ireland. It achieved its independence from Great Britain in 1922 and is to be distinguished from Northern Ireland, the northern six counties that remain a part of the United Kingdom. Hereafter the Republic of Ireland will be referred to as Ireland for simplification.

rated the dual goals, how contradictions were handled, and how it affected the female share of the work force in foreign firms. Examination of documents establishing and maintaining the export-led development process reveals that by 1970 the Irish Industrial Development Authority (IDA), in its role as manager of the export-led development process, was explicitly interested in promoting both of these state goals.

The percentage of the work force that was female in foreign firms is compared to the all-industry average in each manufacturing sector, tracing changes throughout the period. It shows that female shares reflected the relative importance given the two major goals by the Irish state and the manner in which contradictions between them were resolved. The results indicate that the Irish state, via its use of discriminatory employment policies, was able to curtail the use of female labor by multinational corporations, thereby contributing to the lack of change in the aggregate measures of female participation in the labor force.

The conclusion points out the broader theoretical implications of this case study for the literature examining export-led development and the employment of women and for general economic and social theory.

EXPORT-LED DEVELOPMENT AND THE EMPLOYMENT OF WOMEN IN IRELAND

During the latter part of the 1950s, Ireland adopted an export-led development strategy, formalizing the evolution occurring during this decade from the import-substitution strategy established in the 1930s. This shift was substantially motivated by the adverse circumstances occurring in the Irish economy. Ireland's stagnation, high unemployment, and excessive rates of emigration in the 1950s contrasted with the economic recovery and growth most of western Europe was experiencing.[3]

---

3. By the early 1950s, however, the failure of import substitution became increasingly evident and a shift toward increased exports occurred. The world's first free trade zone had been established at Shannon, Ireland, in the late 1940s (Stanton 1979).

Import substitution was limited by the small internal market in Ireland (Long 1980) and by balance of payments deficits that arose when the level of exports could

The export-led development strategy was based on the attraction of foreign direct investment and the widening of trade agreements, which allowed foreign corporations to establish production facilities in Ireland with tariff-free access to the countries in the European Economic Community (EEC). Dramatic changes followed in the institutional structure, sectoral components, and performance levels of the Irish economy.

Institutionally, the profile of the Irish economy was altered by the wider role of the state and the increased presence of multinational corporations. The role of the state in the economy expanded as it aggressively established and pursued a program to attract foreign corporations.[4] The Industrial Development Authority, a semi-autonomous state body, quickly developed a highly attractive incentives package, the major components of which were tax relief for export profits (effective until 1990 for firms entering Ireland through 1980), the reduction of the tax rate on corporate profits to 10 percent for all firms as of 1981, liberal depreciation allowances, and a package of nonrepayable cash grants (of 35 to 50 percent of assets based on regional location). It established promotional facilities abroad and aggressively courted foreign firms that met its social and economic criteria for potential investors.

Ireland was considered an attractive site for foreign direct investment, and by the early 1970s its effort to attract multinational corporations was considered "one of the most highly intensive and

---

not support the increased demand for industrial and consumer imports (NESC 1980:5). The government corrective in the 1950s, a deflationary policy, resulted in stagnation: decreased industrial employment, higher unemployment, and the highest rate of emigration since the 1880s (NESC 1980:5). Social unrest increased. See Kennedy and Dowling (1975:20) for information regarding how low Irish growth rates in the 1950s were relative to those of other western European countries.

The change to export-led development was formalized by two government documents in 1958, *Economic Development* and the first *Programme for Economic Expansion*, which presented the main objectives of the export-led strategy.

4. The Irish government had been active in the economy with the ad hoc establishment in the years following independence of a sector of state-controlled industry that included public transport (buses, the airline, railways, and some shipping), communications, electricity, and some basic industries. Enactment of the export-led development strategy, itself a major undertaking in terms of its arrangements to attract foreign firms, required the state to manage an increasingly complicated and internationally focused macroeconomic policy. In addition, during the period 1961–81, the role of the Irish state in the economy expanded with the increase in the public sector and its correspondingly enlarged role as a direct employer.

organized of its type among competing countries" (National Economic and Social Council 1980:12–13). The financial and trade incentives, combined with a wide range of other subsidies, relatively low labor costs, political stability, and a well-educated work force, made Ireland an attractive competitor for foreign direct investment.[5]

Although there was an influx of foreign firms in Ireland in the 1960s, the largest proportion of total foreign investment for the period 1961–81 came after 1973.[6] Foreign corporations were present in a wide range of industries—those that were growth industries at the time, those that were relatively new to the international scene, and those that set up chiefly low-skill, small-scale production units. Because of the structure of Ireland's incentives packages, foreign firms typically established multiplant operations, often in decentralized locations (Jackson 1983).

Many of the foreign firms locating in Ireland were in manufacturing industries that elsewhere had hired higher proportions of female employees than manufacturing firms in Ireland. (The average share in Ireland was 30 percent in 1970.) For example, there was an influx of electronics firms that had production work forces in Mexico and Southeast Asia that were more than 80 percent female.[7]

The main source of foreign direct investment was the United States. U.S. Department of Commerce data show that, worldwide, Ireland was one of the locations experiencing the fastest rate of growth of U.S. foreign direct investment during the period 1966–

---

5. Ireland offered a wide range of subsidies or allowances such as 100 percent employee training grants, complete freedom to repatriate profits, loan guarantees and interest subsidies, double taxation agreements, advance factory space, duty-free importation of capital equipment, and a variety of after-care support services.

6. The increases after 1973 corresponded to two changes in the strategy. First, EEC membership in 1973 allowed the IDA to offer potential investors tariff-free access to a market of 270 million people. Second, the IDA specifically targeted a few industries as growth industries (electronics, pharmaceuticals, and health care) and vigorously courted them, with the result that by the early 1980s Ireland ranked eighth and fourteenth worldwide in the production of electronics and pharmaceuticals. (Growth in each of these industries was 30 to 40 percent a year compounded annually during the last decade.)

7. According to Joseph Grunwald and Kenneth Flamm, in 1980, 82 percent of electronics production workers in Mexico were female (1985). Rachel Grossman indicates that 90 percent of assembly workers in electronic plants in Penang were women (1980).

77, third only to Singapore and South Korea.[8] The profitability of locating in Ireland is supported by U.S. Department of Commerce data which show that U.S. firms in Ireland earned an average yearly rate of return of 33.7 percent on their manufacturing investment from 1977 to 1980, more than twice the average rate of return on U.S. investment in the EEC (16.8 percent) or in all countries (14 percent).

Corresponding to the increase in foreign firms, Ireland changed from a relatively undeveloped agricultural country into an industrial and service-based economy characterized by a substantial degree of openness. The proportions of gross national product (GNP) and employment arising from the agricultural sector fell from 1961 to 1981, while those due to industry and the service sectors rose.[9]

This period was characterized by a marked break with the economic performance of the past. The average annual growth rate of real gross domestic product (GDP) doubled initially, rising from 2.0 percent during 1949–61 to 4.1 percent for 1961–73 (Nolan 1981:154). Ireland's average rate of growth of GDP of 3.8 percent for the period 1961–79 was among the highest in the Organization for Economic Cooperation and Development (OECD) (Long 1976).

There is widespread agreement among Irish scholars that this sharp change in economic performance was correlated with the adoption of the export-led strategy and the influx of foreign direct investment.[10] A substantial part of the growth in GDP, investment, and exports during this period can be linked to the presence of foreign direct investment.[11] The GDP growth rates were led by 6

---

8. Ireland had a compound annual growth rate of total assets of U.S. foreign direct investment of 27 percent for the 1966–77 period, rising to 41 percent for the years 1977–80 (Grunwald and Flamm 1985).

9. The percentage of total employment in the agricultural sector was cut in half, falling from 36 percent in 1961 to 17 percent in 1981.

Ireland became a much more open economy. Exports rose from 37 percent of GNP in 1962 to 55 percent in 1981, while imports increased from 40 percent to 68 percent. These measures of openness substantially exceeded averages for the European Economic Community (EEC): exports and imports were each 29 percent of GNP for the community as a whole (White 1981). Not surprisingly, the sectoral composition of exports shifted from agricultural to industrial.

10. For example, refer to McAleese 1977a; Fitzgerald 1968; Kennedy and Dowling 1975; Long 1976; NESC 1980:23–27, 29–34; Wickham 1980; Stanton 1981; Coughlan 1980; Jacobsen 1978, 1980.

11. It is hard to estimate precisely the full extent of foreign presence in Ireland

percent annual growth rates in the output of the industrial sector; in turn, three-quarters of the industrial expansion of the 1960s was due to foreign firms (Long 1976). Similarly, an export growth rate of 12 percent a year from 1960 to 1970 was led by the growth in industrial exports of 14 percent; two-thirds of this increase was due to foreign-owned firms[12] (Long 1976; Coughlan 1980). In addition, foreign firms became an increasingly important source of employment, employing one-third of the manufacturing work force (IDA *Annual Report 1982*).[13]

Because Ireland vigorously pursued export-led development—a strategy that has been widely documented as involving increases in the use of female labor—one would assume that the participation of Irish women would have risen during this period. In fact, their labor force participation rate and their share of the labor force exhibited weak responses during this period and remained at relatively low levels. This contrasts sharply with similar measures of

---

for two reasons. First, most of the data are categorized as "new industry" or "grant-aided industry" (these terms will be used here as synonymous although they are technically different). This terminology is misleading, perhaps deliberately so, and it obscures the full role of foreign investment in Ireland.

The term *new industry* includes (1) "domestic" industry ("established Irish and *overseas* firms plus new Irish firms") and (2) "new overseas investment" ("overseas firms which have just commenced operations") (McAleese 1977b:13). Use of *new overseas investment* when discussing foreign direct investment clearly understates actual foreign investment by an amount equal to the overseas component in "domestic" industry.

Second, John Sweeney's research revealed that, in 1972, foreign corporations owned over half of the fixed assets of Irish registered industrial and service companies; however, only 45 percent of these foreign-owned assets appeared in IDA reports accounting for the role of foreign-owned corporations. Many British companies had subsidiaries in Ireland, but only one-third of them had a relationship with the IDA. He hypothesized that those not counted must have been in the older protected industry and were therefore termed "home" industry (NESC 1980:35).

12. For the last half of the 1970s exports were still growing at 10 percent per year, pushed by the 13 percent yearly increase in industrial exports.

13. The growing role of foreign firms in the Irish economy is not without controversy. There are substantial differences of opinion among Irish economists with regard to the net benefits and stability engendered by this process—particularly in light of the high costs of the incentives package and changes in total employment, which fell short of those targeted.

In light of the increasing costs associated with the development strategy, the benefits of attracting foreign direct investment have been questioned. This culminated in an extensive study of the strategy by an outside consultant, *The Telesis Report*. The strategy has never been examined or questioned with respect to its effect on the employment of women.

TABLE 5.1.   Measures of Women's Participation in the Labor Force of
Ireland, 1961–1981

	1961	1966	1971	1975	1979	1981
Participation rate (women aged 15+)[a]	29.4[b]	29.1[b]	28.0[b]	28.5	28.7	29.7
Share of the labor force[c]	26.4	26.3	26.4	27.8	28.9	29.1

Sources: Calculated from tables in *Census of Population in Ireland*, various years; *Labour Force Survey* 1979.
[a]"Gainfully occupied" women aged 15 and over as a percentage of all women aged 15 and over, where "gainfully occupied" includes those "at work" and "unemployed, having lost or given up previous job."
[b]Rates were calculated from ratios in which the data in the numerator were for ages 14+.
[c]Percentage of total employment which is female.

female activity in the labor force in Singapore, another small, export-led economy for which data are available for approximately the same period.

Table 5.1 shows that the labor force participation rate for Irish women was virtually unchanged from 1961 to 1981, remaining at just under 30 percent, and the female share of the Irish labor force increased less than three percentage points.[14] These are strikingly different responses than in Singapore, where, according to table 5.2, both measures nearly doubled during a similar period. The labor force participation rate in Singapore increased to 42 percent in 1979, a level 45 percent higher than in Ireland at the end of this period.[15]

---

14. Census data (the source of information on labor force participation rates and female share of the labor force for all these countries) must be used with a full understanding of their limitations. The data do not distinguish between full-time and part-time workers. In addition, statistics regarding the numbers gainfully occupied may be inaccurate because of the self-reporting of one's principal economic status, the questions asked on census forms, and differences in conventions regarding inclusion of individuals in certain occupations as gainfully employed. Furthermore, there is widespread undercounting of women as unpaid family laborers (on family farms and businesses) and of women in the informal sector. Activities in the underground economy are not picked up by census data, and there is the additional problem that those in home duties are not considered among the economically active in spite of their various productive activities (see Beneria 1981, 1982; Standing 1981:25–54; OECD 1979:21, 23).

15. In addition, comparisons to other western European countries reveal that by 1981 the female share of the labor force in Ireland had become the lowest in these seventeen countries, falling well below the average of 37.3 percent. The female labor force participation rate had become one of the lowest, and changes in each of these

TABLE 5.2. Measures of Women's Participation in the Labor Force of Singapore, 1957–1979

	1957	1970	1975	1979
Participation rate[a]	21.6	29.5	34.9	41.9
Share of the labor force[b]	17.5	23.5	29.6	33.6

Source: Aline K. Wong, "Planned Development, Social Stratification, and the Sexual Division of Labor in Singapore," *Signs* 7 (1981):440.

[a]Economically active women as proportion of total female population aged 15 and over.

[b]Economically active women as proportion of total number of women and men employed.

Aline Wong has shown that these increases in Singapore were related to the pattern of foreign investment (1981).

These results are surprising. The lack of change in Ireland in both the labor force participation rate of women and the female share of the labor force is contrary to expectations regarding the impact of export-led development on the employment of women and is dramatically different from the pattern in Singapore. Although Irish levels of female participation had exceeded those in Singapore around 1960, this was reversed during the development process.[16] The obvious question is why the influx of multinationals did not lead to increases in female participation in Ireland.

THE DUAL AND CONTRADICTORY PURPOSES OF THE IRISH STATE

A survey of Irish social and industrial policy reveals that state personnel saw two primary ways of designing economic and social policy

---

measures were only a small percentage of average increases. Differences between these measures in Irish and western European OECD averages widened during the period of Irish export-led growth (see Pyle 1990).

16. Labor force participation information on women in Ireland has been presented in a variety of Irish sources, some covering substantial amounts of this period (Blackwell 1982, 1983; Garvey 1983; McLernon 1980; Walsh 1982), but none makes any comparison to other export-led countries or examines the impact of export-led growth on the employment of women. Comparisons over time between Ireland and these other countries lead to a more striking perspective on the lack of change in Ireland.

to further their own tenure: the promotion of economic development and the maintenance of traditional familial relationships.[17]

It is widely understood that the Irish government has long been concerned with economic development, from its establishment of the import-substitution policies in the 1930s to its aggressive pursuit of export-led development since 1958. That the maintenance of traditional relations between the sexes has been a major goal of Irish social and economic policy since the early days of the Republic has been less recognized. It can be substantiated by reference to the Constitution of Ireland and to a range of legislation.

The Constitution of 1937, in its specification of fundamental rights, addressed the importance of the family and the role of women in society. According to article 41, "The Family,"

41. 1. 1. The State recognizes the Family as the natural, primary and fundamental unit group of Society, and as a moral institution possessing inalienable and imprescriptible rights antecedent and superior to all positive law.

2. The State, therefore, guarantees to protect the Family in its constitution and authority, as the necessary basis of social order and as indispensible to the welfare of the Nation and the State.

41. 2. 1. In particular, the State recognizes that by her life within the home, woman gives to the State a support without which the common good cannot be achieved.

2. The State shall, therefore, endeavour to ensure that mothers shall not be obliged by economic necessity to engage in labour to the neglect of their duties in the home.

The traditional family was the core institution of the society; women belonged at home, and mothers were not supposed to work. A number of employment and family policies were implemented during these years with this constitutional viewpoint in mind. In 1932, for example, a marriage bar was instituted when the government banned employment of married women as civil service employees. By banning a substantial portion of the female population

---

17. Traditional familial relations are not simply a division of labor between equals but a matter of subordination of women.

from this labor force, the marriage bar dramatically illustrated gender inequality in the workplace.[18]

Similarly, family law and reproductive rights legislation were developed to support what were considered appropriate roles for women. The constitution prohibited divorce, and the sale, advertising or importation of contraceptives was forbidden by law. Males were granted the right of sexual access to their wives, which, combined with the difficulty in obtaining contraceptives, reinforced female subordination in the household by precluding female control over reproduction and via the increased work load for women that the resultant higher fertility rates involved. (This line of analysis is more fully developed in Pyle 1990.)[19]

The clearly defined status of women as subordinate to that of men thus had a long historical precedent. An important part of being a successful politician or bureaucrat and maintaining one's position by reelection or reappointment was to preserve this way of life.

It was within this social context that export-led development in Ireland occurred. Its impact on female employment was therefore mediated by the existence of this other major goal of the state: the preservation of traditional relations between the sexes via both employment policies and family law. Policies designed to preserve traditional male-female relations also affect labor market outcomes. Because of the marriage bar, for example, civil service employers (and others in the private sector who emulated their practices) could not hire married women, and married women could not offer their labor to those arenas of the economy.

The analysis is more complex, however, because these two goals of state policy can be contradictory. Emphasis on the preservation of traditional familial relations can hinder the development process, and, similarly, the promotion of economic growth can undermine traditional relations between the sexes. These contradictions are

18. The marriage ban or marriage bar refers to the policy of compulsory retirement of women from employment upon marriage. It applied to females in clerical jobs in service industries, banks, local authorities, and semistate bodies. The practice was adopted in numerous other sectors. It was phased out over a four-year period (1973–77).

19. A more complete survey of both state employment and family and reproductive rights legislation and the manner in which they reinforce female subordination in the household appears in Pyle 1990.

more pronounced under export-led development than under import substitution because the former depends on attracting foreign firms in industries that tend to hire high proportions of women.

To illustrate the trade-offs involved in meeting these two goals, if women are unable to enter the paid labor force, the export-led development process (which utilizes a predominantly female work force) may be constrained. Similarly, in the absence of structural constraints, increases in the rate of growth of employment during export-led development are accompanied by increases in the labor force participation rate of women, which undermines traditional relations between the sexes. This erosion can happen in a number of ways. According to Elaine McCrate (1985), women become less economically dependent on men as female labor force participation increases. As a result, their options are augmented; for example, increased financial independence may allow women to terminate a marriage. Even when women's wages are too low to permit economic autonomy, their employment can alter traditional gender relations. This can occur via changes in the division of labor in the household as men are pushed to assume more household and child-care responsibilities. Such changes generally entail shifts in relations of power in the household and may be accompanied by other demands by women for increased rights and equality.

The trade-offs between these two goals existed in Ireland. Multinational corporations locating there tended to hire higher proportions of women than the average for Irish industries, presenting a challenge to the maintenance of dual state policy.[20] The effect of export-led development depended on the relative importance given the two major goals by the Irish state and the manner in which the contradictions between them were to be resolved. Resolution of the conflicts had to involve either changes in policies designed to main-

---

20. In addition, an integral part of the Irish export-led development strategy was attainment of membership in the EEC. This was necessary to attract foreign direct investment because it offered foreign firms an export-production platform in Ireland with tariff-free access to markets in the EEC. Membership in the EEC, however, required that Ireland reform social policy to conform with EEC directives on equal pay (1975) and equal treatment with regard to access to employment, vocational training, promotion, and working conditions (1976). One would expect that this dimension of the export-led development program would have enhanced women's participation in the Irish labor force.

tain one goal or the other (and therefore erosion of that goal) or development of new policies to enhance the trade-off.

IMPACT OF EXPORT-LED DEVELOPMENT POLICY ON THE EMPLOYMENT OF WOMEN

The export-led development strategy intensified the contradiction between the dual goals of state policy. Foreign firms locating in Ireland were seeking a financially attractive production platform in the EEC from which to export goods tariff-free to the entire EEC market. A variety of financial incentives (including relatively lower wages) made Ireland attractive in the 1960s. Many firms were said to prefer female workers (Donaldson 1965; Stanton 1981:58, 60–63; Wickham 1982:149) because they were lower-wage workers.[21]

This assertion is confirmed by two different data bases compiled in the 1960s which indicate that foreign firms hired higher proportions of women workers than did domestic firms. Richard Stanton studied the export processing zone at Shannon, Ireland, which consisted almost totally of small foreign-owned enterprises engaged in assembly or simple fabrication (1981:12–20).[22] Table 5.3 shows that in the 1960s the percentage of the work force at the Shannon Industrial Estate that was female exceeded the percentage that was female in the total Irish manufacturing work force.

This was also the case countrywide for manufacturing. According

---

21. The first wave of foreign direct investment consisted largely of firms in the textiles and metals sectors. These sources argued that women were preferred largely because of their lower wages. It was legal to pay female workers less than males until the end of 1975. Loraine Donaldson reports in the early 1960s that "wage rates normally run $29.50 to $36.50 per week for skilled adult men, and $23.60 to $29.50 for unskilled and semiskilled; skilled women receive $15-$20 and unskilled $12-$17. There is a 40–45 hour work week" (1965:114).

This disparity existed in the service sector also. According to the *Annual Report 1967–68* of the Department of Education from December 1964, salaries of national teachers were as follows:

For principals and assistants:

Married men: £770–£31 × 5, £41 × 5, £51 × 4, £52 × 3–£1,490.
Women/single men: £620–£24 × 5, £32 × 5, £41 × 4, £42 × 3–£1,190.

(In 1964, 40 percent of the principals were women, as were 78 percent of the assistants.)

22. The export processing zone established at Shannon in the western part of Ireland in the late 1940s was the first of its kind in the world.

TABLE 5.3.   Percentage Female in Shannon Export Processing Zone and
in Irish Manufacturing, 1960–1971

	Shannon Industrial Estate	Irish Manufacturing
1960	37	
1961	37	33.4
1962	38	
1963	47	
1964	43	
1965	46	
1966	45	31.8
1967	40	
1968	41	
1969	38	
1970	35	
1971	34	30.5

Source: Stanton 1981:13; *Census of Population of Ireland,* various years.

to census data, women's share of manufacturing employment in 1966
was 31.8 percent. By contrast, information collected for *The Survey
of Grant-Aided Industry* reveals that the percentage female in grant-
aided manufacturing industries was 40 percent (1967:43). These
grant-aided industries were largely foreign-owned; in the 1960s,
foreign firms received three-quarters of the funds dispersed under
the Industrial Development Authority New Industries Program.

Further, as shown in table 5.4, on average, grant-aided firms hired
higher percentages of women in every major manufacturing sub-
sector than did the sector as a whole (Farley 1972:19). The probability that this could occur (i.e., that the percentage female in foreign
firms would exceed the percentage in domestic firms) if it was equally
probable for any individual sector that the percentage female in
domestic firms could be above or below the percentage female in
foreign firms is 0.00098. There was thus a significant difference
in the hiring preferences of foreign and domestic firms.[23]

---

23. These enterprises constituted a small percentage of the total manufacturing
labor force in these years, however, and therefore the fact that the percentage of
females in foreign grant-aided firms was higher than the average could only have a
minor impact on aggregate statistics. It was not until the 1970s, when the proportion

TABLE 5.4.   Female Share of Grant-Aided and All Manufacturing in
Ireland, 1966

Sector	Grant-Aided Industries	Manufacturing Industries
Food	47.7	27.8
Drink and tobacco	38.5	20.8
Textiles	59.1	51.6
Clothing and footwear	82.6	71.2
Wood, wood products, furniture	10.6	8.3
Paper and printing	48.6	33.8
Chemicals	31.9	27.8
Clay and cement	28.3	11.9
Metals and engineering	27.8	15.5
Other manufacturing	33.1	31.6

Source: Noel J. J. Farley, "Explanatory Hypotheses for Irish Trade in Manufactured Goods in the Mid-Nineteen Sixties," *Economic and Social Review* 4 (October 1972):19 (based on data in *Census of Population of Ireland, 1966* and *Survey of Grant-Aided Industry* 1967).

In terms of the trade-off between employment and maintenance of traditional relations between the sexes, the events of the 1960s suggest that the increase in the growth of employment accompanying export-led development would result in a weakening of traditional relations as women gained employment opportunities. A major reorganization of the IDA occurred in 1969, however, which resulted in a more sophisticated promotional strategy to attract foreign investment and generate economic growth while, at the same time, circumventing the potential movement of women into the labor market. The IDA formulated a set of economic and social criteria for evaluating proposed industrial projects and for awarding financial incentives at its discretion.[24] Included in these criteria was an explicit statement regarding the sex composition of the new work force,

of total manufacturing employment provided by foreign firms increased, that the percentage of females would have affected manufacturing statistics.

24. As mentioned in note 6, the IDA also targeted specific industrial sectors for development and set up a worldwide network of offices to attract foreign investment with the desired qualifications.

indicating how thoroughly the mandate of the constitution had been integrated into policy making. The *IDA Annual Report 1971/72* (page 27) stated: "We are currently selecting industrial development candidates which will produce goods employing predominantly *men*, have low capital intensity, use local raw materials, have rapid growth potential, and a low probability of technological obsolescence" (emphasis added).[25]

Through the first half of the 1970s the IDA continued to exhibit an explicit interest in the proportions of male jobs created via their new industry grants.[26] They defined "predominantly men." The *Annual Report 1970/71* specified, for example, "In economic terms, the needs are for 11,000 direct jobs to be taken up each year in manufacturing industry, of which over 75% should be for men" (page 15). The *IDA Annual Report 1972/73* (page 12) stated that the IDA had approved new industry grants during the previous year that were expected to generate 10,303 jobs, 75 percent of which were for males. It expressed satisfaction: "The male/female balance was in line with our target" (page 12).

T. S. O'Neill, who at the time was an executive director of the IDA, explained how these objectives were attained in a special issue of *Administration* devoted to the IDA (Spring 1972). IDA policy was to locate "industrial projects which yield a high national economic benefit in relation to the investment involved. A ranking of projects on this basis does not necessarily correspond to a ranking on the basis of commercial profitability. New industrial projects are rated on the... major indicators of economic benefit" (page 42).[27] He explained the process of ranking projects:

---

25. The goals of the IDA (industries that employ predominantly men, have a low capital intensity, low probability of technological obsolescence, and rapid growth potential) are basically incompatible. In general, industries with a low capital intensity do not hire predominantly males and are vulnerable to technological change and foreign competition.

26. This was not simply an internal goal. The IDA placed a twenty-page advertisement in the March 1975 *Fortune* (page 59). Near the beginning, in discussing "Ireland—Incentives for Industry in a Changing Land," it states, "The prime criterion is to provide stable jobs for Irish-men."

27. Refer to IDA Regional Industrial Plans, 1973–1977, part 1, for a complete listing of two categories of IDA objectives:

"A. Objectives deriving directly from the functions and responsibilities of the IDA with respect to industrial development.

B. Objectives deriving from the wider demographic, social and economic goals

Quantified versions of these indicators provide the framework through which the IDA's project selection process is conducted in its initial stages. A project having a high rating on all of these criteria does not necessarily have higher commercial profitability than one with low ratings on all of the criteria. However, the project with high ratings would obviously attract larger incentives per unit of investment since it would deliver higher national economic benefit. (1972:42)

Providing males with employment was deemed an industrial objective that could override the imperatives of commercial profitability (IDA 1972). O'Neill provided an example of the evaluation process and illustrated how funds for economic development were utilized to further broader social goals, such as the provision of employment for males:

> For example, an export-based project involving a product which is at the growth stage of a long life cycle, employs 80% *male* workers of medium skill, and uses Irish raw materials, would attract a higher level of incentive than a *female*-employing, export-based project with a low skill content and using imported materials—even though both projects have the same prospective rate of return on capital employed. (1972:42, emphasis added)

He acknowledged that this process was discriminatory:

> It follows from this discrimination on grounds of economic benefit that it is incorrect to regard the IDA's financial incentives solely as a means of generating projects in which to utilize national resources of capital and labor. Incentives are also the vehicle for the promotion of a product policy for industrial growth. Variations in the rate of incentives to new industrial projects are a key method by which the overall pattern of new industrial expansion is made to conform with national development needs, such as a high *male* content in new job creation, stability and permanence of employment, and use of local raw materials. (42–43, emphasis added)[28]

Evidence that selectivity was exercised appears in other annual reports:

---

which are not within the direct and exclusive field of responsibility of the IDA but which, nevertheless, form part of the framework within which IDA activities are carried out" (page 39).

28. Efforts to obtain a copy of the evaluation forms were met with no response.

The process of selectivity in relation to new industries which we sought to attract to Ireland was further refined during the year. For example, in the textile sector, one in four of the enquiries generated from overseas firms were not pursued by IDA because they did not meet the criteria which IDA employs in screening new industrial proposals (*Annual Report 1974*:3–4).

Since the "textiles, clothing, footwear and leather" sector was a major employer of women, this policy would have had a negative impact on female employment.

The majority of the growth accompanying the export-led development strategy occurred in the 1970s in a social and economic framework designed to provide firms with largely male employees (the 1970s were the decade in which there was growth in total employment and in which there was the largest inflow of foreign firms). The effectiveness of the IDA in achieving this goal (and therefore its corresponding impact on women's employment opportunities) can be examined in three ways: by analyzing the percentage of females in the projects approved in the 1970s, by examining data from a 1974 profile of grant-aided industry, and by surveying unpublished data from the IDA describing the work forces of foreign grant-aided and domestic grant-aided industries for 1973 to 1981.

An analysis of data in IDA annual reports for the five-year period 1970–74, presented in table 5.5, indicates that the IDA kept to its guidelines.[29] Males constituted 74 percent of the estimated full-employment labor force (the number employed when the projects were fully operational) for all projects approved during this period. In contrast, the female share of new employment (26 percent) was well under the female share for all manufacturing (30.5 percent in 1971 and 29.5 in 1975). This profile was a distinct reversal of the pattern of IDA approvals during both the 1952–70 period (also shown in table 5.5)[30] and the 1960s (when the female share in grant-aided firms—40 percent—had exceeded the female share in manufacturing—31.8 percent).

---

29. They stopped publishing data by sex in these categories with the *Annual Report 1975*.

30. The increase in total employment in the eighteen-year period 1952–70 was only 87 percent of the increase in total employment in the five-year period 1970–74.

TABLE 5.5. Sex Composition of IDA-Approved Industrial Projects in Ireland, 1952–1970 and 1970–1974

Year[a]	Projected New Jobs at Full Employment[b]	Number Accounted for in Annual Report	Female	% Female
1970–71	12,487	12,800	2,600	20.3
1971–72	8,734	6,500	1,900	29.2
1972–73	14,139	11,742	2,933	25.0
1973–74	23,316	20,640[c]	5,676	27.5
to 12/74	19,818	17,877[c]	5,080	28.4
Total 1970–74	78,494	69,559	18,189	26.1
Total 1952–70	68,208	70,400	25,800	36.6

Source: Compiled from data in IDA annual reports, various years.
[a]Financial years April 1 to March 31.
[b]According to *Annual Report, 1974—Review of 1970–74*, section 4, page 4.
[c]The number accounted for by sex is below the total because of the omission of data for the midwest region.

Information collected in 1974 for an IDA analysis of grant-aided industry indicates that the tendency observed in the 1960s (for grant-aided industries to hire a higher percentage of women than the national average for each sector) had been eliminated (McAleese 1977b). As shown in table 5.6, there was no longer a clear difference between the sex composition of the labor forces in new industry and in all industry. There were only three sectors in which the percentage of females in new industry exceeded the national average for each sector.[31] Although the categories are defined differently (grant-aided in 1967 in comparison to new industry in 1974), they are comparable.[32]

These results—the low percentage of females employed in the

31. The proportion of female workers by sector (or change in it) reflects not only this aspect of government policy but also the effect of legislation (i.e., protective legislation, training, and apprenticeships) or its absence (i.e., lack of provision for child care, maternity leave, equal pay); however, because I am examining the female share (or change in it) in grant-aided or new industries vis-à-vis all industries, the effects of these other factors (with the possible exception of protective legislation) can be assumed to occur evenly over both sets of data. Variation between them can therefore be attributed to some other factor—for example, the ability of state policy to control access to employment opportunities in manufacturing by sex.
32. Refer to note 11 for discussion of the terms *new industry* and *grant-aided*.

TABLE 5.6.   Female Share of New Industry and All Manufacturing in
Ireland, 1973

Sector	Female Share of New Industry	Female Share of All Manufacturing Industries
Food	22.4%	26.8%
Drink and tobacco	16.3	22.1
Textiles	46.5	47.4
Clothing and footwear	67.7	66.7
Wood, wood products, furniture	11.1	11.2
Paper and printing	32.5	30.2
Chemicals	22.7	24.2
Clay and cement	12.8	12.7
Metals and engineering	23.2	21.3
Other manufacturing	23.8	27.1

Source: Calculated from unpublished data provided by Dermot McAleese.

projects approved in 1970–74 and the elimination of the distinct
differences in the percentage of females employed by foreign industry vis-à-vis the Irish average—suggest that IDA policy was effective during this period in fulfilling its commitment to providing
"predominantly male" employment. The overall female share of new
industry was reduced to 29 percent from its level of 40 percent
(percentage female in grant-aided industry) in 1967, placing it in
line with the overall proportion of women in Irish manufacturing
(29.5 percent in 1975).

The Irish state resolved the problem of the contradiction between
the two goals of state policy and the trade-off this necessitated between the growth of employment and maintenance of traditional
familial relations by developing policies that eased the terms of the
trade-off during these years. The effect of IDA policy specifying the
provision of male employment was to allow a greater growth in
employment without disrupting traditional relations between the
sexes.

Data from the unpublished IDA Employment Survey suggest,
however, that control by the IDA of the sex composition of the
employment provided by foreign firms weakened in the latter half

of the 1970s.[33] Figure 5.1 shows that the female share of the foreign grant-aided work force exceeded that of the domestic grant-aided work force in all years but that since 1975 the gap has widened from 3.6 percentage points to more than 10. The percentage of females in the foreign grant-aided work force rose to 36 percent in 1981 and fell to under 26 percent in domestic grant-aided industry. (The figure also reveals the growing importance of foreign firms in providing manufacturing employment, which rose from 22 percent in 1973 to more than 30 percent in 1981.)

Further detailed investigation of subsectors is presented in table 5.7, which lists the top twenty foreign grant-aided industrial sectors in descending order by the total number of women employed.[34] A comparison of the percentage of females in foreign grant-aided firms with the percentage of females in domestic grant-aided firms for the entire period shows that in three-quarters of the sectors the percentage of females in foreign grant-aided firms exceeded that of domestic grant-aided firms for all the years involved.

This change in IDA control over the sex composition of new employment reflected a revised assessment of the relative importance of the state's two goals and the appropriate manner in which to resolve the problem of the trade-offs between them. By the latter part of the 1970s, there is evidence that the IDA recognized the conflict between its efforts to generate employment and state policies

---

33. This is a set of unpublished IDA employment data for detailed industrial subsectors for 1973–83. This information differs from previous data sets (1) by the use of the NACE industrial classification, (2) by the use of foreign and indigenous categories as well, as (3) by the redefinition of *foreign* and *domestic* to solve the problem mentioned earlier in these definitions (see note 11).

Understood as a unique data base, it can be used to examine employment differences (and trends in them) between foreign firms (widely taken to desire larger proportions of women in their work forces) and domestic (which had a smaller percentage of females than the EEC average in most sectors) in light of the IDA's desire to provide largely male employment in the new industries.

The survey has been changed retroactively, however, to pick up companies that should have been included. Therefore, the file on 1974 is not the same data file used in the 1977 *Profile* by McAleese. Accordingly, this data set cannot be compared to the information regarding the percentage female in grant-aided sectors in 1967 or in new industry in 1974.

34. There are nineteen other sectors but all employ fewer than one thousand women.

FIGURE 5.1.   Percentage Female in the Foreign Grant-Aided Work
Force, Domestic Grant-Aided Work Force, and All Industry in Ireland,
1973–1981

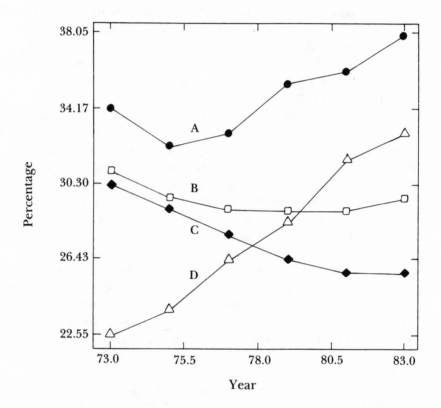

A = % of the foreign grant-aided work force which is female
B = % of all industrial work force which is female
C = % of the domestic grant-aided work force which is female
D = % of industrial employment which is in foreign grant-aided firms

Source: IDA Employment Survey 1983.

TABLE 5.7.   Female Share of Foreign Grant-Aided and Domestic
Grant-Aided Industry in Ireland, 1973–1981

NACE Sectors	% Foreign 1981	1973		1981	
		PPFGA	PFDGA	PFFGA	PFDGA
Electrical engineering	63.8	43.8	38.8	50.8	29.6
Computer/office machinery	80.4	62.7	58.7	49.7	36.1
Health-care products	92.0	35.3	0.0	54.7	18.2
Metal products	23.3	20.8	13.5	20.7	9.9
Textiles	45.5	35.5	38.3	20.0	37.7
Pharmaceutical chemicals	76.2	39.6	22.9	26.9	37.6
Clothing	22.6	83.6	78.1	84.5	78.9
Alcoholic beverages	54.8	18.9	13.6	17.1	13.2
Chocolate and sugar confection	46.7	50.8	22.8	42.2	22.3
Rubber products	76.1	17.6	12.1	16.8	12.9
Mechanical engineering	48.6	11.7	9.0	10.3	10.7
Motor vehicles and parts	41.2	10.8	8.5	17.8	8.4
Plastic products	48.5	22.2	29.9	27.9	20.9
Chemical, oil, tar	34.4	9.1	11.8	11.9	10.6
Manmade fibers	97.2	14.7	9.1	19.3	3.1
Toys, sports, instruments	49.9	60.0	31.3	53.6	38.8
Other means of transport	56.8	7.1	4.3	5.4	5.4
Other food	43.4	44.8	28.4	39.9	38.5
Footwear	34.4	55.8	50.8	58.3	52.1
Instrument engineering	71.4	36.2	29.5	57.4	29.0

Source: Compiled from information in the IDA Employment Survey, 1973–83.
   NACE = classification of manufacturing subsectors; % Foreign = percentage of
employment in the sector in foreign firms; PFFGA = percentage of the work force
which is female in foreign grant-aided firms; PFDGA = percentage female in domestic grant-aided firms.

regarding women's economic roles. The IDA policy of attracting
foreign industry and providing males with employment brought the
contradiction between the dual objectives of the Irish government
to center stage—and left the Irish government with a difficult trade-
off. Foreign firms likely to locate in Ireland were in industries that
hired substantial numbers of female workers. On the one hand, to
the extent the IDA specified preference for providing employment
for men, the influx of foreign capital was likely to be dampened and

the growth of employment restricted. On the other hand, to abandon the specification that males would be hired could enhance the growth of employment for women, undermining traditional relations between the sexes.

The trade-offs were difficult since the legitimacy of the government depended on generation of employment and on preserving traditional familial relations. IDA personnel were aware of the critical importance of generating large yearly tallies of new jobs. Providing employment opportunities was a major political issue in this labor-surplus economy, with its increasing population of working age. In addition, there was substantial expense involved in maintaining the extensive financial incentives program to attract foreign investment. The IDA had to present detailed annual reports and was increasingly held accountable for funds spent and employment generated.

It became evident that to attract foreign capital—the engine of employment generation—more was needed than the handsome financial incentives packages offered by the IDA. Foreign firms needed freedom to hire any workers they wanted. The IDA recognized that certain state policies designed to preserve traditional roles between the sexes were hindering its efforts to stimulate the growth of employment and the accumulation process. The choice was clear: to prevent a stalling of the export-led development process, the IDA had to reverse its explicit position regarding women.

Thus, in 1978, the IDA lobbied for the repeal of protective legislation prohibiting women from working at night, arguing that it had "proved to be a serious problem for us in our promotional work abroad in relation to female employing industries such as electronics and textiles" (Employment Equality Agency 1978:29). In addition, beginning with the *Annual Report 1975*, it dropped the provision of predominantly male employment from its list of objectives and no longer reported by sex the number of jobs at full employment in approved projects.[35] In 1979, even housewives were acknowledged

35. Frances Ruane refers to a 1979 IDA publication as mentioning provision of male employment as an objective (1980). My research could not verify this, and in some instances I found the phrase "men and women" (1978–82 Industrial Plan:17).

The IDA may have been under dual pressure to eliminate explicit references to this blatantly discriminatory policy regarding the sex of net new employment. The

to be a source of employees for foreign firms by the IDA. An IDA survey of the recruitment pattern of the work force in new industry indicated that housewives comprised about 8 percent of its labor force (IDA *Annual Report 1979*:2).

In spite of the recognition by the IDA in the later 1970s that *explicit* policies limiting the availability of female workers were to its disadvantage in generating new employment, it continued to pursue the goal of providing employment for males on an ad hoc and informal basis as individual situations allowed. Richard Stanton cited an IDA executive, for example, who in 1977 described "resolute bargaining by the Authority to persuade a new investor, proposing a 90 percent female work force, to cut this percentage" (1981:66).

In the early 1980s, the head of an IDA office in the United States stated in an interview that the financial incentives structures at that time were flexible and that more benefits were offered a prospective investor if the project fit certain criteria. One was the proposed sex of the work force. According to this official, a company proposing to hire more males was, all things being equal, offered more than a company seeking largely females (1982 interview with the author). The procedure outlined by O'Neill in 1972 was still used in the early 1980s.

The overall effect of such ad hoc procedures can best be gauged by comparing the percentage of females in foreign grant-aided firms in the key sectors in Ireland with the percentage in foreign firms in these same sectors in other export-led countries. Unfortunately, the availability of this type of information is limited; data exist in comparable form only for the electronics industry.[36]

Results of a 1981 survey by James Wickham and Peter Murray indicate that 72 percent of noncraft production workers in the Irish electronics industry were women and that 51 percent of the total work force in the electronics industry was female (1983). Evidence from other countries indicates that this figure is low. For example, Joseph Grunwald and Kenneth Flamm have shown that in 1980, 82

---

condition of joining the EEC—that Irish employment policy be changed to correspond with community equal employment legislation—may have also been a factor.

36. An accurate comparison requires employment of comparable industrial categories and data reflecting the type of production at that location.

percent of the electronics production workers in Mexico were female (1985). The proportion was even higher in Malaysia. Rachel Grossman indicates that 90 percent of the assembly workers in electronics plants in Penang were women (1980).[37] (In all cases, the production units referred to were largely foreign-owned.)

This suggests that the IDA's efforts to provide largely male employment remained relatively effective even though they were somewhat weakened in the late 1970s by the necessity to promote the development process. It is likely that informal pressures by the IDA dampened the tendencies of foreign firms in many industries to hire high percentages of women.

CONCLUSIONS

From 1961 to 1981 the employment opportunities for Irish women were shaped not only by the process of export-led development operating in a competitive market environment but also by the structure of state policy, which in addition to economic growth had as an objective the preservation of familial relations as outlined in the Constitution of Ireland. These goals were contradictory and involved difficult trade-offs for Irish state personnel.

The position of women in the labor market in Ireland during this period therefore reflected the impact of policies designed to attain each of these objectives and the manner in which contradictions between these objectives were resolved. Only by incorporating the role of state personnel, their objectives, and the impact of their policies into the analysis can this situation be understood.

The experience of the 1960s indicated that export-led growth would enhance female employment opportunities and alter traditional economic roles. The political economy of Ireland was more complex than a competitive economy, however; state personnel wished to promote job opportunities while maintaining traditional familial relations and designed policies to these ends. In the 1970s, when the influx of multinational corporations occurred, the state

37. Additionally, a survey of U.S. electronics firms in Malaysia reveals that 60 percent of the total work force is female, in comparison to the 51 percent in Ireland (Ramzi 1983).

was able to achieve these goals by planning to provide largely male employment and by the selective use of financial incentives to implement this plan.

By the late 1970s, the contradictions between the two major policies had intensified. IDA personnel realized that their efforts to increase employment growth were hampered by constraints on the availability of female workers. Although they had to defer to the fundamental need for net new employment, they were still able to influence the sex composition of the labor force in foreign-owned firms through ad hoc bargaining and discretionary use of funds.

The problem arising from the trade-off between the two major goals of the state was diminished during the 1970s, when discriminatory programs and practices allowed greater growth without jeopardizing traditional relations between the sexes.[38] Through explicit and informal policies, the Irish state was able to curtail use of female labor by multinational firms, contributing to the unexpectedly lackluster measures of women's labor force activity throughout the period.[39]

This case study has broader theoretical implications both for the literature examining the economic role of women during export-led development and for general economic and social theory. According to the literature on export-led growth, women are incorporated into the labor force as economic development occurs. To the extent that this literature discusses the role of the state, it is to focus primarily

---

38. The trade-off possibilities between the two goals of state policy were also reinforced by a broader range of government policies: employment policies such as the marriage bar, protective legislation, and the implementation of training programs and apprenticeships; and family policies that perpetuated unequal relations in the household (prohibition on divorce, limited access to contraception, laws regarding abuse). All of these had an adverse impact on labor market decisions regarding women during this period. For development of this broader argument, see Pyle 1990.

Although state personnel were forced to change some discriminatory employment policies in the mid- to late 1970s by the imperatives of the export-led development process, discriminatory employment practices persisted. This, in combination with virtually no substantive change in family law, meant that the freedom of women to enter the labor market remained constrained.

39. Contradictions between the goals of economic growth and the reproduction of traditional familial relations notwithstanding, my broader research indicates that state employment and family policies designed to maintain traditional relations between the sexes were the mechanism that kept measures of women's participation in the labor force relatively low in Ireland.

on its promotion of the development strategy; the fact that state personnel may also wish to perpetuate traditional familial relations is not incorporated into the analysis. The alternative approach developed in this chapter recognizes that structural impediments to the expected trend in female labor force participation may exist in the form of discriminatory state policy.

It is commonly accepted in the general literature that economic issues are subjects of interest for state personnel concerned with perpetuating their tenure.[40] Less understood is that maintenance of traditional relations between the sexes can be a major goal of state policy. Because state policies taken as a whole may not be gender-neutral, this case study reveals the importance of integrating the state into any analysis of the employment of women.[41]

---

40. This is also a relevant dimension to add to the analysis of the subordination and exploitation of women.

41. For example, see Nordhaus 1973 or Downs 1957.

6

WOMEN'S WORK AND WOMEN'S PLACE IN THE JAPANESE ECONOMIC MIRACLE

Larry S. Carney and Charlotte G. O'Kelly

The swiftness and scope of the economic growth and transformation of Japan in the postwar period has been likened to a "miracle." From the devastations of defeat in World War II, Japan has become the second most productive core economy in the capitalist world system and now challenges the United States for international technological supremacy.

Although most discussions of Japanese economic development have acknowledged the importance of female workers in the early stages of modernization, until recently few have given much attention to the vital role women have played in the post–World War II economy and in Japan's adaptation to structural changes in the world market.[1]

This chapter links three lines of arguments. (1) The ongoing political and social construction of female subordination has been a diffuse but important means by which state and capital have established and maintained the core position of the Japanese economy in the world system. (2) The historical struggles between capital and labor, mediated by both the repressive and reformist initiatives of the state, have taken place within a framework of ideological as-

---

1. Among recent contributions that analyze more fully the characteristics and functions of female labor in present-day Japan are Sheridan 1984, Y. Kawashima 1987, Fujita 1987 and 1988, and Kaji 1986.

sumptions that continuously have affirmed the peripheral and dependent character of female participation in the labor force. (3) The organizational features of contemporary Japanese capitalism have developed not only on the basis of the assumption of male dominance but have continuously reproduced this dominance in new, albeit contradictory, forms.

GENDER AND THE POLITICAL ECONOMY OF JAPANESE MODERNIZATION BEFORE 1945

Despite the sweeping changes in Japanese society in the post–World War II period, the characteristics and functions of female labor are still deeply rooted in the structural and ideological transformations that took place during the initial period of modernization beginning with the establishment of the Meiji state in the late nineteenth century and ending with the surrender in 1945.

The Meiji state (1868–1912) emerged as a response of aristocratic, military, and civil elites to the encroachment of Western powers.[2] The samurai bureaucrats who rose to political ascendancy at that time were preoccupied with maintaining the sovereignty and independence of the Japanese nation within a world system dominated by imperialist rivalries. They quickly perceived that a powerful military based upon an indigenously controlled industrial economy was the key to attaining and maintaining autonomy within this system.

The Meiji political project (and its continuation in other forms after 1912) was a supremely nationalist—or, as it has sometimes been called, an "ultranationalist" (Maruyama 1963)—complex of political responses and strategies. Its nationalism involved far more, however, than the simple exaltation of the Japanese as a nation and people. It entailed the "modernization of tradition": the elaboration of

---

2. A brief and useful compilation of source materials on the Meiji period may be found in Livingston, Moore, and Oldfather 1973. A nonmainstream treatment that we continue to find useful, despite some disagreements with its interpretive apparatus, is Halliday 1975. A recent major contribution to the historical understanding of Meiji ideology is Gluck 1985. Our own view on this subject is substantially in accord with Hirai's 1987 critique of Gluck. Arnason 1987 and 1988 and Ooms 1987 provide useful theoretical guidance for the study of state and ideology in Japanese history. From another perspective, Silberman 1982 addresses issues germane to our interpretation of the Meiji state.

themes and symbols of the supposed "uniqueness," even the supe-
riority, of Japanese culture—its traditions and values—as means of
ideologically implementing new forms of political legitimation, institutional innovation, and social domination directed toward modernizing Japanese society and its economy.

The Political Samuraization of
Family Relations and the State

At the heart of the emergent ideological mythification that informed
the Meiji project was what came to be known as *tennoism*, the "Emperor system." The reconstruction of the socialized Emperor as an
institution and symbol through which they could implement the
modernization of Japanese society was a commonly held goal among
ascendant Meiji elites, however much they may have differed regarding the form this implementation should take.[3] The Emperor,
presented as the divine bearer of a 2,500-year-old "unbroken" line
of succession to the Japanese throne, the essence of the Japanese
people and their traditions, was the primary ideological symbol
through which the state not only advanced its strategies to modernize
but through which it repressed and coopted opposing political and
social forces. At the same time, *tennoism* was itself embedded in a
much larger field of political-cultural discourse and practice in which
the contours and contents of national consciousness were reshaped
to legitimate both new forms of internal domination and resistance
to (Western) and embracement of (Japanese) imperialist expansion.
This field provided the ground not only for the modernization of
"traditional" Japanese thought but also the modernization of "traditional" Japanese social institutions.

Debate and bureaucratic infighting concerning institutional reform in Meiji Japan centered on the creation of new forms of government, civil and criminal law, the military and the police, the
educational system, and, not least, the family and place of women
within the family. Embryonic political movements for the liberation
of women did appear in Meiji Japan. But because they were inev-

---

3. Fujitani 1986 provides an excellent description of the (often literally architec-
tural) construction of the Emperor as a modern sacral institution and symbol of power.

itably linked to more diffuse culturally emancipatory, democratic, "popular," civil libertarian, socialist, or anarchist movements, they met not only official repression but also official and extra-official condemnation and repudiation as being "Western" in origin, as lying outside the spirit of *wa* or "harmony" that was projected as defining Japanese society and the "national polity" (Hane 1988; Sievers 1983; Nolte 1983b).

The subjugation of women in early modern Japan did not end, however, with the repression of conscious and active feminism. At the more pervasive levels of cultural and institutional reconstruction, women and their relationships to men became deeply and repressively implicated in the political project through which Japan became defined to itself as well as to others in the inter-imperialist arena.[4] Definitive for the gender dimensions of this reconstruction was the Meiji political debate over the "Japanese family system." One of the most remarkable paradoxes of the Meiji ideological reconstruction of Japanese society from a historical perspective is that *politically* the "traditional Japanese family" was largely a product of modernization.

The family system that was codified into law in the 1898 Meiji Civil Code was modeled primarily on the historical experience of the samurai warrior class. The Meiji juridical view of the family was constructed on an ideological base that presupposed the structural and psychological subsumption of women in the family and the fundamental ordering of their status in society on the basis of their relationships to male kin, most particularly to father, husband, eldest son, or eldest brother. In no sense were women conceived as independent citizens, breadwinners, producers, or workers, except in the most residual and contingent of circumstances.

Actual family structure in pre-Meiji Japan varied over time and by region, level of urbanization, and social class. At the same time, there is no denying that the kinship, household property, inheritance, and descent complex known as the *ie* had historically evolved

---

4. For the political dimensions of family change under modernization in Japan and their implications for macrosocietal forms of social control, see Kawamura 1983, Ueno 1987, Sievers 1983, R. Smith 1983, Nolte 1983a, Shibukawa 1971, Kano 1986, and Hani 1948.

in ways that in many respects may be described as a peculiarly Japanese adaptive form of domestic and communal organization (Paulson 1983). But within the larger historical framework of Meiji ideological and institutional innovation, the significance of the juridical samuraization of Japanese family relations lay in its utility as an instrument of social control and the "Japanization" of the relations between the citizen and the modern state. In the words of Japanese sociologist Fujiko Isono.

> [The] system of the [*ie*] was made the authorized system of the Japanese family *after* modernization and . . . the ideas and ethics of the *ie* were propagated through the modern system of compulsory education to social classes in which the relationships among family members had been far less authoritarian. (1964:42)

The highly articulated political-cultural construct of the "traditional Japanese family system" that emerged from the Meiji project became paradigmatic of a more diffuse mythification of social relations. The patterns of gender, age, and generational stratification embodied in the idealized version of the *ie* provided a basis for the ideological "familization" of the state. The state, in turn, clothed in the ideological garb of patriarchal familism, became the political and cultural instrument by which actual family and gender relations became more rigidly patriarchal. In the expanded Meiji ideology of the *ie*, the Emperor was the Father of the people; and the entire Japanese social structure was idealized as a national family ("the family state") in which all hierarchical authority structures could be legitimated on the basis of familistic imagery focused on male dominance and filial obedience. The *ie* system of family life was officially conceived as continuous with the kinds of authority relations that ideally should obtain in all aspects of Japanese society, as, for example, between landlords and tenants, employers and workers, teachers and pupils, military officers and recruits, officials and citizens.[5]

The structures and cultural perspectives of male dominance and authoritarian familism, new strategies of social and political

---

5. For the development of familistic business ideologies of labor relations on the part of Japanese business and industrial elites, see Marshall 1967.

domination, and elite efforts to achieve national unification and
accelerated modernization in the world system were thus fused
in the institutional and cultural transformations that informed
the Meiji project and its political successors until 1945. In the
conclusion of this chapter, we argue that the incorporation of
gender ideology into more comprehensive nationalist ideologies
available for the advancement of economic development and social control is by no means a lapsed practice in Japanese politics,
although the forms of this incorporation have experienced significant changes.

The Prewar Female Labor Force:
Structure and Ideology

The political samuraization of Japanese family life not only denied
women equality with men within prewar Japan's legal order and its
highly restricted democratic institutions. It also refined and enforced
the ideological and practical framework of family and gender relations that preserved women as an encapsulated peripheral labor
force within an expanding modern economy.

Beginning in the late nineteenth century, modern Japanese industry developed a characteristic dual structure, in the organization of both production and the labor market (Broadbridge
1966; Taira 1970; Jones 1976–77). In the early and intermediate
phases, there was a very small core sector of permanent workers.
These workers were lodged principally in large-scale and highly
oligopolistic units and sectors of production. The masses of peripheral workers, however, bore the brunt of the contradictions
and human depredations of capital accumulation and the development process. Until 1930, the peripheral sector of unskilled
industrial labor was made up principally of women, most of
whom were young and of rural origin. This peripheral sector
was utterly vital to Japan's early development as a modern and
eventually core economy in the world system (Kusano 1973;
Jones 1976–77).

In the early textile industries, young single women, many actually
children, were housed in squalid company dormitories and worked
either twelve-hour shifts, alternating day and night shifts every other

week, or as many as sixteen hours or more in single day shifts. They worked under crowded and often dangerous conditions, were subject to harsh discipline, and suffered a high incidence of serious and often fatal disease and injury. The women were usually recruited from rural villages and bound by contracts signed by their fathers for three to five years. These contracts involved a lump payment or "loan" to the father to be repaid out of deductions from the wages of his daughter. Deductions were also made for room and board, casualty insurance, and a compulsory payment to a company savings account. Little was left for the women. They were paid on a modified piece-work basis, while men working in the same industry were paid fixed wages. Their incomes were typically pitiable, well below those of their male co-workers, who themselves by no means constituted a labor aristocracy. Despite tight security, many of these women successfully fled their bondage; some went on to mount the first industrial strikes in Japan (Saxonhouse 1973; Kidd 1978; Hane 1982; Tsurumi 1986).

Not until the 1930s and the further development of heavy industry did the number of men exceed that of women as industrial workers, and only then did a truly permanent industrial labor force become rooted in Japanese society. With the establishment of this permanent work force in the factories and the growth of the office economy associated with the expansion of industry and commerce, the core, "lifetime employment" sector of the male labor force became more prominent, although it did not become a major aspect of the system until after World War II. Women not only continued to labor in industry almost entirely outside this sector, but their labor continued to be culturally defined as contingent. In fact, it represented an indispensable contribution of low-wage labor to the economy. The ideological nexus that masked this contradiction continued to be cast essentially within the framework of the Meiji political reconstruction of Japanese family "traditions": the only legitimate social roles for women were as wives and mothers; work outside the home or domestic economy was justified as an interlude before marriage, but in no way could it obviate women's fundamental status in society. Women were defined as human beings whose destinies were irrevocably embedded in the family (Sievers 1983.)

This ideology was reinforced from the beginnings of the 1930s through World War II as the nationalistic militarization of Japanese society spread and deepened with the expansion of Japanese imperialism throughout Asia. Thomas R. H. Havens has demonstrated that the ideological ascendancy of the idea that women were defined by their essential social function as wives and mothers actually inhibited the rational use of female labor on the Japanese home front during World War II. Female labor force participation rose in Japan during the war, but not nearly so much as in the United States, the Soviet Union, and Great Britain. Even the notoriously sexist Nazi regime made much greater use of female labor during the war than did Tojo's Japan. The major policy bias was to avoid, as much as possible, the use of *married* women as extra-domestic workers (Havens 1975).

Gender and the Labor Movement:
The Contradictions of Protectionism

With a few notable (and noble) exceptions, the prewar male-dominated labor movements—themselves persistently harassed, repressed, and delegitimated by the state—made little effort to incorporate female workers as equals (Tsurumi 1984). This phenomenon cannot be fully explained by the "hegemony" of male chauvinism or male economic self-interest, although these factors were certainly of considerable consequence. A broader perspective must include consideration of the severe restrictions on the political options available to labor in its struggle with capital. Detailed discussion of this subject lies beyond the scope of this chapter, but the contradictions faced by labor with respect to the division of the work force by gender can be illustrated by the prewar reformist debate over workplace protection.[6] This debate was to have considerable historical consequence for the positioning of female labor after 1945.

All prewar attempts to establish a body of law that would secure labor's right to organize and bargain collectively, including those initiated by reformist elements in the state, proved unsuccessful. The limitations of its political representation and the ever-present threat of repression pushed labor toward firm-specific strategies of con-

---

6. The following discussion relies heavily on Nomura 1978.

frontation with capital that could not be institutionalized at the level of law and judiciary practice. Insofar as a statutory basis for the protection of labor did emerge, much of it was focused on issues of workplace health and safety and restrictions on the length and ordering of the workday. The entire debate over these issues was shaped by the ramifications of interimperialist competition. It was also permeated by considerations of gender. Japan's rival imperialist powers in the West (particularly in the context of the deliberations of the International Labor Organization after its founding in 1919) persistently accused Japan of implementing its industrial advance in the world system on the basis of the exploitation of cheap labor ("social dumping"). Predictably, the characteristic response of the Japanese state and Japanese capitalists was that Westerners did not understand the "harmony" and "family feelings" that existed between employers and employees in Japan and the "beautiful Japanese customs" that informed their relationships (Nomura 1978; Crawcour 1978).

Because of their prominence, vulnerability, and well-documented exploitation in Japan's chief export industries (particularly silk reeling and textiles) and the pervasiveness of cross-national gender ideologies of female "weakness," women workers became the chief objects of the international controversy concerning workplace reform. The fledgling protectionist labor regime that emerged in Japan during the first decades of the twentieth century was, therefore, focused to a large degree on the status of women. Enforcement lagged well behind this legislation, but the interimperialist context of conflict and debate over the "labor question" served to give primacy to the question of protection of *female* labor—rather than of the working class. Indeed, ideologically, women were defined *out* of the working class: female workers were daughters who were potentially (and sometimes actually) mothers who (sometimes) worked but not "real" workers on par with men. As such, women needed special protection. The ideological and practical embeddedness of women in the family unit again determined the prevailing views of their status in the labor force, even when that status seemed deceptively elevated to one of privilege. Japanese labor reformers, both male and female, did not escape the consequences of the mystifications involved in this view of peripheral female labor. Japanese women *were* in dire need of protection in the workplace; but in the Japanese and international context of the time, the most socially resonant ideologies available to advance such protection were those of gender and family, not of class.

These issues were to be raised again within a framework of very similar assumptions and contradictions in the post–World War II period.

FEMALE LABOR IN THE
POSTWAR JAPANESE POLITICAL ECONOMY

The early intentions of the Allied occupation under General Douglass MacArthur were to dismantle much of Japan's already badly damaged industrial establishment, to distribute much of it through Northeast and Southeast Asia, and to turn Japan, at least for a number of years, into a disarmed semi-agrarian state (Schaller 1985). With the advent of the Cold War, however, and a clearer recognition of the economic implications of U.S. hegemony in the world system, a sharp turnabout took place in U.S. policy. As part of an emerging system of worldwide anticommunism and the effort to secure the foundations for the rapid expansion of a world market based on a new international division of labor, the United States chose to stimulate Japan's economic recovery and reindustrialization. Japan was to become America's chief anticommunist ally in the Pacific. The Korean War launched what was to become known as the "Japanese economic miracle," which lasted from the early 1950s to the beginnings of the 1970s.

During the 1960s and early 1970s, Japan's real gross national product grew an average of more than 10 percent a year. This astonishing economic expansion featured a close association between the state and big business; intense competition among collaborative "enterprise groups," which brought manufacturing, commercial, and financial firms into close association with one another in the oligopolistic sector; and, after the final crushing of the leftist labor confederations in the 1950s, increasingly collaborative relationships between organized labor and management (Gayn 1948; Moore 1983; A. Gordon 1985).

Structural Dualism and the
Lifetime Employment System

The expansion and structural transformation of the Japanese economy were characterized by the persistence and increased complexity of structural dualism. Growth in output and productivity of oligopolistic firms came increasingly to depend on the maintenance of quasi-paternalistic ties to intricate networks of intermediate and especially small-scale suppliers, subcontractors, distributors, and dealers whose flexibility, dependence, and market vulnerability permitted large firms to externalize many of the short-run risks and costs of competition, economic growth, and structural transformation. As much as their collaborative relations with the state, other oligopolistic firms, and their company unions, the shaping and regulation of dependent networks of small and intermediate-sized firms allowed technologically and organizationally sophisticated large Japanese corporations to become "long-term planners" in domestic and world markets.[7]

Structural dualism has, however, not been confined to interorganizational relations based on firm size. Within large-scale organizations themselves, different systems of labor relations have been developed that have also had the effect of making the best of Japan's large and intermediate-sized corporations supremely adaptive to the exigencies of global competition. It is in the complex relationships among core and peripheral systems of labor both between firms of different sizes and within firms, particularly larger ones, that the intersection of economic organization and gender has determined the structure of women's work and the parameters of women's place in the postwar Japanese economic miracle.

The essential framework for the organization of core labor in the Japanese economy has been determined by the historical evolution of what has come to be known as the "lifetime employment system" (LTES). Although the LTES was not institutionalized as a "system" until the 1950s, antecedents are found in a number of developments

---

7. Dore 1986 provides an overview and case study of these networks. A particularly revealing empirical account of another case is Pascale and Rohlen 1983. The role of subcontractors is described in *Focus Japan* (1978).

that characterized the struggle between capital and labor in the pre-war period (Crawcour 1978; A. Gordon 1985; Yoshino 1968). It was from the beginning a constructed system, and although its architects belonged exclusively neither to capital nor labor, the environment in which it was built in both the prewar and early postwar period (with the important exception of the first year and a half of the Occupation) was one of almost unrelieved repression by both capital and state of all truly politically adversarial forms of labor organization.

Although often described as the supposed product of "traditional" paternalistic features of Japanese culture, the familistic ideologies with which the LTES is commonly infused are also of modern invention and serve to obscure the rational and historically negotiated foundations on which it rests. In its present form it represents a historical "compromise" between large corporate capital and the relatively pacified post-1950s labor movements to maintain relative job security and in-firm job mobility for a circumscribed sector of labor in exchange for that sector's collaboration with capital's efforts to plan long range and to maintain organizational control of the workplace (Taira 1970).

The fact that the LTES has probably never included more than a third of the Japanese labor force at any one time (and probably now includes more nearly one-fourth) is not merely a result of the relative weakness of organized labor. It also reflects the underlying organizational logic of the post-1950s Japanese political economy itself: institutionally protected labor presupposed the structural "flexibility" and "adaptability" of relatively unprotected labor.

The essential features of the LTES have been widely described—as well as frequently idealized and reified—in the literature on Japanese management and labor relations.[8] Of crucial importance to the present analysis, however, is the fact that the LTES as the primary form of organization of core labor presupposes a quite specific model of the family and socially prescriptive gender division of labor. Male workers are expected to become responsible breadwinners (heads of families) *and* to be on call for sustained and "loyal" participation

---

8. For varying accounts of the system, see Yoshino 1968, Taira 1970, Carney and O'Kelly 1987, and especially Inagami 1988.

in the workplace, not subject to demands on their time and energies for familial responsibilities (Carney and O'Kelly 1987). The not-so-hidden assumed prerequisite for the maintenance of this availability and commitment by the core male worker is the confinement of women in the primary roles of housewife and mother.

In the early postwar period, even before the consolidation of the LTES, the contradictory and repressive (for women) implications of the gender division of labor implied by the LTES had already revealed themselves in the efforts of labor reformists to define the parameters of that other role for women demanded by Japanese capital: that of extra-domestic worker.

The Debate over "Protection of Motherhood"

The dilemmas and contradictions that were to face women working outside the home in the postwar period were clearly anticipated in the debates and political conflicts that surrounded the introduction of new labor legislation. Policy during the early years of the Occupation was, on balance, strongly on the side of the emancipation of labor and the formation of strong activist unions as loci for the democratic challenge of what were perceived to be the still-strong authoritarian or "fascist" tendencies of the Japanese ruling class (Nomura 1978). Within this framework, Japanese advocates of labor reform both seized upon and created opportunities to implement long-repressed programs of legal and institutional empowerment of the working classes. Women as workers were also to be emancipated within the framework of these reformist projects, given equal rights with male workers, and offered special encouragement and education to help them overcome their supposed cultural legacy of passivity with respect to labor issues.

But these programmatic concerns were counterbalanced by other preoccupations, namely those centered on specific protectionist labor legislation for female workers—or, as it was known in Japanese parlance, "the protection of motherhood"—and whether women were to be segmentally organized into "women's sections" in the newly legalized unions. Both Japanese and Occupation reformers, male and female, were split on these issues, but the eventual outcome of the implementation of policy, the reconstruction of law, and the institutionalization of practice was to reaffirm the *contingent* character and ultimately the *marginality* of female labor.

Issues related to the prewar reformist debate concerning the protection of female labor received renewed attention in the first year and a half of the Occupation. Although some labor advocates expressed fears that an overly protectionist regime would have the result of making women second-class citizens in the labor market, the Labor Standards Law, passed originally in 1947, severely restricted the conditions under which women could work outside the home. The prewar preoccupation with the protection of women as putative wives and mothers continued to dominate the consideration of gender in labor politics. Legal restrictions on the use of female labor were widely and plausibly viewed as barriers against the return of prewar patterns of exploitation. Nevertheless, these limitations inevitably had the effect of encapsulating female workers in the labor force as a gender-defined army of peripheral labor. Equal pay for equal work was ostensibly guaranteed (although never widely enforced). But women—with certain exceptions such as nurses and those working in restaurants and entertainment places—were forbidden from working between the hours of 10 P.M. and 5 A.M. ("no midnight labor"); from working overtime for more than two hours a day, six hours a week, or 150 hours a year; from performing various forms of "dangerous" work (working at heights above forty-five meters and lifting heavy weights); and from working underground. They were guaranteed the right to maternity leave, menstrual leave, and two breast-feeding breaks each workday (Cook and Hayashi 1980).

Rationales for most of these protections were patent and compelling, given prewar experience and the place of women in Japanese society. But unaccompanied by more comprehensive protectionist legislation for the working class as a whole or legal guarantees of women's right to exercise primary roles as workers, these regulations placed women at a clear *legal* disadvantage in securing permanent employment at the core of the Japanese labor force. Indeed, thousands of female workers in such industries as railway transport lost their jobs almost immediately on the implementation of the Labor Standards Law, as employers argued that they were unable to comply with its protectionist measures for women. These workers protested vigorously, pleading for legal exceptions for their occupations, but generally to no avail (Nomura 1978).

Women in the Postwar Labor Force: The Parameters of Participation

The forced withdrawal of women from the labor force because of the impact of the Labor Standards Act was part of a larger picture of general decline in female labor force participation lasting until the mid-1970s. In 1955, the participation rate for women fifteen years and older still stood at 56.7 percent. By 1975, it had reached its postwar low of 45.7 percent.[9]

But the percentage declines in labor force participation masked important changes in the composition of the female labor force. With rapid industrialization, the number of farm households declined dramatically, removing large numbers of female family workers from employment; rising educational mobility drastically reduced the supply of younger workers; and with the rapid decline in the birth rate after 1947, the twenty-to-twenty-four-year-old age group, the group with the highest participation rate, eventually declined in its relative position in the labor force. The numbers of self-employed women remained fairly stagnant over the period. In contrast, the numbers and relative proportions of paid female employees increased dramatically, from a total of 5,310,000 (31.2 percent of the females employed) in 1955 to 11,670,000 (59.8 percent of the females employed) in 1975 (Japan Institute of Labor 1981). After 1975, the labor force participation of women began to rise, reaching 48.6 percent in 1987. In the latter year, paid female employees numbered 16,150,000 or 66.5 percent of the female labor force. Women were 39.9 percent of the total labor force and 36.5 percent of paid employees.[10] Behind these figures lies the reality of women's place in the rapidly changing economy of postwar Japan: women's increasing importance as a structurally circumscribed group of non-lifetime workers and flexible labor reserve, strategically necessary to the maintenance of the restricted lifetime employment system and

---

9. The 1955 and 1975 figures are taken from Japan Institute of Labor 1981.
10. 1987 figures are from Japan Ministry of Labor 1988.

the facilitation of structural transition in a rapidly changing economy.

As Japan moved toward the advanced stages of industrialization, the rapid expansion of the tertiary sector of the economy, especially wholesale and retail trade and services, increased both the variety of available positions and the level of demand for female workers. By 1986, about 39 percent of working women were employed as clerical and sales personnel. In addition, the expansion of the modern economy created an increasing number of "female-specific" professional positions, such as teachers, pharmacists, and laboratory assistants; 10.7 percent of the female labor force were employed in jobs classified as "professional and technical" in 1986. Moreover, compared to most other advanced industrial nations, Japan's industry continued to call upon large numbers of female production workers; 22 percent of working women in 1986 still worked in the "craftsmen and production process" sector.[11] These figures reflect in part the continued importance of small-scale industry in the Japanese economy; but female workers, especially the young and unmarried, have also been widely used in the most advanced sectors (electronics and computer) of the postwar Japanese economy.[12]

The young and unmarried are not the only women who work outside the home in contemporary Japan. In recent years there has been a dramatic influx of married women back into the labor force. As late as 1960, only 25 percent of the paid female labor force were married. By 1987, the figure had reached 58.7 percent (Japan Ministry of Labor 1988). An additional 9.1 percent were divorced or widowed. Through the 1950s, the female participation rate displayed a "spiked" curve, with women in their late teens and early twenties at the apex. Today, the curve is "M-shaped"—the two peaks occur-

---

11. The figures for 1986 are from the *Japan Statistical Yearbook 1986* (1987).

12. During the 1960s and 1970s, the employment conditions of young, unmarried female workers in the electronics industry recalled some of the oppressive features of those of the "mill-girl" of the prewar period (Kaji 1973; Shiozawa 1977). Although conditions have generally improved considerably in recent years, a great deal of factory as well as office work (particularly in jobs created by automation) in which women are involved continue to receive their share of public exposure with regard to the prevalence of burnout, occupational disease, and worker demoralization (Agora Japan n.d.; Agora Japan 1985; Hiroki 1986). For current employment conditions of women as production workers in high-tech firms, see Fujita 1988.

ring in the twenty-to-twenty-four and forty-to-forty-nine age groups. The difference is attributable to returned married workers. In 1983, "working wives" outnumbered full-time housewives for the first time.

The main reasons for this transformation have been the following:

1. From 1960 to the oil crisis of 1973, Japan's booming economy faced increasingly difficult labor shortages. As a result, there was an increase not only in the beginning wages of male entrants to the labor force but in the demand for female workers.

2. These changes were part of a deeper structural change in labor demand: the exhaustion of plentiful supplies of cheap male labor from the countryside whose low wages were determined largely by market forces and its replacement by cheap female labor from both rural and urban areas whose lower wages are determined mainly by the operations of the gender stratification system.

3. With the onset of the slow growth period in the 1970s, increasing pressure was put on the LTES. Expansion of the numbers involved in this system has been partially restrained both by the cyclical hiring of full-time young female recruits, most of whom will leave the labor force (at least temporarily) after a few years, and by the hiring of mid–life entry married female workers who fall effectively outside the LTES.

4. The combination of the advancing longevity of the Japanese population and low birth rates has produced a constantly aging labor force. This has meant greater costs to firms in maintaining the LTES (where length of service is the major factor that determines wage increments) and increased difficulty in implementing the lock-step promotion patterns characteristic of the system. Firms have responded by laying off older workers and by creating incentives and sanctions designed to induce them to "volunteer" for early retirement. Female workers, especially mid-entry ones, who lie outside the LTES, have often replaced such workers in function, but not in status.

5. Within a general context of diminished economic growth in the world as a whole, the Japanese economy is experiencing a rapid structural transformation as Japanese firms and the Japanese government seek to command the competitive heights in the struggle for supremacy in the world market for high-technology goods and services. The processes of automation and reorganization of work

that attend this transformation have placed added strain on the LTES, not only because they have led to the elimination of specific types of labor but also because there is a need for greater fluidity in many areas of the labor market. Again, the flexible employment of female workers, who can make no claims on the expected rewards of the LTES, involves both cost and organizational advantages.

6. On the side of labor supply, the overwhelming factor pushing wives into the labor force has been the effects of slower growth on the family budget. Not only have the usual sizable increments in annual income characteristic of the period of rapid growth disappeared for most Japanese male heads of households, but their average real earnings have actually experienced periods of decline since the mid-1970s. In the face of soaring costs for housing and the increasingly onerous financial demands of their children's education, more and more wives have felt they have no choice but to work after their children enter school.[13]

In light of these developments, it is not surprising that a major feature of the growth in female employment in Japan has been not only the ascendancy of married workers but also the increasing importance of women working part time or on a "temporary" basis.

"Part time" in Japan is an elusive concept; from the standpoint of Japanese management, deliberately so. The government statistical agencies, following standard international practices, classify part-time workers as those working fewer than thirty-five hours per week. In fact, sizable proportions of those *classified* as part-timers actually work more than thirty-five hours per week, often as many or more hours than regular "standard" workers, and are employed continuously for years at the same firm, albeit without long-range contracts

---

13. The most detailed study of this phenomenon is Shioji 1980. There is no doubt that, as in the United States and elsewhere, more and more wives look to employment outside the home as an alternative to isolation in the household and restriction to a life dominated by interaction with children and other women. But also as elsewhere, this motivation to work outside the home has so far been of less importance than that born of the perception of economic necessity. As more and more married women do work, however, and as the service sector continues to expand, providing more and greater varieties of opportunities, working as a way to achieve "emancipation" is becoming more and more common in contemporary Japan, reinforced by the imagery of the "career" woman prominent in the media.

(Beauchamp 1985). These anomalies point to an important feature of the Japanese system of labor relations: workers, especially females, can be classified in a variety of ways, irrespective of the job performed and hours worked, as a means of buffering the effects of the LTES, lowering costs, and creating flexibility of labor. Different categories of workers doing the same work and working the same hours may earn very different wages, benefit from or be deprived of important fringe benefits, receive very different bonuses, or perhaps no bonuses at all, and enjoy very different levels of job security.

This same elasticity of classification applies to so-called "temporary" employees, who often perform very demanding full-time work requiring considerable skill, on a short-term contract basis, constantly subject to renewal but without guarantee, and without realizing the wages or accruing the benefits of the lifetime employee. Temporary employees also include the fast-growing army of "dispatched" workers, those supplied to firms by third parties (i.e., "manpower" agencies). The vast majority of these employees are women[14] (Watanabe 1985).

Also of considerable, if declining, importance in the Japanese peripheral labor force are off-site piece workers or so-called "industrial home workers" (*naishoku*), who work in their own homes or at other places of choice, addressing envelopes, assembling industrial inputs, finishing goods, packing, sewing, or performing a wide variety of other tasks. *Naishoku* work through contractors, and although they are officially classified as "self-employed," they must be distinguished from those members of the labor force who actually operate small businesses on their own account.

---

14. Statistical agencies of the Japanese government define temporary workers as those who are contracted (directly at the place of employment or through agency hire) for a specific period of one month to one year. They stand in contrast to "regular employees" (those who have a contract for an unspecified period of duration or for a period of more than one year) and "casual" or "day" workers (those who are employed on a daily basis or for a period of less than a month). "Part-timers" may be "regular," "temporary," or "day" workers. "Standard" workers are those who have worked continuously with one employer since entering the labor force upon completion of their formal education. It should be emphasized that this complex nomenclature implies not only, or even primarily, a convenient system of classification, but also fairly rigid differentials of wages and salaries, bonuses, fringe benefits, opportunities for promotion, job security, and social status.

Those Far from the Core:
Some Statistical Approximations

If we view owners of small businesses, family workers, wage earners
in small businesses, and part-time, temporary, and day and home
industrial workers as comprising the most visible and flexible elements of the peripheral labor force, we may draw the following
statistical portrait of nonagricultural female peripheral workers.[15]

Self-employed.   In 1986, self-employed owners of small businesses still constituted 11.2 percent of the labor force outside agriculture.[16] Women represented only 25.7 percent of small-business
proprietors and, significantly, only 18.7 percent of those who employed other workers.

Family Workers.   While males own the vast majority of small businesses, the more than 3 million nonproprietor family members (6.3
percent of the total 1986 labor force) who work in them are overwhelmingly female (82 percent). Thirteen percent of all female
workers outside agriculture fall into this category.

Workers in Small Firms.   Half of all workers in the private sector
are employed in small firms with fewer than thirty workers, but the
relative percentage of female workers (56.5 percent in 1986) is
higher than it is for males (46.3 percent). Forty-three percent of all
workers in small firms are female. Among paid employees, 43 percent of females (35 percent of males) work in small firms. Contract
earnings and extra payments for all *regular* employees who work in
firms with fewer than thirty workers average only 70 percent of

15. Unless otherwise noted, the percentage figures contained in the following
statistical portrait represent our own calculations based on tabular data presented in
Annual Report on the Labour Force Survey (1987). This portrait is necessarily imprecise
because of problems of undercounting in the data as well as the crudity of the
categories involved. Nevertheless, as in the more detailed analysis along the same
lines carried out by Y. Kawashima (1987), the overall picture is indicative, and no
doubt an underestimate, of the scope and range of the outer fringes of peripheral-
ization of the female labor force.
16. On the statistical problems of estimating the size of the small-business sector,
see Patrick and Rohlen 1987.

those who work in firms with thirty workers or more; but female earnings (regular workers) in small firms average only 53 percent of male earnings in this category (*Japan Statistical Yearbook 1986* 1987). Twenty-four percent of all female paid employees actually work in firms that employ only one to nine persons (males, 18.6 percent). Paid female employment by firm size is highly differentiated by age and marital status. In 1986, 48 percent of married employees worked in small firms, while only 26 percent of unmarried employees twenty to twenty-nine years of age (the age bracket that includes the majority of single female wage and salary earners) worked in such firms.

Part-timers.   Even recognizing the ambiguities of definition, part-time female employees are the growing edge of employment expansion in Japan today, and their statistical portrait is a truly remarkable index of gender stratification in the work force. Even though their actual incidence is no doubt underestimated,[17] official government surveys reveal that they are now about 23 percent of the paid female labor force (as opposed to 5 percent of males), up from about 9 percent at the beginning of the 1960s. They are 70 percent of the total paid part-time labor force. Most of these women are married, their average age in 1983 was 41.7 years, and more than two-thirds of them were over the age of thirty-five (Beauchamp 1985). Almost one-third of the net increase in female paid labor from 1960 to 1986 was accounted for by part-timers. In recent years this proportion has been even more dramatic, accounting for 42.6 percent of the net increase between 1979 and 1986. More than 13 percent of the *total* net increase in paid employment between 1960 and 1986 was made up of female part-time labor; the figure was 23 percent between 1979 and 1986. Over half of all female part-time employees are found in firms with fewer than thirty employees. The advantages of hiring such workers are as obvious for employers as is the inferiority of their position to regular employees. Eighty per-

---

17. The percentage figures in this section are all based on the official government definition of a part-time worker, that is, one who works an average of fewer than thirty-five hours per week. The size of the labor force *classified by employers* as "part time" is difficult to calculate with precision but is known to be significantly larger than that encompassed by the official definition.

cent of Japanese businesses rely to one degree or another on part-time labor (Beauchamp 1985). No longer are they hired to "assist" full-time workers, which was the prevailing custom in the past. Now they are fully integrated into the standard assignment of work tasks in the firm. With respect to the relative rewards they reap from their work, a government survey carried out in the early 1980s reported the following findings: (1) More than half of all the part-time workers received no paid holidays. (2) Although 65 percent of all firms paid bonuses to part-time workers, these averaged only 20 percent of the bonuses paid to standard workers. (3) Less than 10 percent of part-timers who worked for their employers *on a continuous basis* were included in the companies' retirement plans. The figure for "temporary" part-timers was less than 4 percent. (4) Less than 40 percent of part-timers working on a continuous basis were included in company health insurance programs (Beauchamp 1985).[18]

Temporary Workers.   Government figures also probably considerably underestimate the numbers of temporary workers. But there can be no doubt of the importance of such workers in helping the Japanese economy to adjust both to short-run changes in the business cycle and to long-term structural change. Temporary employees have represented a rather constant 3 percent of the officially recorded male paid labor force in recent years; but among females, the percentage rose from 12.7 percent in 1979 to 15 percent in 1986. Seventy-four percent of all temporary employees are women. Over 26 percent of the net increase in the paid female labor force between 1979 and 1986 was accounted for by female temporaries (full and part time); and 13.8 percent of the net increase in the total paid labor force during that period was due to additions of temporaries. Of particular significance are the marked year-to-year fluctuations in the hiring of temporaries due to movements in the business cycle, which varied within a range of annual increments of between 0.4 and 10.4 percent during the period 1980–86.

---

18. According to government calculations, an average thirty-five-year-old male with a high school education earned about four times the annual income of a female "part-timer" who worked the same amount of time (M. Kawashima 1985).

Day Workers. Day workers are particularly subject to under-counting but still officially represented 3.9 percent of the paid female nonagricultural labor force in 1986, down from 4.5 percent in 1979. The absolute number of female day workers remained constant over this period, while the total for males declined by more than 13 percent. Over 30 percent of female day workers are employed in manufacturing, and over 27 percent are employed in retail trade and eating and drinking places. The expansion of the latter sectors in the overall economy accounts for the lack of decline in the number of female workers in this category.

Home Industrial Workers. Official counts of industrial home workers in Japan have declined rapidly in recent years, registering almost a 50 percent drop since 1973. It is well known, however, that such workers figure prominently in the "invisible labor force" that does not enter into government statistics. In 1987, 1,025,000 were officially recorded, 93 percent of them women (4.2 percent of all female workers). If counted as paid employees (which officially they are not), they would represent 6 percent of the paid female labor force (Japan Ministry of Labor 1988). Female home industrial workers earn less than 60 percent of the average hourly wage of female part-timers (Japan Ministry of Labor 1988). They work completely outside the wage, benefit, and security system of the LTES but have an average duration of employment almost equal to that of female permanent employees (Y. Kawashima 1987).

Those Nearer the Core:
Institutional Exclusion

If one were to aggregate the categories of small business owners and family, temporary, day, and home workers—an exercise that would exclude "regular" part-timers—as a first approximation of the number of females in the peripheral labor force, one would find that in 1986, 39.1 percent of female workers in manufacturing, 44.3 percent in wholesale and retail trade and eating and drinking places, and 34.0 percent in services would be subsumed under these categories (*Annual Report on the Labour Force Survey* 1987). This crude exercise overlooks the impact of firm size on employment status; but even more important, it does not deal with those dimensions of work status that partially or totally exclude the majority of female "regular" workers from the benefits and protections of the LTES. A major case in point has been the widespread practice in the postwar period of subjecting young women from both the assembly line and office to involuntary "retirement."

Before the late 1960s, companies routinely enforced mandatory retirement for women upon marriage, birth of the first child, or at a "customary" age, such as twenty-four, twenty-five, or thirty. Women workers, often backed by dissident unions or by the Japan Communist party, fought these policies in the courts. Not until 1966 did the first landmark case establish a legal precedent for a reversal of these policies. In the aftermath of that decision, a number of court cases have been won by women challenging mandatory retirement because of marriage, pregnancy, or age. Such policies are, however, still widely implemented on an informal basis. Intense pressure is often brought to bear on those who fail to conform, and complainants still resort to the courts.

Throughout the postwar period the legal arguments of the firms involved in these cases have reflected the often reiterated public posture of their managers toward female workers: that women workers (1) by and large carry out supplementary and relatively unskilled labor; (2) usually work at jobs that require little training and that can easily be filled by the many inexperienced female job seekers coming out of the schools each year; (3) perform work that cannot rationally be remunerated on an ascending basis over time, which would be necessary if they were to remain on the job and receive wage increases according to educational credentials and years of service under the LTES; (4) represent unjustified costs to the firm if they are employed on a continuous basis, because of the existing protective legislation, which, among other things, requires maternity leave and special protections for women who work while pregnant; (5) as wives and mothers tend to be preoccupied with the responsibilities of housekeeping and child rearing, which lowers their job commitment and efficiency; and (6) within the framework of Japanese society are *expected* to accommodate their work careers to their primary roles as wives and mothers (Cook and Hayashi 1980).

Formal and informal policies of mandatory retirement have effectively excluded millions of young female workers from attaining
the securities and benefits of the LTES. As a persistent institutional
feature of Japanese employment practices in the postwar period,
these policies have had a major effect on the structuring of female
"career expectations" and the formation of women's attitudes toward
continuous work outside the domestic sphere. Employers often argue that most young women *voluntarily* leave the work force upon
marriage or the initiation of motherhood (i.e., they "want to"). But
the origins of the institutionalization of such "voluntary" behavior
can only be mystified when the behavior itself is analyzed apart from
the essentially coercive framework in which it has emerged and become culturally legitimated.

Quite apart from overt pressures to leave the work force at an
early age, female white-collar workers in particular confront a work
environment that reinforces at every turn the definition of their jobs
as temporary and that provides little room for expecting responsibilities, remuneration, or levels of self-fulfillment that approach
those available to men.[19]

In the white-collar workplace, Japanese women are expected to
assume a subordinate position appropriate to the gender hierarchy
and female gender roles. The process begins at the hiring stage,
when companies often recruit based on age and appearance rather
than merit. Once hired, a young woman faces stereotypical gender-
based job assignments. Whatever the formal position, female employees are usually expected to serve tea to male co-workers, greet
guests, do housekeeping chores around the office, and arrive early
to clean the desks of male employees, as well as their own. Skilled
secretarial work is often assigned to the lowest-ranking males on the
career escalator in a manner similar to the old apprenticeship
pattern.

Unlike male workers, females do not usually get extensive on-the-
job training in more substantive areas (Inoue 1985). They are not
rotated around the company so that they may gain a broad view of

19. For more extended treatments of the problems faced by female white-collar
and managerial personnel, see Rohlen 1974, McLendon 1983, Kaminski and Paiz
1984, Steinhoff and Tanaka 1986–87, and Carney and O'Kelly 1987.

its operations and are rarely transferred or given assignments requiring travel. These practices severely limit the women's usefulness
to their companies. Even women who formally hold managerial positions typically do not get such exposure; they are hired for a specific
set of skills, and their position in the company is tied exclusively to
their area of expertise.

Even when men and women receive the same base salary, male
employees commonly receive higher biannual bonuses than the females, and housing allowances and dependency allowances are provided primarily to married men. Male employees may also remain
on the job late into the evening, demonstrating their commitment
to the company, in a manner rarely available to married women,
who are expected to use their evenings to fulfill their child-rearing
and domestic responsibilities. Similar restraints restrict the opportunity of women, especially married women, to socialize after-hours
with co-workers and superiors.

At a more fundamental level, female aspirants to managerial or
professional achievement in Japanese corporations have to confront
the fact that the LTES itself presupposes, organizationally as well as
ideologically, the functional necessities of gender exclusion in the
workplace. In 1984, in the midst of a national debate on the passage
of an equal opportunity employment law, a Japanese journalist made
the revealing comment that the granting of equal employment rights
to women "may well destroy the lifetime employment system and
the seniority wage system, the very basis of the stability of Japanese
corporations" (Tayama 1984:883). In fact, the debate pursuant to
the passage of this law, the eventual form of the law itself, as well
as the corporate responses to it underscore the tenacity of institutionalized male dominance in the Japanese corporate economy, both
structurally and ideologically.

The New Equal Opportunity Law: Corporate Cooptation

The United Nation's International Year of the Woman in 1975 became the occasion for groups concerned with women's rights both
inside and outside of Japan to mobilize to pressure the Japanese

government to legislate an equal opportunity law.[20] The government's eventual decision to ratify the International Convention on the Elimination of All Forms of Discrimination against Women made the enactment of some version of such a law politically mandatory. Predictably, heated debate concerning various forms of proposed legislation centered on whether the law would maintain the regime of protective legislation for women in the workplace or whether most of these restrictions would be abolished in exchange for "equality" in the labor market.

Corporate Japan had long been opposed to the restrictive protectionist regime, while not hesitating to use its existence as a legitimation for discriminating against women in employment practices. Most (but not all) women's groups fought to maintain, or even expand, female protectionist legislation while vigorously supporting the passage of a law that would clearly proscribe discriminatory practices in hiring, promotion, retention, and training. The eventual legislation, passed in April 1985 and taking effect one year later, did prohibit gender discrimination in all these areas; but it also abolished or reduced many of the major restrictions contained in the corpus of "protection of motherhood" laws and regulations.

At the same time, the new law was congruent with the favored "consultative" strategies of Japanese elites in the use of the state to manage social change. While doing away with much of the protectionist regime, it only "obliged" employers "to make efforts" to end discrimination, provided no penalties for violations, and offered a nonenforceable mediatory process as the essential means by which aggrieved female workers could seek redress. Initial corporate responses to the law indicate that, in the Japanese context, it presents no real obstacle to capital's efforts to rationalize labor's "adaptation" to economic restructuring while preserving the "benefits" of institutionalized male domination. Perhaps the most indicative response has been the increased use of what is variously called "channeling management," "ramified career systems," or "personnel career track

---

20. For discussions of the Equal Opportunity Employment Law and the political debates surrounding its introduction and passage, see Kaji 1986, Hayashi 1986, and Centre for Asian Women's Workers' Fellowship 1987a, b.

systems." These systems were introduced at the end of the 1970s by several large Japanese trading companies. They have become increasingly common in the 1980s in large-scale corporations of all kinds, but particularly those in finance and banking (*Japan Times* 1986; M. Gordon 1986). Under these systems, all new white-collar employees (and usually younger workers who were already employed at the point of initiation of the system) are given the option of choosing a "track" that will define their conditions of employment. Typically, the system provides two or three tracks—prospective administrative officers/clerical staff, executive officers/technical staff, or "professional"/clerical staff. Usually the system is nominally applied to both men and women.

Ostensibly based on the choice of the individual to follow or not to follow a career path, these systems offer no fundamental challenge to the *organizational* hierarchy of the firm, which effectively turns initial "choice" into occupational destiny, most particularly with respect to the gender-specific sorting mechanisms for subordinate workers. Critics (Centre for Asian Women Workers' Fellowship 1987a) of the tracking systems have pointed out that the prevailing practices of testing, administrative review, and supervisory "guidance" have done little to encourage women to opt for the elite tracks and have turned away sizable numbers of women who have tried to enter them. At the same time, there has been no discernible movement of males into the type of "clerical" work customarily performed by females. It is clear that some women committed to professional/managerial careers have already benefited from these systems and that more will benefit in the future. What is revealing about the nature of such systems, however, is that they seem clearly to assume that on the basis of the "inclination" of most female white-collar workers—enhanced by formal and informal means of review and selection—the fundamental gender hierarchy of the workplace and the prevailing linkages between work and family life can be maintained, while at the same time judicious use can be made of a limited number of well-trained, highly skilled, and ambitious female professionals/managers. Again, Japan seems to be developing a more formal set of institutional mechanisms of gender stratification in the workplace to accomplish what is achieved by less visible means elsewhere.

Conclusion: State, Ideology, and the Management of Structural Change

Although Japan experienced its own version of the baby boom during 1947–49, economic recovery, the subsequent sustained period of high economic growth, rapid urbanization, government-sponsored family limitation programs (including almost unrestricted access to legal abortions), and the emergence of a highly competitive system of universal education and a chronic shortage of urban living space all worked to produce a demographic revolution of astonishing proportions. With this revolution came the accelerated nuclearization of Japanese family life. Of particular importance from the standpoint of the drafting of new cultural models of family relations for the society at large was the spread of family forms predicated on the male career trajectories and work demands of the LTES, especially as they applied to white-collar workers (Imada and Imada 1982).

But despite these developments and the fact that the constitution imposed by the Occupation in 1947 swept away the juridical foundations of the *ie,* creating legal equality between men and women in marriage, the "Japanese family system" as national ideology has not disappeared. Of particular importance to this analysis is the political-cultural transmutation of the concept of the "traditional" Japanese family to embrace the nuclear family ideal of women defined as essentially (house)wives and mothers for whom abstention from continuous full-time participation in the labor force outside the home is regarded not only as a familial duty (and necessity) but a fulfillment of unique national-cultural ideals. From this perspective, women as wives and mothers are seen as "in service" to the nation, a kind of long-suffering and dedicated army of wifely and maternal soldiers who are the domestic counterparts of the husbands who wage economic war in the world system. Government and economic elites have promulgated such imagery, as have the media, academic literature, and the educational system; but the imagery itself is reflective of pervasively institutionalized patterns of everyday symbolic interaction in Japanese society. Douglas Lummis describes a vignette that illustrates the effective synthesis of nationalist and gender ideologies that informed the Japanese public's response to

the exigencies of international competition during the peak years of
postwar economic expansion:

> I attended a wedding and a reception several years ago in a hotel, and
> one of the things that impressed me was the speech by the matchmaker.
> . . . He began at the level of international economics, and Japan's supreme
> position. He said he had recently been to England and had seen for himself
> the social causes of the decline in the British economy, and so had learned
> the secret of Japan's success in the great war between capitalist countries
> for economic supremacy. It was, he said, the dedication of each worker
> to his company, and beneath that, the absolute foundation of all of it, the
> fact that Japanese wives accept that their husbands belong to their com-
> panies, and will not interfere with the companies' primary power over
> their husbands. In other words, Japanese wives will not and must not
> complain when their husbands have no vacations, when their husbands
> come home late, etc., etc., etc. And so his whole speech, beginning with
> international economics and working down step by step to the family, was
> in the end addressed to the bride, telling her, ordering her, putting the
> weight not only of the people gathered there, but of the whole country
> on her, to be obedient to the company. It was as if it was the analysis of
> a radical feminist turned upside down. (Kogawa and Lummis 1985:51)

The linkages between gender stratification and the celebrated Japanese "work ethic" are seldom explored by foreign observers of
Japanese society, but they are well understood by the Japanese themselves (Atsumi 1988).

It would be disingenuous to infer from Lummis's or other de-
scriptions of genderized political economic ideology in postwar Japan
that Japanese women live in a benighted state of psychological ab-
jection in the family. For most, this is simply not the case. What is
important in the present context is that the incorporation of family-
gender ideology of this kind into the prevailing forms of national
discourse concerning the challenges and dilemmas facing Japan in
the competitive world system serves not only to reinforce the *ideal*—
that the place of women is "in the home"—but also, in a more complex way, to legitimate their encapsulation in the labor force as a
flexible army of peripheral workers while masking the systematic
violation of the ideal that takes place at the level of institutionalized
practice.

The ideologies of women's place do not drift unattended in the world of Japanese business and the Japanese state. They are put to use to facilitate the realization of male elites' visions of the Japanese future and of the place of Japan in the ranks of nations. The present form of incorporation of women in the Japanese labor force was anticipated by Japanese planners not merely as the working out of the operations of the "invisible hand" of the marketplace but as a planning strategy in which gender subordination could be utilized as a resource to rationalize economic transition. In 1963, a report of the prestigious and influential Economic Council, an advisory agency to the prime minister, made the following proposals to Japanese industry as means of dealing with the future labor needs of the economy:

1. To use extensively young, unmarried female workers in simple jobs.
2. To use only a small number of educated women in supervisory positions.
3. To return to their families women of a suitable age for marriage.
4. To rehire persons (e.g. women) of middle age. (Perry 1976:193)

Six years later, a study commission of the joint Committee of the Council on the Labor Force in the Economy stated that in order to sustain high rates of growth, 8.4 million new workers had to be "recruited from a labor force which has not yet been drafted, mainly housewives" (Kaji 1973:377).

In another vein, today in the late 1980s, government bureaucrats, politicians, journalists, and academics continue a campaign ("Perfecting the Foundations of the Family") begun in the mid-1970s to extol and promote the strengthening of the "Japanese welfare society," an effort, inspired by the politics of fiscal retrenchment, to maintain wives, mothers, and daughters as the principal (unpaid) angels of support for the sick, the handicapped, and especially the aged of Japanese society (Watanuki 1986; Hayashi 1986; Kitazawa 1986). This political-ideological project should bear a particular pathos for women when viewed in light of projections by government economic planners that, because of economic restructuring, the ratio for 1985 of six full-time workers in the labor force to one part-time worker will fall to three to one by the beginning of the 1990s (M. Kawashima 1985).

Currently, most women in Japan, as well as government and industry, seem to accept as normative the phased participation pattern of work outside the home represented by the M curve. In this sense, the earlier postwar Japanese version of the "two-sphere" doctrine—the husband as exclusive breadwinner, the wife as full-time child rearer and homemaker—appears to have been modified to allow women to return to the labor force at least part time after their children have entered school. Comparatively few Japanese women express a desire for a full-time "career" that will extend throughout their married and child-bearing years (Japan. Prime Minister's Office 1984).

But in Japan, as elsewhere, stability and shifts in normative orientations and "career choices" are notoriously difficult to separate from realistic expectations within the limitations imposed by the social arrangements and cultural milieux in which individuals live out their lives. Trends indicate that under current economic conditions of slow growth and structural transition, a growing proportion of Japanese women are working continuously through both the initial stages of marriage and child rearing, whatever the prevailing images of the "ideal." At the same time, younger women who have left the work force temporarily are returning at earlier ages than did the cohorts of women born before them (Holden 1983). The M curve is definitely beginning to flatten, as it already has in other advanced industrial societies. How will working wives and mothers react over time to continuous discrimination and restriction of opportunity in the workplace, factors of which they are clearly conscious but which they have not yet vigorously protested on a mass basis?[21]

In the midst of the structural changes taking place in the Japanese economy, women's values and aspirations are also changing. Although discrimination and lack of opportunity in the world of work outside the home may not yet be salient preoccupations for the majority of Japanese women, they are certainly becoming concerns for more and more women, especially those who are younger and

---

21. On Japanese women's consciousness of gender inequality in the workplace as well as in society at large, see Japan. Prime Minister's Office 1983. Mackie 1988 provides a contextual analysis of the politics of feminism in Japan today.

more educated. Furthermore, married women are becoming increasingly concerned with the quality of their relationships with their husbands and with the burdens imposed by their lack of involvement in domestic work and child rearing (O'Kelly and Carney 1986). Along these two vectors, one would anticipate the contradictions and conflicts as well as the new aspirations that will provide the context for whatever challenge to "women's place" may emerge in Japanese society in the near future. It is in response to these structural and attitudinal changes that one would also anticipate future efforts on the part of Japanese elites to elaborate ideologically and politically the connections between gender and nationality as a resource for economic advance in the world system.

PART III

RESISTANCE AND AMBIVALENCE

7

"THEIR LOGIC AGAINST THEM": CONTRADICTIONS IN SEX, RACE, AND CLASS IN SILICON VALLEY

Karen J. Hossfeld

The bosses here have this type of reasoning like a seesaw. One day it's "you're paid less because women are different than men," or "immigrants need less to get by." The next day it's "you're all just workers here—no special treatment just because you're female or foreigners."

Well, they think they're pretty clever with their doubletalk, and that we're just a bunch of dumb aliens. But it takes two to use a seesaw. What we're gradually figuring out here is *how to use their own logic against them.*

—Filipina circuit board assembler in Silicon Valley (emphasis added)

This chapter examines how contradictory ideologies about sex, race, class, and nationality are used as forms of both labor control and labor resistance in the capitalist workplace today. Specifically, I look at the workplace relationships between Third World immigrant women production workers and their predominantly white male managers in high-tech manufacturing industry in Silicon Valley, California. My findings indicate that in workplaces where managers and workers are divided by sex and race, class struggle can and does take gender- and race-specific forms. Managers encourage women immigrant workers to identify with their gender,

---

This chapter draws from a forthcoming book to be published by the University of California Press.

racial, and national identities when the managers want to "distract" the workers from their *class* concerns about working conditions. Similarly, when workers have workplace needs that actually *are* defined by gender, nationality, or race, managers tend to deny these identities and to stress the workers' generic class position. Immigrant women workers have learned to redeploy their managers' gender and racial tactics to their own advantage, however, in order to gain more control over their jobs. As the Filipina worker quoted at the beginning of the chapter so aptly said, they have learned to use managers' "own logic against them."

One of the objectives of this chapter is to expand traditional definitions of workplace resistance and control. All too frequently, these definitions have failed to consider the dynamics of gender and racial diversity. Another goal is to add to current theoretical debates about the changing conditions of capitalist, patriarchal, and national labor arrangements. My empirical data verify what Diane Elson and Ruth Pearson (1981a), Maria Patricia Fernandez-Kelly (1983), June Nash and Fernandez-Kelly (1983), Helen Safa (1981), and many others have documented: namely, that the "new" international division of labor is increasingly based on gender, as well as class and nation. In addition, my findings confirm what Rachel Grossman (1979), Lenny Siegel (1980), and Linda Lim (1978) have each suggested: that high-tech industry is at the forefront of these trends toward a globalized, "gendered" labor division. Finally, I hope to inform strategic questions posed by organizers and workers who are faced with the struggle against this increasingly hierarchical and fragmented division of labor.

This chapter draws from a larger study of the articulation of sex, race, class, and nationality in the lives of immigrant women high-tech workers (Hossfeld 1988b). Empirical data draw on more than two hundred interviews conducted between 1982 and 1986 with Silicon Valley workers; their family members, employers, and managers; and labor and community organizers. Extensive in-depth interviews were conducted with eighty-four immigrant women, representing twenty-one Third World nationalities, and with forty-one employers and managers, who represented twenty-three firms. All but five of these management representatives were U.S.-born white males. All of the workers and managers were employed in

Santa Clara County, California, firms that engaged in some aspect of semiconductor "chip" manufacturing. I observed production at nineteen of these firms.

Before turning to the findings of my field research, I briefly situate the global context of Silicon Valley's highly stratified division of labor and identify the class structure and demographic features of its high-tech industry.

SILICON VALLEY

The Prototype

"Silicon Valley" refers to the microelectronics-based high-tech industrial region located just south of San Francisco in Santa Clara County, California. The area has been heralded as an economic panacea and as a regional prototype for localities around the globe that seek rapid economic growth and incorporation into the international market. Representatives from more than two thousand local and national governments, from People's Republic of China delegations to the queen of England, have visited the valley in search of a model for their own industrial revitalization. They have been awed by the sparkling, clean-looking facilities and the exuberant young executives who claim to have made riches overnight.[1] But the much-fetishized Silicon Valley "model" that so many seek to emulate implies more than just the potential promise of jobs, revenue, growth, and participation in the technological "revolution."

The development of the microelectronics industry in its current form involves highly problematic relations of production that extend both inside and outside the workplace. Microelectronics is the "way of the future" not only technologically but, as developed under capitalism, in its work arrangements and social relationships, which are predicated on sharp divisions according to sex, race, class, and nation. Not only the *technology* of microelectronics but the structure of its industries as well are important tools in the capitalist economy's constant search for new permutations in the division of labor. What

---

1. For a comprehensive analytical description of the development of Silicon Valley as a region and an industry, see Saxenian 1981.

Silicon Valley is all about, then, is more than laser technology, video games, and illusory hottubs for the masses; it is about class structure, class struggle, and the division of labor.

The media have been much enamored with the computer "revolution" in general and in particular with the imagery and ideology of the industry's preponderance of "self-made" millionaires. But for every young, white boy-wonder who made his first million tinkering in the garage (as folklore says the founders of the Apple Computer Company, Steve Jobs and Steve Wozniak, did), there are scores of low-paid immigrant women workers. These women from Mexico, China, Vietnam, Korea, the Philippines, and other Third World countries prop up the computer revolution, in what amounts to a very *un*revolutionary industrial division of labor.

Since the 1960s, the large U.S. microelectronics manufacturers have been shifting production facilities to "offshore" locations, primarily in Southeast Asia, but also in Mexico, Puerto Rico, and other locations in both the Third World and Europe. Assembly work has been particularly easy to shift abroad since the materials involved are light in weight, small in size, and of relatively low per-unit value. Materials and assembled products are thus easy to transport. Assembly requires little special equipment or skilled labor when performed manually: the work involves relatively low capital investment but is labor-intensive. Frequently, semiconductors are manufactured in the United States, shipped abroad, where they are assembled and sometimes tested, and then shipped back to the United States for final inspection, packaging, and distribution. Increasingly, any one circuit board on the U.S. market represents labor performed in several countries.

The major motivating force in shifting production has been to cut labor costs. Assembly workers in most Third World high-tech outposts are paid only a few dollars a day. According to my informants at the American Electronics Association, assembly workers in the Philippines, for example, earn one-tenth of what they do in Silicon Valley. But which countries the companies choose to go to has depended on other labor and investment considerations as well. The Singapore government, for example, has actively courted multinational high-tech firms and has offered them economic and tax incentives. The governments of Singapore, Korea, and the Philippines have strongly discouraged and in some cases outlawed labor organizing and strikes (although the "investment climate" in the Philippines may change under Corazon Aquino's government). In a global economy that is short on both capital and jobs, microelectronics firms have been able to shop around the world for the most advantageous labor market conditions.

The skewed division of labor based on gender and race is even more pronounced in offshore sites than in Silicon Valley. Invariably, offshore assembly plants employ young women almost exclusively, the figurative if not the literal sisters of Third World immigrants who work in Silicon Valley. With no Equal Employment Opportunity Commission (EEOC) or other state watchdogs and no unions with bargaining power, firms are free to discriminate openly according to sex, age, and marital status.

Although most low-paying, high-tech jobs are sent to the periphery and semiperiphery of the world economy, firms continue to employ production workers in Silicon Valley to meet the ongoing need for quickly available prototypic and short-term projects. Thus, during the 1980s, the *percentage* of production work done in the valley declined drastically, as the industry expanded, but the number of production jobs did not decrease significantly. Although most manufacturing done on-site in Silicon Valley involves "higher-tech" stages of the production process, the assembly work that immigrant women engage in closely resembles the same "low-tech" labor done by their "sisters" overseas.

What Silicon Valley offers the numerous other "Silicon dales" and "deserts" that are springing up around the world is not only a model of technological know-how and development, but also—and equally important—a model of labor control based on highly stratified divisions of race, sex, and class. This study suggests that this division of labor stratifies not only Singapore and San Francisco—core and periphery—but workers within the core metropole itself.

Class Structure and the Division of Labor

Close to 200,000 people—one out of every four employees in the San Jose Metropolitan Statistical Area labor force—work in Silicon

Valley's microelectronics industry. There are more than 800 manufacturing firms that hire ten or more people each, including 120
"large" firms that each count over 250 employees. An even larger
number of small firms hire fewer than ten employees apiece. Approximately half of this high-tech labor force—100,000 employees—
works in production-related work: at least half of these workers—
an estimated 50,000 to 70,000—are in low-paying, semiskilled operative jobs (Siegel and Borock 1982; *Annual Planning Information*
1983).[2]

The division of labor within the industry is dramatically skewed
according to gender and race. Although women account for close
to half of the total paid labor force in Santa Clara County both inside
and outside the industry, only 18 percent of the managers, 17 percent of the professional employees, and 25 percent of the technicians
are female. Conversely, women hold at least 68 percent and by some
reports as many as 85 to 90 percent of the valley's high-tech operative
jobs. In the companies examined in my study, women made up an
average of 90 percent of the assembly and operative workers. Only
rarely do they work as production managers or supervisors, the
management area that works most closely with the operatives.

Similar disparities exist vis-à-vis minority employment. According
to the 1980 census, 26.51 percent of the civilian work force of Santa
Clara County was composed of racial minorities. Fifteen percent
were Hispanic (all races); 7.5 percent were Asian–Pacific Islanders;
3 percent were Black; 0.5 percent were Native-American; and 0.2
percent were listed as "other races—not Hispanic" (*Annual Planning
Information* 1983:96–97). Over 75 percent of the Hispanics were of
Mexican descent. Of the 102,000 Asian–Pacific Islanders counted in
the 1980 census as living in the area, roughly 28 percent were Filipino
or of Filipino descent; 22 percent each were Japanese and Chinese:
11 percent were Vietnamese; 6 percent were Korean; 5 percent were
Asian Indian; and less than 2 percent each were of other national
origins (*Annual Planning Information* 1983:64).

---

2. These production jobs include the following U.S. Department of Labor occupational titles: semiconductor processor; semiconductor assembler; electronics assembler; and electronics tester. Entry-level wages for these jobs in Silicon Valley in 1984
were $4.00 to $5.50; wages for workers with one to two years or more experience
were $5.50 to $8.00 an hour, with testers sometimes earning up to $9.50.

Since the census was taken, influxes of refugees from Indochina have quadrupled the number of Vietnamese, Laotians, and Cambodians in the area: as of early 1984, there were an estimated forty-five thousand Southeast Asian refugees in Santa Clara County, as well as a smaller but growing number of refugees from other regions such as Central America. I have talked with Silicon Valley production workers from at least thirty Third World nations. In addition to the largest groups, whose members are from Mexico, Vietnam, the Philippines, and Korea, workers hail from China, Cambodia, Laos, Thailand, Malaysia, Indonesia, India, Pakistan, Iran, Ethiopia, Haiti, Cuba, El Salvador, Nicaragua, Guatemala, and Venezuela. There are also small groups from southern Europe, particularly Portugal and Greece.

Within the microelectronics industry, 12 percent of the managers, 16 percent of the professionals, and 18 percent of the technicians are minorities—although they are concentrated at the lower-paying and less powerful ends of these categories. An estimated 50 to 75 percent of the operative jobs are thought to be held by minorities.[3] My study suggests that the figure may be closer to 80 percent.

Both employers and workers interviewed in this study agreed that the lower the skill and pay level of the job, the higher the percentage of Third World immigrant women who were employed. Thus assembly work, which is the least skilled and lowest-paying production job, tends to be done predominantly by Third World women. Entry-level production workers, who work in job categories such as semiconductor processing and assembly, earn an average of $4.50 to $5.50 an hour; experienced workers in these jobs earn from $5.50 to $8.50. At the subcontracting assembly plants I observed, immigrant women accounted for 75 to 100 percent of the production labor force. At only one of these plants did white males account for more than 2 percent of the production workers. More than 90 percent of the managers and owners at these businesses were white males, however.

---

3. "Minority" is the term used by the California Employment Development Department and the U.S. Department of Labor publications in reference to people of color. The statistics do not distinguish between immigrants and nonimmigrants within racial and ethnic groupings.

This occupational structure is typical of the industry's division of labor nationwide. The percentage of women of color in operative jobs is fairly standardized throughout various high-tech centers; what varies is *which* minority groups are employed, not the job categories in which they are employed.[4]

Obviously, there is tremendous cultural and historical variation both between and within the diverse national groups that my informants represent. Here I emphasize their commonalities. Their collective experience is based on their jobs, present class status, recent uprooting, and immigration. Many are racial and ethnic minorities for the first time. Finally, they have in common their gender and their membership in family households.

LABOR CONTROL ON THE SHOP FLOOR

Gender and Racial Logic

In Silicon Valley production shops, the ideological battleground is an important arena of class struggle for labor control. Management frequently calls upon ideologies and arrangements concerning sex and race, as well as class, to manipulate worker consciousness and to legitimate the hierarchical division of labor. Management taps both traditional popular stereotypes about the presumed lack of status and limited abilities of women, minorities, and immigrants and the workers' own fears, concerns, and sense of priorities as immigrant women.

But despite management's success in disempowering and devaluing labor, immigrant women workers have co-opted some of these ideologies and have developed others of their own, playing on management's prejudices to the workers' own advantage. In so doing, the workers turn the "logic" of capital against managers, as they do the intertwining logics of patriarchy and racism. The following section examines this sex- and race-based logic and how it affects class

---

4. In North Carolina's Research Triangle, for example, Blacks account for most minority employment, whereas in Albuquerque and Texas, Hispanics provide the bulk of the production labor force. Silicon Valley has perhaps the most racially diverse production force, although Hispanics—both immigrant and nonimmigrant—still account for the majority.

structure and struggle. I then focus on women's resistance to this manipulation and their use of gender and racial logics for their own advantage.

From interviews with Silicon Valley managers and employers, it is evident that high-tech firms find immigrant women particularly appealing workers not only because they are "cheap" and considered easily "expendable" but also because management can draw on and further exploit preexisting patriarchal and racist ideologies and arrangements that have affected these women's consciousness and realities. In their dealings with the women, managers fragment the women's multifaceted identities into falsely separated categories of "worker," "ethnic," and "woman." The effect is to increase and play off the workers' vulnerabilities and splinter their consciousness. But I also found limited examples of the women drawing strength from their multifaceted experiences and developing a unified consciousness with which to confront their oppressions. These instances of how the workers have manipulated management's ideology are important not only in their own right but as models. To date, though, management holds the balance of power in this ideological struggle.

I label management's tactics "gender-specific" and "racial-specific" forms of labor control and struggle, or gender and racial "logic." I use the term *capital logic* to refer to strategies by capitalists to increase profit maximization. Enforcement by employers of a highly stratified class division of labor as a form of labor control is one such strategy. Similarly, I use the terms *gender logic* and *racial logic* to refer to strategies to promote gender and racial hierarchies. Here I am concerned primarily with the ways in which employers and managers devise and incorporate gender and racial logic in the interests of capital logic. Attempts to legitimate inequality form my main examples.

I focus primarily on managers' "gender-specific" tactics because management uses race-specific (il)logic much less directly in dealing with workers. Management clearly draws on racist assumptions in hiring and dealing with its work force, but usually it makes an effort to conceal its racism from workers. Management recognizes, to varying degrees, that the appearance of blatant racism against workers is not acceptable, mainly because immigrants have not sufficiently internalized racism to respond to it positively. Off the shop floor, however, the managers' brutal and open racism toward workers was apparent during "private" interviews. Managers' comments demonstrate that racism is a leading factor in capital logic but that management typically disguises racist logic by using the more socially acceptable "immigrant logic." Both American and immigrant workers tend to accept capital's relegation of immigrants to secondary status in the labor market.

Conversely, "gender logic" is much less disguised: management uses it freely and directly to control workers. Patriarchal and sexist ideology is *not* considered inappropriate. Because women workers themselves have already internalized patriarchal ideology, they are more likely to "agree" with or at least accept it than they are racist assumptions. This chapter documents a wide range of sexist assumptions that management employs in order to control and divide workers.

Gender Ideology

A growing number of historical and contemporary studies illustrate the interconnections between patriarchy and capitalism in defining both the daily lives of working women and the nature of work arrangements in general. Sallie Westwood, for example, suggests that on-the-job exploitation of women workers is rooted in part in patriarchal ideology. Westwood states that ideologies "play a vital part in calling forth a sense of self linked to class and gender as well as race. Thus, a patriarchal ideology intervenes on the shopfloor culture to make anew the conditions of work under capitalism" (1985:6).

One way in which patriarchal ideology affects workplace culture is through the "gendering" of workers—what Westwood refers to as "the social construction of masculinity and femininity on the shop floor" (page 6). The forms of work culture that managers encourage, and that women workers choose to develop, are those that reaffirm traditional forms of femininity. This occurs in spite of the fact that, or more likely because, the women are engaged in roles that are traditionally defined as nonfeminine: factory work and wage earning. My data suggest that although factory work and wage earning are indeed traditions long held by working-class women, the dominant *ideology* that such tasks are "unfeminine" is equally traditional. For example, I asked one Silicon Valley assembler who worked a

double shift to support a large family how she found time and finances to obtain elaborate manicures, makeup, and hair stylings. She
said that they were priorities because they "restored [her] sense of
femininity." Another production worker said that factory work
"makes me feel like I'm not a lady, so I have to try to compensate."

This ideology about what constitutes proper identity and behavior
for women is multileveled. First, women workers have a clear sense
that wage earning and factory work in general are not considered
"feminine." This definition of "feminine" derives from an upper-
class reality in which women traditionally did not need (and men
often did not allow them) to earn incomes. The reality for a production worker who comes from a long line of factory women does
not negate the dominant ideology that influences her to say, "At
work I feel stripped of my womanhood. I feel like I'm not a lady
anymore. It makes me feel... unattractive and unfeminine."

Second, women may feel "unwomanly" at work because they are
away from home and family, which conflicts with ideologies, albeit
changing ones, that they should be home. And third, earning wages
at all is considered "unwifely" by some women, by their husbands,
or both because it strips men of their identity as "breadwinner."

On the shop floor, managers encourage workers to associate "femininity" with something contradictory to factory work. They also
encourage women workers to "compensate" for their perceived loss
of femininity. This strategy on the part of management serves to
devalue women's productive worth.

Under contemporary U.S. capitalism, ideological legitimation of
women's societal roles and of their related secondary position in the
division of labor is already strong outside the workplace. Management thus does not need to devote extreme efforts to developing
new sexist ideologies within the workplace in order to legitimate the
gender division of labor. Instead, managers can call on and reinforce
preexisting ideology. Nonetheless, new forms of gender ideology
are frequently introduced. These old and new ideologies are dis-
seminated both on an individual basis, from a manager to a worker
or workers, and on a collective basis, through company programs,
policies, and practices. Specific examples of informal ways in which
individual managers encourage gender identification, such as flirting, dating, sexual harassment, and promoting "feminine" behavior,

are given below. The most widespread company practice that encourages engenderment, of course, is hiring discrimination and job segregation based on sex.

An example of a company policy that divides workers by gender is found in a regulation one large firm has regarding color-coding of smocks that all employees in the manufacturing division are required to wear. While the men's smocks are color-coded according to occupation, the women's are color-coded by sex, regardless of occupation. This is a classic demonstration of management's encouragement of male workers to identify according to job and class and its discouragement of women from doing the same. Regardless of what women do as workers, the underlying message reads, they are nevertheless primarily women. The same company has other practices and programs that convey the same message. Their company newsletter, for example, includes a column entitled "Ladies' Corner," which runs features on cooking and fashion tips for "the working gal." A manager at this plant says that such "gender tactics," as I call them, are designed to "boost morale by reminding the gals that even though they do unfeminine work, they really are still feminine." But although some women workers may value femininity, in the work world, management identifies feminine traits as legitimation for devaluation.

In some places, management offers "refeminization" perks to help women feel "compensated" for their perceived "defeminization" on the job. A prime example is the now well-documented makeup sessions and beauty pageants for young women workers sponsored by multinational electronics corporations at their Southeast Asian plants (Grossman 1979; Ong 1985). While such events are unusual in Silicon Valley, male managers frequently use flirting and dating as "refeminization" strategies. Flirting and dating in and of themselves certainly cannot be construed as capitalist plots to control workers; however, when they are used as false compensation for and to divert women from poor working conditions and workplace alienation, they in effect serve as a form of labor control. In a society where women are taught that their femininity is more important than other aspects of their lives—such as how they relate to their work—flirting can be divisive. And when undesired, flirting can also develop into a form of sexual harassment, which causes further workplace alienation.

One young Chinese production worker told me that she and a co-worker avoided filing complaints about illegal and unsafe working conditions because they did not want to annoy their white male supervisor, whom they enjoyed having flirt with them. These two women would never join a union, they told me, because the same supervisor told them that all women who join unions "are a bunch of tough, big-mouthed dykes." Certainly these women have the option of ignoring this man's opinions. But that is not easy, given the one-sided power he has over them not only because he is their supervisor, but because of his age, race, and class.

When women workers stress their "feminine" and female characteristics as being counter to their waged work, a contradictory set of results can occur. On one hand, the women may legitimate their own devaluation as workers, and, in seeking identity and solace in their "femininity," discard any interest in improving their working conditions. On the other hand, if turning to their identities as female, mother, mate, and such allows them to feel self-esteem in one arena of their lives, that self-esteem may transfer to other arenas. The outcome is contingent on the ways in which the women define and experience themselves as female or "feminine." Femininity in white American capitalist culture is traditionally defined as passive and ineffectual, as Susan Brownmiller explores (1984). But there is also a female tradition of resistance.

The women I interviewed rarely pose their womanhood or their self-perceived femininity as attributes meriting higher pay or better treatment. They expect *differential* treatment because they are women, but "differential" inevitably means lower paid in the work world. The women present their self-defined female attributes as creating additional needs that detract from their financial value. Femininity, although its definition varies among individuals and ethnic groups, is generally viewed as something that subtracts from a woman's market value, even though a majority of women consider it personally desirable.

In general, both the women and men I interviewed believe that women have many needs and skills discernible from those of male workers, but they accept the ideology that such specialness renders them less deserving than men of special treatment, wages, promotions, and status. Conversely, both the men and women viewed men's special needs and skills as rendering men *more* deserving. Two of the classic perceived sex differentials cited by employers in electronics illustrate this point. First, although Silicon Valley employers consistently repeat the old refrain that women are better able than men to perform work requiring manual skills, strong hand-eye coordination, and extreme patience, they nonetheless find it appropriate to pay workers who have these skills (women) less than workers who supposedly do not have them (men). Second, employers say that higher entry-level jobs, wages, and promotions rightly belong to heads of households, but in practice they give such jobs only to men, regardless of their household situation, and exclude women, regardless of theirs.

When a man expresses special needs that result from his structural position in the family—such as head of household—he is often "compensated," yet when a woman expresses a special need resulting from her traditional structural position in the family—child care or *her* position as head of household—she is told that such issues are not of concern to the employer or, in the case of child care, that it detracts from her focus on her work and thus devalues her productive contribution. This is a clear illustration of Heidi Hartmann's definition of patriarchy: social relationships between men, which, although hierarchical, such as those between employer and worker, have a material base that benefits men and oppresses women (1976).

Definitions of femininity and masculinity not only affect the workplace but are in turn affected by it. Gender is produced and reproduced in and through the workplace, as well as outside it. Gender identities and relationships are formed on the work floor both by the labor process organized under capitalism and by workers' resistance to that labor process. "Femininity" in its various permutations is not something all-bad and all-disempowering: women find strength, pride, and creativity in some of its forms. But the ideological counterpositioning of "feminine" as weak, powerless, and submissive and of "masculine" as strong, powerful, and dominant raises yet another problem in the workplace: sexual harassment. For reasons of space, I will not discuss this here. I turn now to one of the other tenets of women workers' multitiered consciousness that employers find advantageous: gender logic that poses women's work as "secondary."

THE LOGIC OF "SECONDARY" WORK

Central to gender-specific capital logic is the assumption that women's paid work is both secondary and temporary. More than 70 percent of the employers and 80 percent of the women workers I interviewed stated that a woman's primary jobs are those of wife, mother, and homemaker, even when she works full time in the paid labor force. Because employers view women's primary job as in the home, and they assume that, prototypically, every woman is connected to a man who is bringing in a larger paycheck, they claim that women do not need to earn a full living wage. Employers repeatedly asserted that they believed the low-level jobs were filled only by women because men could not afford to or would not work for such low wages.

Indeed, many of the women would not survive on what they earned unless they pooled resources. For some, especially the nonimmigrants, low wages did mean dependency on men—or at least on family networks and household units. None of the women I interviewed—immigrant or nonimmigrant—lived alone. Yet most of them would be financially better off without their menfolk. For most of the immigrant women, their low wages were the most substantial and steady source of their family's income. *Eighty percent of the immigrant women workers in my study were the largest per annum earners in their households.*

Even when their wages were primary—the main or only family income—the women still considered men to be the major breadwinners. The women considered their waged work as secondary, both in economic value and as a source of identity. Although most agreed that women and men who do exactly the same jobs should be paid the same, they had little expectation that as women they would be eligible for higher-paying "male" jobs. While some of these women—particularly the Asians—believed they could overcome racial and class barriers in the capitalist division of labor, few viewed gender as a division that could be changed. While they may believe that hard work can overcome many obstacles and raise their *families'* socioeconomic class standing, they do not feel that their position in the gender division of labor will change. Many, of course, expect or hope for better jobs for themselves—and others expect or hope to leave the paid labor force altogether—but few wish to enter traditional male jobs or to have jobs that are higher in status or earnings than the men in their families.

The majority of women who are earning more than their male family members view their situation negatively and hope it will change soon. They do not want to earn less than they currently do; rather, they want their menfolk to earn more. This was true of women in all the ethnic groups. The exceptions—a vocal minority— were mainly Mexicanas. Lupe, a high-tech worker in her twenties, explained:

> Some of the girls I work with are ridiculous—they think if they earn more than their husbands it will hurt the men's pride. They play up to the machismo. . . . I guess it's not entirely ridiculous, because some of them regularly come in with black eyes and bruises, so the men are something they have to reckon with. But, my God, if I had a man like that I would leave. . . .
>
> My boyfriend's smart enough to realize that we need my paycheck to feed us and my kids. He usually brings home less than I do, and we're both damn grateful for every cent that either of us makes. When I got a raise he was very happy—I think he feels more relieved, not more resentful. But then, he's not a very typical man, no? Anyway, he'd probably change if we got married and had kids of his own—that's when they start wanting to be the king of their castle.

A Korean immigrant woman in her thirties told how her husband was so adamant that she not earn more than he and that the men in the household be the family's main supporters that each time she cashed her paycheck she gave some of her earnings to her teenaged son to turn over to the father as part of his earnings from his part-time job. She was upset about putting her son in a position of being deceitful to his father, but both mother and son agreed it was the only alternative to the father's otherwise dangerous, violent outbursts.

As in the rest of America, in most cases, the men earned more in those households where both the women and men worked regularly. In many of the families, however, the men tended to work less regularly than the women and to have higher unemployment rates. While most of the families vocally blamed very real socioeconomic conditions for the unemployment, such as declines in "male" in-

dustrial sector jobs, many women also felt that their husbands took
out their resentment on their families. A young Mexicana, who went
to a shelter for battered women after her husband repeatedly beat
her, described her extreme situation:

> He knows it's not his fault or my fault that he lost his job: they laid off
> almost his whole shift. But he acts like I keep my job just to spite him,
> and it's gotten so I'm so scared of him. Sometimes I think he'd rather kill
> me or have us starve than watch me go to work and bring home pay. He
> doesn't want to hurt me, but he is so hurt inside because he feels he has
> failed as a man.

Certainly not all laid-off married men go to the extreme of beating
their wives, but the majority of married women workers whose husbands had gone through periods of unemployment said that the
men treated other family members significantly worse when they
were out of work. When capitalism rejects male workers, they often
use patriarchal channels to vent their anxieties. In a world where
men are defined by their control over their environment, losing
control in one arena, such as that of the work world, may lead them
to tighten control in another arena in which they still have power—
the family. This classic cycle is not unique to Third World immigrant
communities, but as male unemployment increases in these communities, so may the cycle of male violence.

Even some of the women who recognize the importance of their
economic role feel that their status and identity as wage earners are
less important than those of men. Many of the women feel that men
work not only for income but for respect and dignity. They see their
own work as less noble. Although some said they derive satisfaction
from their ability to hold a job, none of the women considered her
job to be a primary part of her identity or a source of self-esteem.
These women see themselves as responsible primarily for the welfare
of their families: their main identity is as mother, wife, sister, and
daughter, not as worker. Their waged work is seen as an extension
of caring for their families. It is not a question of *choosing* to work—
they do so out of economic necessity.

When I asked whether their husbands' and fathers' waged work
could also be viewed as an extension of familial duties, the women

indicated that they definitely perceived a difference. Men's paid labor outside the home was seen as integral both to the men's self-definition and to their responsibility vis-à-vis the family; conversely, women's labor force participation was seen as contradictory both to the women's self-image and to their definitions of female responsibility.

Many immigrant women see their wage contribution to the family's economic survival not only as secondary but as *temporary*, even when they have held their jobs for several years. They expect to quit their production jobs after they have saved enough money to go to school, stay home full time, or open a family business. In actuality, however, most of them barely earn enough to live on, let alone to save, and women who think they are signing on for a brief stint may end up staying in the industry for years.

That these workers view their jobs as temporary has important ramifications for both employers and unions, as well as for the workers themselves. When workers believe they are on board a company for a short time, they are more likely to put up with poor working conditions, because they see them as short term. A Mexican woman who used to work in wafer fabrication reflected on the consequences of such rationalization:

> I worked in that place for four years, and it was really bad—the chemicals knocked you out, and the pay was very low. My friends and me, though, we never made a big deal about it, because we kept thinking we were going to quit soon anyway, so why bother. . . . We didn't really think of it as our career or anything—just as something we had to do until our fortune changed. It's not exactly the kind of work a girl dreams of herself doing.
>
> My friend was engaged when we started working there, and she thought she was going to get married any day, and then she'd quit. Then, after she was married, she thought she'd quit as soon as she got pregnant. . . . She has two kids now, and she's still there. Now she's saying she'll quit real soon, because her husband's going to get a better job any time now, and she'll finally get to stay home, like she wants.

Ironically, these women's jobs may turn out to be only temporary, but for different reasons and with different consequences than they planned. Industry analysts predict that within the next decade the majority of Silicon Valley production jobs may well be automated out of existence (Carey 1984). Certainly for some of the immigrant women, their dreams of setting aside money for occupational training or children's schooling or to open a family business or finance relatives' immigration expenses do come true, but not for most. Nonetheless, almost without exception, the women production workers I interviewed—both immigrant and nonimmigrant—saw their present jobs as temporary.

Employers are thus at an advantage in hiring these women at low wages and with little job security. They can play on the women's *own* consciousness as wives and mothers whose primary identities are defined by home and familial roles. While the division of labor prompts the workers to believe that women's waged work is less valuable than men's, the women workers themselves arrive in Silicon Valley with this ideology already internalized.

A young Filipina woman, who was hired at a walk-in interview at an electronics production facility, experienced a striking example of the contradictions confronting immigrant women workers in the valley. Neither she nor her husband, who was hired the same day, had any previous related work experience or degrees. Yet her husband was offered an entry-level job as a technician, while she was offered an assembly job paying three dollars per hour less. The personnel manager told her husband that he would "find [the technician job] more interesting than assembly work." The woman had said in the interview that she wanted to be considered for a higher-paying job because she had two children to support. The manager refused to consider her for a different job, she said, and told her that "it will work out fine for you, though, because with your husband's job, and you *helping out* [emphasis added] you'll have a nice little family income."

The same manager told me on a separate occasion that the company preferred to hire members of the same families because it meant that workers' relatives would be more supportive about their working and the combined incomes would put less financial strain on individual workers. This concern over workers and their families dissipated, however, when the Filipino couple split up, leaving the wife with only the "helping-out" pay instead of the "nice little family income." When the woman requested a higher-paying job so she could support her family, the same manager told her that "family concerns were out of place at work" and did not promote her.

This incident suggests that a woman's family identity is considered important when it is advantageous to employers and irrelevant when it is disadvantageous. Similarly, managers encourage women workers to identify themselves primarily as workers or as women, depending on the circumstances. At one plant where I interviewed both managers and workers, males and females were openly separated by the company's hiring policy: entry-level jobs for females were in assembly, and entry-level jobs for males were as technicians. As at the plant where the Filipino couple worked, neither the "male" nor the "female" entry-level jobs required previous experience or training, but the "male" job paid significantly more.

Apparently, the employers at this plant *did* see differences between male and female workers, despite their claims to the contrary. Yet, when the women workers asked for "special treatment" because of these differences, the employers' attitudes rapidly changed. When the first quality circle[5] was introduced in one production unit at this plant, the workers, all of whom were women, were told to suggest ways to improve the quality of work. The most frequently mentioned concern of all the women production workers I met was the lack of decent child-care facilities. The company replied that child care was not a quality of work–related issue but a "special women's concern" that was none of the company's business.

A Portuguese worker succinctly described the tendency among employers to play on and then deny such gender logic:

> The boss tells us not to bring our "women's problems" with us to work if we want to be treated equal. What does he mean by that? I am working here *because* of my "women's problems"—because I am a woman. Working here *creates* my " women's problems." I need this job because I am a woman and have children to feed. And I'll probably get fired because I am a woman and need to spend more time with my children. I am only one

---

5. Quality circles are introduced by management for the stated goals of increasing both employee satisfaction and production efficiency by giving workers input into decision-making processes.

person—and I bring my whole self to work with me. So what does he mean, don't bring my "women's problems" here?

As this woman's words so vividly illustrate, divisions of labor and of lives are intricately interwoven. Any attempts to organize the women workers of Silicon Valley—by unions, communities, political or social groups and by the women themselves—must deal with the articulation of gender, race, and class inequalities in their lives.

RESISTANCE ON THE SHOP FLOOR

There is little incidence in Silicon Valley production shops of *formal* labor militancy among the immigrant women, as evidenced by either union participation or collectively planned mass actions such as strikes. Filing formal grievances is not common in these workers' shop culture. Union activity is very limited, and both workers and managers claim that the incidence of complaints and disturbances on the shop floor is lower than in other industries. Pacing of production to restrict output does occur, and there are occasionally "informal" incidents, such as spontaneous slowdowns and sabotage. But these actions are rare and usually small in scale. Definitions of workplace militancy and resistance vary, of course, according to the observer's cultural background, but by their *own* definitions, the women do not frequently engage in traditional forms of labor militancy.

There is, however, an important, although often subtle, arena in which the women do engage in struggle with management: the ideological battleground. Just as employers and managers harness racist, sexist, and class-based logic to manipulate and control workers, so too workers use this logic against management. In the ideological arena, the women do not merely accept or react to the biased assumptions of managers: they also develop gender-, class-, and race-based logic of their own when it is to their advantage. The goal of these struggles is not simply ideological victory but concrete changes in working conditions. Further, in Silicon Valley, immigrant women workers have found that managers respond more to workers' needs when they are couched in ethnic or gender terms, rather than in class and labor terms. Thus, class struggle on the shop floor is often disguised as arguments about the proper place and appropriate behavior of women, racial minorities, and immigrants.

When asked directly, immigrant women workers typically deny that they engage in any form of workplace resistance or efforts to control their working conditions. This denial reflects not only workers' needs to protect clandestine activities, but also their consciousness about what constitutes resistance and control. In their conversations with friends and co-workers, the women joke about how they outfoxed their managers with female or ethnic "wisdom." Yet most of the women do not view their often elaborate efforts to manipulate their managers' behavior as forms of struggle. Rather, they think of their tactics "just as ways to get by," as several workers phrased it. It is from casual references to these tactics that a portrait of worker logic and resistance emerges.

The workers overwhelmingly agreed that the challenges to management in which they could and did engage were on a small-scale, individual, or small-group level. Several women said they engaged in forms of resistance that they considered "quiet" and unobtrusive: acts that would make a difference to the woman and possibly her co-workers but that management would probably not recognize as resistance. Only rarely was resistance collectively articulated.

The vast majority of these women clearly wish to avoid antagonizing management. Thus, rather than engaging in confrontational resistance strategies, they develop less obvious forms than, say, work stoppages, filing grievances, and straightforwardly refusing to perform certain tasks, all of which have frequently been observed in other industrial manufacturing sectors. Because the more "quiet" forms of resistance and struggle for workplace control engaged in by the women in Silicon Valley are often so discrete and the workers are uncomfortable discussing them, it is probable that there are more such acts and they are broader in scope than my examples imply. As a Chinese woman in her forties who has worked as an operative in the valley for six years explained:

> Everybody who does this job does things to get through the day, to make it bearable. There are some women who will tell you they never do any-

thing unproper or sneaky, but you are not to believe them. The ones that look the most demure are always up to something. . . . There's not anybody here who has never purposefully broken something, slowed down work, told fibs to the supervisor, or some such thing. And there's probably no one but me with my big mouth who would admit it!

As discussed above, it is clear that managers have found effective ways to play off workers' gender, racial, and immigrant conscious-ness. At the same time, white male managers in particular often have striking misconceptions about the gender and cultural experiences of their workers, and workers can thus frequently confuse them with bogus claims about the women's special needs. Workers can also use real claims that supervisors have tried to co-opt.

A Salvadorean woman, fed up with her supervisor for referring to his Hispanic workers as "mamacitas" and "little mothers" and with admonishing them to "work faster if you want your children to eat," had her husband bring both her own children and several nieces and nephews to pick her up one day. She lined all the children up in front of the supervisor and asked him how fast she would have to work to feed all those mouths. One of the children had been coached, and he told the supervisor that his mother was so tired from working that she did not have time to play with them anymore. The guilt-ridden supervisor, astonished by the large number of chil-dren and the responsibility they entailed, eased up on his admon-ishments and speed-up efforts and started treating the woman with more consideration.

The most frequently mentioned acts of resistance against man-agement and work arrangements were ones that played on the white male managers' consciousness—both false and real—about gender and ethnic culture. Frequently mentioned examples involved work-ers who turned management's ideologies against them by exploiting their male supervisors' misconceptions about "female problems." A white chip tester testified:

It's pretty ironic because management seems to have this idea that male supervisors handle female workers better than female supervisors. You know, we're supposed to turn to mush whenever he's around and respect his authority or something. But this one guy we got now lets us walk all over him. He thinks females are flighty and irresponsible because of our hormones—so we make sure to have as many hormone problems as we can. I'd say we each take hormone breaks several times a day. My next plan is to convince him that menstrual blood will turn the solvents bad, so on those days we have to stay in the lunchroom!

A Filipina woman production worker recounted another example:

The boss told us girls that we're not strong enough to do the heavy work in the men's jobs—and those jobs pay more, too. So, I suddenly realized that gosh, us little weak little things shouldn't be lifting all those heavy boxes of circuit board parts we're supposed to carry back and forth all the time—and I stopped doing it.
    The boss no longer uses that "it's too heavy for you girls" line anymore ...but I can tell he's working on a new one. That's okay; I got plenty of responses.

A Mexican wafer fabricator, whose unit supervisor was notorious for the "refeminization" perks discussed above, told of how she manipulated the male supervisor's gender logic to disguise what was really an issue of class struggle:

I was getting really sick from all the chemicals we have to work with, and I was getting a rash from them on my arms. [The manager] kept saying I was exaggerating and gave the usual line about you can't prove what caused the rash. One day we had to use an especially harsh solvent, and I made up this story about being in my sister's wedding. I told him that the solvents would ruin my manicure, and I'd be a mess for the wedding. Can you believe it? He let me off the work! This guy wouldn't pay attention to my rash, but when my manicure was at stake, he let me go!

Of course, letting this worker avoid chemicals for one day because of a special circumstance is more advantageous to management than allowing her and others to avoid the work permanently because of health risks. Nonetheless, the worker was able to carve out a small piece of bargaining power by playing off her manager's gender logic. The contradiction of these tactics that play up feminine frailty is that they achieve short-term, individual goals at the risk of reinforcing damaging stereotypes about women, including the stereotype that women workers are not as productive as men. From the workers' point of view, however, the women are simply using the prejudices of the powerful to the advantages of the weak.

Another "manicure" story resulted in a more major workplace change at one of the large plants. Two women fabricator operatives, one Portuguese and one Chicana, applied for higher-paying technician jobs whereupon their unit supervisor told them that the jobs were too "rough" for women and that the work would "ruin their nails." The women's response was to pull off their rubber gloves and show him what the solvents and dopants had done to their nails, despite the gloves. (One of the most common chemicals used in chip manufacturing is acetone, the key ingredient in nail polish removal. It also eats right through "protective" rubber gloves.) After additional goading and bargaining, the supervisor provisionally let them transfer to technician work.

Although the above are isolated examples, they represent tactics that workers can use either to challenge or play off sexist ideology that employers use to legitimate women's low position in the segregated division of labor. Certainly there are not enough instances of such behavior to challenge the inequality between worker and boss, but they do demonstrate to managers that gender logic cannot always be counted on to legitimate inequality between male and female workers. And dissolving divisions between workers *is* a threat to management hegemony.

RACIAL AND ETHNIC LOGIC

Typically, high-tech firms in Silicon Valley hire production workers from a wide spectrum of national groups. If their lack of a common language (both linguistically and culturally) serves to fragment the labor force, capital benefits. Conversely, management may find it more difficult to control workers with whom it cannot communicate precisely. Several workers said they have feigned a language barrier in order to avoid taking instructions; they have also called forth cultural taboos—both real and feigned—to avoid undesirable situations. One Haitian woman, who took a lot of kidding from her employer about voodoo and black magic, insisted that she could not work the night shift because evil spirits were out then. Because she was a good worker, the employer let her switch to days. When I tried to establish whether she believed the evil spirits were real or imagined, she laughed and said, "Does it matter? The result is the same: I can be home at night with my kids."

Management in several plants believed that racial and national diversity minimized solidarity. According to one supervisor, workers were forbidden from sitting next to people of their own nationality (i.e., language group) in order to "cut down on the chatting." Workers quickly found two ways to reverse this decision, using management's own class, racial, and gender logic. Chinese women workers told the supervisor that if they were not "chaperoned" by other Chinese women, their families would not let them continue to work there. Vietnamese women told him that the younger Vietnamese women would not work hard unless they were under the eyes of the older workers and that a group of newly hired Vietnamese workers would not learn to do the job right unless they had someone who spoke their language to explain it to them. Both of these arguments could also be interpreted as examples of older workers wanting to control younger ones in a generational hierarchy, but this was not the case. Afterwards both the Chinese and the Vietnamese women laughed among themselves at their cleverness. Nor did they forget the support needs of workers from other ethnic groups: they argued with the supervisor that the same customs and needs held true for many of the language groups represented, and the restriction was rescinded.

Another example of a large-scale demonstration of interethnic solidarity on the shop floor involved workers playing off supervisors' stereotypes regarding the superior work of Asians over Mexicans. The incident was precipitated when a young Mexicana, newly assigned to an assembly unit in which a new circuit board was being assembled, fell behind in her quota. The supervisor berated her with racial slurs about Mexicans' "laziness" and "stupidity" and told her to sit next to and "watch the Orientals." As a group, the Asian women she was stationed next to slowed down their production, thereby setting the average quota on the new boards at a slower than usual pace. The women were in fits of laughter after work because the supervisor had assumed that the speed set by the Asians was the fastest possible, since they were the "best" workers.

Hispanic workers also turn management's anti-Mexican prejudices against them, as a Salvadorean woman explained:

> First of all, the bosses think everyone from Latin American is Mexican, and they think all Mexicans are dumb. So, whenever they try to speed up production, or give us something we don't want to do, we just act dumb. It's not as if you act smart and you get a promotion or a bonus anyway.

A Mexicana operative confided, "They [management] assume we don't understand much English, but we understand when we want to."

A Chinese woman, who was under five feet tall and who identified her age by saying she was a "grandmother," laughingly told how she had her white male supervisor "wrapped around [her] finger." She consciously played into his stereotype that Asian women are small, timid, and obedient by frequently smiling at and bowing to him and doing her job carefully. But when she had a special need, to take a day or a few hours off, for example, she would put on her best guileless, ingratiating look and, full of apologies, usually obtained it. She also served as a voice for co-workers whom the supervisor considered more abrasive. On one occasion, when three white women in her unit complained about poor lighting and headaches, the supervisor became irritated and did not respond to their complaint. Later that week the Chinese "grandmother" approached him, saying that she was concerned that poor lighting was limiting the workers' productivity. The lighting was quickly improved. This incident illustrates that managers can and do respond to workers' demands when they result in increased productivity.

Some workers see strategies to improve and control their work processes and environments as contradictory and as "Uncle Tomming." Two friends, both Filipinas, debated this issue. One argued that "acting like a China doll" only reinforced white employers' stereotypes, while the other said that countering the stereotype would not change their situation, so they might as well use the stereotype to their advantage. The same analysis applies to women workers who consciously encourage male managers to view women as different from men in their abilities and characteristics. For women and minority workers, the need for short-term gains and benefits and for long-term equal treatment is a constant contradiction. And for the majority of workers, short-term tactics are unlikely to result in long-term equality.

POTENTIAL FOR ORGANIZING

Obviously, the lesson here for organizing is contradictory. Testimonies such as the ones given in these pages clearly document that immigrant women are not docile, servile people who always follow orders, as many employers interviewed for this study claimed. Orchestrating major actions such as family migration so that they could take control of and better their lives has helped these women develop leadership and survival skills. Because of these qualities, many of the women I interviewed struck me as potentially effective labor and community organizers and rank-and-file leaders. Yet almost none of them were interested in collective organizing, because of time limitations and family constraints and because of their lack of confidence in labor unions, the feminist movement, and community organizations. Many were simply too worn out from trying to make ends meet and caring for their families. And for some, the level of inequality and exploitation on the shop floor did not seem that bad, compared to their past experiences. A Salvadorean woman I interviewed exemplified this predicament. Her job as a solderer required her to work with a microscope all day, causing her to develop severe eye and back strain. Although she was losing her eyesight and went home exhausted after working overtime, she told me she was still very happy to be in the United States and very grateful to her employer. "I have nothing to complain about," she told me. "It is such a luxury to know that when I go home all of my children will still be alive." After losing two sons to government-backed terrorist death squads in El Salvador, her work life in Silicon Valley was indeed an improvement.

Nonetheless, their past torment does not reduce the job insecurity, poor working conditions, pay inequality, and discrimination so many immigrant workers in Silicon Valley experience in their jobs. In fact, as informants' testimonies suggest, in many cases, past hardships have rendered them less likely to organize collectively. At the same time, individual acts of resistance do not succeed on their own in changing the structured inequality of the division of labor. Most of these actions remain at the agitation level and lack the coordination needed to give workers real bargaining power. And, as mentioned, individual strategies that workers have devised can be contradictory. Simultaneous to winning short-run victories, they can also reinforce both gender and racial stereotypes in the long run. Further, because many of these victories are isolated and individual, they can often be divisive. For workers to gain both greater workplace control *and* combat sexism and racism, organized *collective* strategies hold greater possibilities.

Neither organized labor nor feminist or immigrant community organizations have prioritized the needs of Silicon Valley's immigrant women workers.[6] As of 1989, for example, not a single full-time paid labor union organizer was assigned to the local high-tech industry. Given that Silicon Valley is the center of the largest and fastest-growing manufacturing industry in the country, this is, as one long-time local organizer, Mike Eisenscher, put it, "a frightening condemnation of the labor movement" (1987). That union leadership has also failed to mark for attention a work force that is dominated by women of color is equally disheartening.

My findings indicate that Silicon Valley's immigrant women workers have a great deal to gain from organizing, but also a great deal to contribute. They have their numeric strength, but also a wealth of creativity, insight, and experience that could be a shot in the arm to the stagnating national labor movement. They also have a great deal to teach—and learn from—feminist and ethnic community movements. But until these or new alternative movements learn to speak and listen to these women, the women will continue to struggle

---

6. One of the few organizations that *has* included immigrant women workers and that addresses their needs is the Silicon Valley Toxics Coalition. This group effectively addresses itself to improving residential and occupational health and safety hazards posed by the highly toxic local high-tech industry.

on their own, individually and in small groups. In their struggle for better jobs and better lives, one of the most effective tactics they have is their own resourcefulness in manipulating management's "own logic against them."

8

WOMEN AND THE EXPORT INDUSTRY IN TAIWAN: THE MUTING OF CLASS CONSCIOUSNESS

Rita S. Gallin

Since the 1960s, a new form of industrialization—export-oriented manufacturing—has taken root throughout much of the Third World. The origins of this phenomenon are well known (Worsley 1984), especially for Taiwan, which as the "economic miracle" has been in the forefront of development through export (Gold 1986; Ho 1978; Lin 1973). The flow of women into the labor force has facilitated this "miracle" (Chiang and Ku 1985:7–8; Galenson 1979:395; Greenhalgh 1985:273). Between 1956 and 1973, the proportion of female workers in Taiwan increased from 20 to 40 percent (Greenhalgh 1985:273), and in 1986, women accounted for 45 percent of the labor force (DGBAS 1987:6). Most of these women were young and unmarried. In 1986, for example, 48 percent were between the ages of fifteen and twenty-nine (DGBAS 1987:13), and 58 percent were unmarried (DGBAS 1987:102–3).

In 1986, most of the jobs (65 percent) these women held were in the manufacturing sector (calculated from DGBAS 1987:35–37), were waged rather than salaried positions, and paid less, on average, than equivalent jobs held by men.[1] Most also were deskilled, mo-

---

1. No figures are provided in DGBAS for the proportion of supervisory and nonsupervisory positions held by women and men in the manufacturing sector. If one

notonous, dead-end positions that offered few benefits to their in-cumbents—and thus were exceedingly unattractive to men seeking work with opportunities for advancement. Industrialization in Tai-wan, then, was and continues to be fueled by a large reserve of women who are willing to work at lackluster jobs for low wages.

The situation of female workers in Taiwan is not unique. A sub-stantial body of literature documents similar processes at work else-where in the developing world (e.g., Elson and Pearson 1981b; Fernandez-Kelly 1983; Fuentes and Ehrenreich 1983; Lim 1981, 1985; Nash and Fernandez-Kelly 1983; North-South Institute 1985). What is unique in Taiwan is the lack of labor militancy among female workers. In contrast to their counterparts elsewhere (Blake 1984; Halim 1983; Lim 1981, 1985), women in Taiwan's industrial sector have not organized to effect changes in their working conditions. The purpose of this chapter is to explore the reasons for this quiescence.

My approach to the subject is guided by the belief that women's participation in labor struggles is dependent on the emergence of their class consciousness. Following Helen I. Safa's lead, I define class consciousness "as a cumulative process by which women rec-ognize they are exploited, . . . recognize the source of their exploi-tation, . . . and are willing and able to organize and mobilize in their own interests" (1976:71). In Taiwan, the articulation of government policies and managerial practices appears to combine with family processes to inhibit the formation of class consciousness among the women.

This chapter is based on direct research with women in Taiwan (see, for example, Gallin 1984a and 1984b) and on an interpretation of the literature. Although I have not explored the topic of women's class consciousness in the field, the close fit of the data to the liter-ature leads me to expect that my argument will continue to hold; it may need to be updated, however, as new data are developed.

The chapter begins with a description of the development of

---

assumes that salaried jobs are likely to be supervisory positions, then the data indicate that in 1986 men constituted two-thirds (64 percent) of the supervisors in manufac-turing (DGBAS 1987:35). Moreover, the ratio of female supervisors' salaries to those of male supervisors was 0.75. The comparable ratio of wages for female and male production workers was 0.79 (DGBAS 1987:667).

export-oriented industrialization in Taiwan and of the traditional Chinese family to establish the context for the material that follows. I then discuss state policy and managerial practices in Taiwan and examine how they have interacted with family processes to mute women's class consciousness. In the concluding section, I consider how women could unite to work toward improvement of their common condition.

DEVELOPMENT IN TAIWAN

When the Chinese nationalist government retreated to Taiwan in 1949, it found a primarily agricultural island marked by conditions that were not consistently favorable to development. The strategies it adopted to foster economic growth have been documented in detail elsewhere (Ho 1978; Lin 1973). Here it need only be emphasized that the government initially strengthened agriculture to provide a base for industrialization, pursued a strategy of import substitution for a brief period during the 1950s, and then in the 1960s adopted a policy of industrialization through export.

The latter policy produced dramatic changes in Taiwan's economic structure. The contribution of agriculture to the net domestic product declined from 36 percent in 1952 to 7 percent in 1986, while that of industry rose from 18 to 47 percent over the same period. Trade expanded greatly, increasing in value from U.S. $303 million in 1952 to U.S. $64 billion in 1986. The contribution of exports to the volume of trade also rose dramatically, from U.S. $116 million (38 percent) in 1952 to U.S. $40 billion (63 percent) in 1986 (Lu 1987:2).

Two industries accounted for a large proportion of this growth: textiles (including apparel) and electronics. The textile industry, for example, expanded its share of exports from 6 percent in 1956 to 29 percent in 1976. Expansion in electronics was even more rapid. In 1979, "the exports of textiles and electronics amounted to U.S. $6.5 billion, about 41 percent of total exports" (Kuo et al. 1981:23–24). In combination with food processing, these two industries "accounted for almost half of the total labor absorbed into manufacturing" during the 1960s and 1970s (page 14).

The textile industry was the first to respond to the government's

1960 reforms to stimulate local and foreign investment.[2] Indigenous entrepreneurs had both experience in the local market and the capacity to take advantage of the new opportunities created. Nevertheless, because they were neither part of an international trade network nor familiar with Western tastes, a division of labor emerged. Local industrialists produced goods, and foreigners provided the "know-how" and marketed the products globally. By contrast, the electronics industry had virtually no base on Taiwan, and foreign capital and technology had to be imported to establish the industry. As a result, the electronics sector was and still is dominated by a few very large transnational corporations (TNCs) that serve as assemblers and by a mass of small, local suppliers. In addition, other TNCs maintain considerable leverage over local suppliers.

In the mid–1960s, when "the relaxation of cold war tensions facilitated general expansion of world trade" (Gold 1986:79), TNCs began to stream into Taiwan. In response to the island's comparative advantage, first one TNC and then others set up export factories throughout the island, as well as in the export processing zone (EPZ), established in 1966 in Kaohsiung, a southern port city. (Two other EPZs were opened in 1971: one near Kaohsiung and the other in the center of the island at Taichung.)

By 1973, the cities, towns, and rural areas of the island were dotted with factories, and Taiwan's economy was made up of a small "modern" sector of large enterprises and a massive "traditional" sector of small and medium-sized factories.[3] Large-scale enterprises have tended to be located in Taiwan's three EPZs and in the outlying areas of its large cities. They produce directly for export, either as subsidiaries of TNCs or as contractors for foreign firms. Small and medium-sized factories, by contrast, are dispersed throughout the island; as early as 1971, 50 percent of Taiwan's industrial and commercial enterprises and 55 percent of its manufacturing firms were

2. For discussions of the 1960 reforms, see Gold 1986:76–78; Ho 1978:107–8, 239; Jacoby 1966:134–35; and Lin 1973:chap. 5. Detailed information on the development of the textile and electronics industries can be found in Gold 1986:78–87, which is the source of the material presented in the following two paragraphs.

3. Following Ho (1976:57), "small" is defined as fewer than ten workers, "medium" as ten to ninety-nine workers, and "large" as one hundred workers or more. The definition of size appears arbitrary to those studying Taiwan. Richard Stites (1982:248), for example, defines small as one hundred or fewer workers, while Gold (1986:141, n. 16) defines large as more than three hundred workers.

located in rural areas (Ho 1976:17).[4] They produce directly for mass marketers (such as K-Mart) or foreign firms (such as Arrow and Jantzen), or they act as agents for foreign firms by subcontracting work to small firms or home workers. (Many small firms also produce goods for the domestic market.)

Regardless of the size of the firm, the preferred employee in the manufacturing sector is female. Young, single women make up the largest proportion of the labor force in Taiwan's EPZs, for example, constituting 77.6 percent of all factory workers in the three zones in mid–1977 (Arrigo 1980:25). These women represented only a fraction of the labor force employed in the industry, however.[5] In 1986, women held the majority (52.8 percent) of waged jobs in the manufacturing sector (DGBAS 1987:35) and constituted three-quarters (75.7 percent) of the waged labor force in the clothing manufacturing industry (page 57) and two-thirds (67.6 percent) in the electronic products manufacturing industry (page 85).

In summary, in response to problems encountered in its import-substitution policy, the government switched in the 1960s to export-oriented industrialization based on foreign and local investment and low-cost female labor. The Taiwan "miracle" is the product of high-volume exports that, in turn, are the product of having a continuing supply of female workers. Despite a 1973 government decision to promote capital-intensive industries in response to competition from lower-wage countries, the bulk of Taiwan's exports continues to be labor-intensive goods, produced primarily by women.

THE TRADITIONAL CHINESE FAMILY

The basic unit of Chinese society is the family, which has always been a cooperative enterprise and the fundamental provider of eco-

---

4. The dispersal of industry to the countryside has been explained as a product of industry's desire to be near the sources of low-cost labor and raw materials (Ho 1976). While true, the government did not act to protect agricultural land until the goal of industrialization had been achieved and farm productivity had declined. In November 1975, the government promulgated a law barring the use of certain agricultural lands (i.e., grades 1–24) for purposes other than farming. (Before this law, only land graded 1–12 had been so regulated.)

5. Calculations based on figures Linda Gail Arrigo provides in her text and data in her table 1 (1980:25–26) suggest that less than 10 percent of the female labor force was employed in EPZs in mid–1977.

nomic and social security for the individual. It also was—and continues to be—highly patriarchal.

China's patrilineal kinship structure recognizes only male children as descent group members with rights to the family's property.[6] In the past, and to a large extent today, residence was patrilocal; when a woman married, she left her natal home to live as a member of her husband's family, severing her formal ties with her father's household. Parents considered daughters a liability—household members who drained family resources as children and withdrew their assets (domestic labor and earning power) when they married. Sons, in contrast, steadily contributed to the family's economic security during its growth and expansion and provided a source of support in old age. Not surprisingly, parents strongly preferred male children.

Members of the older generation also strongly favored arranged marriages. Marriages brought a new member into the household, joined two people in order to produce children, and established an alliance between families. The needs of the family therefore took precedence over the desires of the individual in the selection of a mate. When parents arranged marriages, they attempted to recruit women who would be compliant, capable workers; who would produce heirs for the group; and who were from families willing to forge bonds of cooperation and obligation.

Life in the family was dominated by an authoritarian hierarchy based on gender, generation, and age. The oldest male had the highest status; the status of women, although it increased with age and the birth of sons, was lower than that of any man. The desires of women were subjugated to those of men, just as the wishes of the young were subjugated to those of the old. The older generation socialized women from birth to accept their inferiority and subordination to males and to observe the "three obediences" to father, husband, and sons. Family members took women's labor for granted, even though women's work was necessary for the maintenance of

---

6. The government of Taiwan has attempted to alter the traditional pattern of inheritance by providing women with institutionalized access to the property of their families of origin. Nevertheless, customary law continues to be applied in practice, and women seldom claim their inheritance. Instead, they accept their dowries as patrimony.

the household. Reproductive capacity, rather than work or economic contributions, defined women's status. Women were brought into the family for the purpose of bearing and rearing a new generation; whatever their other achievements, their position in the family depended on fulfilling this expectation. Women, in short, had no real control over their lives. Social and economic marginality marked their experience.

STATE POLICY AND EMPLOYERS' STRATEGIES TOWARD LABOR

Because Taiwan's economy is so heavily dependent on foreign capital and trade, the government must maintain a favorable investment climate, including political stability and low wage rates, to ensure that capital does not seek a cheap labor force elsewhere. Taiwan is also inextricably linked to the capitalist world economy and therefore extremely vulnerable to international market fluctuations. Accordingly, the government must maintain an elastic labor force responsive to the demands of business cycles. By pursuing policies that create an ideological and economic environment attractive to foreign investors, Taiwan has sought to ensure its comparative advantage in the world economy.

One way this advantage has been maintained is by sustaining and perpetuating, through the educational system and the mass media, a traditional patriarchal ideology. Women's primary roles are defined as those of wife and mother, and the purpose of their education is to produce better mothers (Diamond 1975:5–18, 37). Accordingly, they are socialized into norms of hard work, compliance, and subordination to the interests of the patriliny and are provided less education and training than men.[7] This traditional ideology effec-

---

7. According to Susan Greenhalgh, the government, "well aware of the links between education and development, in 1963 . . . made six years of primary education free and compulsory, and in 1968–69 . . . added three more years (junior middle school) of free schooling" (1985:272). Yet, although educational opportunities in Taiwan are relatively gender-neutral—"the ratio of girl to boy graduates was .97 at the junior level" in the early 1980s (page 272)—parents practice "systematic discrimination against daughters" (page 303) and "educational investments vary by sex" (page 302). In this sense, then, the patriarchal family is the fundamental source of women's subordination and the major reproducer of traditional hierarchies. The government,

tively shapes them into the kind of labor force industry requires—
that is, one that is docile, minimally trained, tractable, and willing
to accept low pay, lackluster jobs, and irregular work depending on
the exigencies of the economy.

At the same time, the government has ensured political stability
by pursuing restrictive policies toward labor unions.[8] Until July 15,
1987, Taiwan was under martial law, on the grounds that the province was engaged in a civil war, and this "myth" was used to justify
government policies. The lifting of "emergency controls" did not
affect the government's stance toward unions, however (Lin 1987:4).
Although strikes are permitted, they are legal only if all affected
workers vote to strike and wages in the affected industry fall below
exceedingly low government standards (Luce and Rumpf 1985:26–
27).[9] In addition, an industrial plant must employ a minimum of
fifty workers for it to be organized, and industrial unions are prohibited from crossing factory lines to organize workers (Galenson
1979:426–27).

Given these government policies and the nature of Taiwan's economy, industries have considerable latitude in choosing strategies that
will encourage productivity and discourage labor unrest. As might
be expected, the wage structures and working conditions in "modern" and "traditional" sectors have few similarities. Large enterprises
offer relatively high wages and generous fringe benefits (such as
subsidized meals and housing, work clothing, transportation, and
bonuses) (Galenson 1979:421–25), and many have recreational facilities and programs (Kung 1983:109). Work in a large factory is
usually based on a formal contractual agreement, is organized along
complex hierarchical lines, and, in the case of electronics, is per-

---

however, uses and perpetuates traditional hierarchical ideology to maintain and justify
the employment practices that underpin the island's political economy.

8. There is a dearth of information about labor unions in Taiwan, but Walter
Galenson (1979:425–32) provides some material on their structure and operation,
while Don Luce and Roger Rumpf (1985) briefly describe how they are controlled
by the government.

9. Unlike most developing nations, the government of Taiwan has not intervened
to any real extent in the determination of wages (Galenson 1979:414). Although a
minimum wage rate has been in effect since 1956, this minimum has always been
lower than actual rates of pay (pages 419–20). To circumvent the restrictions on
strikes, employees sometimes will not report for work, explaining their absence with
excuses such as "it's a holiday" (personal communication, Yeh Chuen-rong, 1987).

formed in relatively clean and well-lighted settings (pages 93, 59–60).[10] Large firms tend to be unionized, but management usually dominates in these organizations; all employees except top management belong to the union, and supervisory officials frequently hold union positions as elected officers (Galenson 1979:431).

Medium-sized firms, in comparison, offer lower wages and fewer benefits; however, workers who receive standard wages can increase their take-home pay by working overtime (Stites 1982:256), and those who are paid piece rates can earn more by increasing their speed. Because half the manufacturing firms in Taiwan employ fewer than twenty people (Gates 1979:402), most medium-sized firms are not unionized. Work, therefore, is usually based on an informal contractual agreement and is organized into only a few positions. These factories tend to be dirty and dark.[11]

To lower their costs, medium-sized firms frequently subcontract some production tasks to home workers or to small firms, often family businesses using unpaid family labor and hired labor. The hired workers in such firms receive "low wages, work long hours . . . [under conditions of] danger, noise, [and] health-threatening pollution" and often must provide "personal services exacted by the owners' families" (Gates 1979:402). Nevertheless, the wages of such workers are appreciably higher than those of uncontracted home workers, who work irregularly on a piece-rate basis and receive no fringe benefits.

THE MUTING OF CLASS CONSCIOUSNESS

As the preceding discussion suggests, the complex reasons underlying the nonemergence of women's class consciousness in Taiwan are rooted in government policies—both active and inactive—and

---

10. An indigenous entrepreneur who operates a factory employing two hundred people told me that his company does not tell employees at the time they are hired what their monthly wages will be. "When they get their first pay check," he reported, "they know that's what they'll be making."

11. See Stites 1982:253–56 for a description of factory workers' perceptions of these differences. According to his informants (pages 255–56), the work routine in small factories is "informal" and relationships between employers and employees are "personalized." My informants did not always report this to be the case, however (Gallin 1989).

managerial practices (see also Blake 1984; Halim 1983; Fernandez-Kelly 1983:144–50.) First, restrictive policies toward unions have hindered their ability to unify workers in defense of their interests. The limitations on strikes have severely handicapped the unions' ability to win concessions for the workers they represent and have thereby prevented them from organizing workers to take action against their exploitative working conditions. The government's rules regulating the number of workers required to organize an industrial union also make it impossible for large numbers of workers to improve their situation through collective bargaining. And the government's prohibition against area unions tends to isolate women in individual factories, making it difficult for them to realize their common position as workers.

Second, the Taiwanese government did nothing to prevent encroachment by industry into agricultural land until after the province had industrialized, thereby facilitating the dispersal of industry throughout the island's towns and rural areas and, consequently, causing the geographical dispersal of women. This broad distribution of industry has encapsulated women in separate work settings, obscuring their shared problems.

Third, government actions taken in the early 1960s to stimulate local and foreign investments prompted the development of both "modern" and "traditional" sectors within the economy and gave license to enterprises to devise sectoral-specific incentives to control labor. As a result, women, set apart in different sectors of the economy, have been regulated by a variety of practices that forestall the formation of a sense of collectivity.

Differences in the wage structures and working conditions in the "modern" and "traditional" sectors tend to translate into status distinctions, so that jobs in the "modern" sector are described as "high status" while those in the "traditional" sector are characterized as "low status." Such distinctions act to divide women by obfuscating their collective problems and creating the perception that their problems are isolated and individual.

Within sectors, industries also employ techniques that separate workers. Large industries divide the production process into a myriad of functions, each performed by someone with a different title. Workers are thus demarcated into small categories, which fosters individual, rather than group, identification. Large industries that provide special recreational activities and programs for their employees further nurture workers' identification with the firm rather than with one another.

Medium-sized firms, in contrast, have neither the labor force nor the capital to support complex work organization or to provide fringe benefits. Nevertheless, management techniques are used that serve to undermine the development of women's working-class con-·sciousness. The "personalized" relationships and "informal" work routine (Stites 1982:255) of the factory promote a "team spirit," for example, while piece rates promote individual initiative and competitiveness. Moreover, the common practice of subcontracting jobs to home workers effectively isolates these workers from other workers, men as well as women.

Finally, the inability of small firms to conduce to a workers' alliance needs no discussion. Hill Gates's (1979:402) graphic description of the work settings in small firms leaves little doubt that women employed in such businesses are unable to recognize their collective deprivation and to organize in an effort to change it.

The lack of a collective identity among working women, then, can be traced to the articulation of government policies and managerial practices. Yet this articulation provides only a partial explanation for its absence insofar as women exposed to similar conditions in other countries have mobilized in their own behalf (Fuentes and Ehrenreich 1983). The unwillingness of working women in Taiwan to resist economic injustices must reflect other influences as well.

As noted above, working women in Taiwan are not a homogeneous group. Both married and single women are in the industrial labor force. They are separated by generation and class, yet they share one element in common—the ideological precepts that govern their lives.

Women are expected to conform to traditional norms: to bear and rear children, to contribute their labor to the family enterprise, and to function as family members whose welfare and social standing are bound up with the unit's success. Socialized in norms of hard work, compliance, and subordination to the interests of the patriliny, women accept the expectation that they will sell their labor power to repay the costs of their rearing and to reproduce the family group.

Provided with only a modicum of education and training, they subscribe to the belief that they will attain security and upward mobility not through a career but through marriage and the advancement of the family economy.[12] Patriarchal ideology, in sum, binds women to the family and inhibits both their commitment to work and their solidarity.

It is not surprising, then, that the women do not recognize that they are exploited or organize to challenge the sources of that exploitation, for they are viewing their work experience through the refracting prism of traditional ideology; their dead-end, low-paying jobs offer neither an alternative to marriage nor an alternative to a locked-in dependency relationship. Single women must work to accumulate money for a dowry, which will secure a husband whom they hope will provide social mobility. Married women must work to earn money for a budget that will secure their families' subsistence or "fortunes."[13] The need to hold on to a job or the drive toward upward mobility thus inhibits the emergence of class consciousness.

CONCLUSIONS

Evidence exists that Taiwan's working women are not totally unaware of the exploitative nature of their jobs (Kung 1983:176); the predominant expression of worker discontent in Taiwan is labor turnover, and the rates among women are high (Gold 1986:89). The separation rate in 1986 for all employees, male and female, was 3 percent (DGBAS 1987:8). In the clothing manufacturing industry—in which the labor force was dominated by women—the separation rate was 3.8 percent in the same year (DGBAS 1987:214, table 37). Moreover, evidence exists that some working women also "recognize the source of their exploitation ... and are willing and able to organize ... in their own interests" (Safa 1976:71). Early in 1987, for

---

12. See Kung 1983:171–80, Greenhalgh 1985, and Gallin 1984a for an expanded discussion of these points.

13. Some married women as well as single women *must* work to satisfy their families' needs for money. The percentage of households that are headed by poor women is lower in Taiwan than in other countries; the marriage rate is high, the divorce rate is low, and most women are members of "intact" families. As one of my informants reported, "I have to work to make money for the household necessities and to pay the children's school expenses. I was born to do these things. I must do these things."

example, women workers went on "strike" at the Taichung export processing zone after three union representatives were fired for "pressing . . . [the women's] opposition to a reduction in holiday time ordered by management" (Goldstein 1987:56). Given the narrow focus of the protest, however, the women's action was most likely spontaneous and short-lived, rather than the result of a longer-term plan to change the existing system.

Whether women workers in Taiwan will organize in the future is impossible to predict.[14] Nevertheless, history shows that Chinese women have been able to articulate their class interests and to unify politically. In 1927, for example, women comprised 58.6 percent of the factory workers in Shanghai, China's main industrial center and the country's "most important center of strike action" (Chesneaux 1968:378). Almost half of these women workers were employed in Shanghai's largest industry, cotton (Honig 1985), which had been hit by the greatest number of strikes, in both relative and absolute terms, between 1919 and 1927 (Chesneaux 1968:379).

There is little material available to explain this labor militancy. Emily Honig's (1985) discussion of the sisterhoods organized by female workers in Shanghai's cotton mills during the 1920s suggests one way such class consciousness could be mobilized. According to Honig, these sisterhoods were traditional mutual aid associations, rather than "political" ones. In the view of the Chinese Communist party (CCP), however, they were "potentially revolutionary organizations" (page 712), and the CCP used them to organize female workers (pages 711–13).

Although factory workers in contemporary Taiwan have not organized to the extent of the sisterhoods in the 1920s, they have formed groups based on region and dialect to exchange tangible and intangible support (Kung 1983:79–81). These solidarity groups may represent the building blocks on which women's individual discontents can be converted into collective action (see also Milkman

---

14. The organization of women is closely linked to the political situation in Taiwan. Yenlin Ku (1988) argues that the lifting of martial law represents an opportunity to effect improvement in their situation, but she writes, "How to capitalize on this new situation to open more channels of agitation for change, and more importantly, how to raise female consciousness in general, are the challenges facing today's feminists in Taiwan" (page 186). The discussion that follows suggests one strategy.

1985; Safa 1976). As the Chinese case shows, such groupings can mobilize women's understanding of their position in the economic and social systems, the forces that create and perpetuate them, and the possibilities for change. Armed with this understanding, female workers can define their collective situation as unacceptable and organize to change the structures that limit them.

9

MAQUILADORA WOMEN:
A NEW CATEGORY OF WORKERS?

Susan Tiano

Export processing industrialization is a recent stage in the process of international capitalist expansion. It involves transferring the labor-intensive phases of production to Third World nations that possess an abundant supply of low-waged labor. In contrast to earlier forms of foreign investment, women constitute the bulk of the labor force in export zones throughout the world. Mexico established an export zone along its northern frontier in 1965 in order to achieve a number of development goals, including abating the rising unemployment troubling the region. Yet unemployment continued to rise during the first two decades of the Border Industrialization Program. One explanation for the program's inability to alleviate joblessness in the region emphasizes the gender composition of the labor force in export zones. This argument stresses the "structural imbalance" between the nature of northern Mexico's unemployment problems and the type of worker recruited for jobs in export processing. The thesis is that unemployment in the Third World is essentially a male problem, while most workers involved in export processing are women (Martinez 1978:132; Fernandez 1977:141;

An earlier version of this paper was presented at the Association of Borderlands Scholars meeting, Fort Worth, Texas, April 1985. The data for this study were collected in collaboration with Karen Bracken. Bob Fiala's and Paul Steele's comments on an earlier version of this paper are much appreciated.

Woog 1980:51,101). This "conventional thesis," that unemployment
is not a problem for northern Mexican women, assumes that women
need not enter the labor force because their households are adequately supported by male breadwinners, or that women who need
jobs to support themselves and their families are able to secure them.
A related argument is that export-processing industries have exacerbated male unemployment by mobilizing into the labor force a
new, previously economically inactive category of workers—
women—who otherwise would be in the household or in school
(Martinez 1978:132; Safa 1980:13; Fernandez-Kelly 1983:45;
Fuentes and Ehrenreich 1983:28). This discussion examines these
claims using data from a study of assembly-processing workers in
Mexicali, Mexico.

EXPORT PROCESSING AND THE BORDER
INDUSTRIALIZATION PROGRAM

Export-processing industrialization is a strategy developed by corporations to lower costs by reorganizing production on a global scale.
By establishing factories in export zones, transnational corporations
can decrease production costs by employing Third World workers
whose wage scales and benefit levels are considerably below those in
advanced industrial countries. The resulting geographical division
of labor parallels the segmentation of the production process into
discrete stages, the more labor intensive of which are further de-
composed through scientific management principles into simple, re-
petitive tasks requiring minimal skill and training. Transnational
corporations transfer these deskilled tasks to the export zones, while
retaining in their home countries activities requiring skilled labor,
rapidly innovating technologies, and capital-intensive production
techniques (Evans 1979:28). Research and development, product
design, and basic component fabrication typically occur in the home
country; the components are then shipped to the export zone for
additional processing, assembly, and testing; the finished product is
reexported for distribution in the home country and other parts of
the world (Frobel et al. 1980; Grunwald and Flamm 1985).
　The export-processing strategy, conceived during the years after

World War II, came into widespread use during the 1960s and 1970s. First employed by U.S.-based companies in response to growing competition for American markets, it has subsequently been adopted by firms headquartered in western Europe, Japan, and elsewhere that produce for consumers throughout the world. Export processing is particularly suitable for highly competitive industries whose labor costs constitute a large share of their operating budgets. Three such industries, which account for a considerable proportion of the investment in export processing throughout the world, are the textile and garment and electronics industries.

From the perspective of Third World governments, export-led industrialization has become a primary strategy for national development (Sklair 1989:17). Throughout the last three decades, increasing numbers of countries have encouraged it as a way of alleviating trade imbalances, providing jobs for underemployed populations, stimulating domestic industrialization, and promoting capital accumulation. Hoping to model the spectacular growth of Singapore, South Korea, Taiwan, and Hong Kong, growing numbers of Third World states have established export-processing zones within their borders in order to attract foreign investors. Enticements to firms locating within these export zones have included tax exemptions, inexpensive electricity rates, and the provision of roads, buildings, and other physical infrastructures. Some governments have attempted to increase their nation's comparative advantage by waiving worker-protection legislation that increases labor costs (Safa 1980:16). In 1975, seventy-nine of these zones were in operation, and thirty-nine more were under construction, in developing nations (Frobel et al. 1980:304). Between 1963 and 1985, the proportion of the world's manufactured exports accounted for by developing countries increased from 4.3 to 12.4 percent (Sklair 1989:15).

The transformation wrought by export processing is highlighted by comparing it to previous forms of foreign investment. In contrast to its characteristically passive role in earlier epochs, the Third World state is playing a more active part in stimulating foreign investment by granting incentives to foreign firms and enacting policies that stabilize wage rates and maintain political stability (Evans 1979:43– 50; Enloe 1983:410–11). Moreover, the contribution and composition of the Third World labor force differs from that of earlier periods, when a predominantly male work force extracted raw materials for export to core country markets. Workers within the new international division of labor are involved in manufacturing, and most, particularly within the "light" industries such as textiles and electronics, are young women (Grossman 1979:3; Enloe 1983:409; Ward 1988b:18). Women, typically aged sixteen to twenty-four, constitute 80 to 90 percent of the export-processing labor force in Mexico, Southeast Asia, and other export platform nations (Grossman 1979:3). Within a single generation, the process has created a female proletariat in export zones throughout the world (Lim 1981:186; Safa 1986:68).

The northern Mexican border region is a leading site for export-processing industrialization. Currently, over half of the imports entering the United States from less developed nations under the export-processing tariff provisions come from this region (Fernandez-Kelly 1983:34).[1] The Mexican state established this export zone in 1965, with the authorization of the Border Industrialization Program (BIP). In addition to fostering industrial development along the border, the program was intended to abate the high unemployment in the region, resulting in part from the termination of the *bracero* (guest worker) program (Bustamante 1983:242).[2] The BIP offers a number of incentives to foreign firms,

---

1. Although they were not designed specifically to augment export-led investment, items 806.3 and 807 of the U.S. tariff schedules have stimulated U.S. companies to export raw materials, equipment, and components for assembly by foreign subsidiaries or subcontractors. According to these provisions, tariff duties apply only to the product value added outside the United States, most of which is contributed by relatively inexpensive foreign labor (Fernandez 1977:36; Woog 1980:16–18).

2. The *bracero* program was constituted in August 1942 by the U.S. and Mexican governments to regulate Mexican labor migration to the U.S. Southwest. The program was intended to alleviate the shortage of unskilled agricultural laborers made acute by World War II and to regulate the long-running flow of undocumented immigration from Mexico. Although the program accomplished the first objective, it fell short on the second. To appease an American public alarmed by the continuing flow of undocumented immigrants, the U.S. Congress unilaterally cancelled the program in December 1964, despite protest from Mexico, whose labor market could not absorb the two hundred thousand workers abruptly expelled from the United States. The Mexican border region, whose population was already swollen by the steady stream of interior migrants hoping to serve as *braceros*, received the bulk of this return migration. Unemployment rates in many northern Mexican cities reached 50 percent, threatening economic and political stability in the region. The BIP was one response to this crisis (Fernandez-Kelly 1983:26; Sklair 1989).

including exemptions both from duties and regulations on the importation of raw materials and capital equipment and from taxes associated with profits, sales, and dividends (Fernandez 1977:135; Pena 1982:11). Moreover, the region's proximity to U.S.-based companies and markets, the active promotional efforts of officials on both sides of the border, and a series of currency devaluations that have made Mexican labor costs some of the lowest in the world have contributed to the program's growth. By 1979, the BIP (more commonly known as the maquiladora or maquila program) included more than 472 maquilas (assembly plants), employing 99,122 workers (Pena 1980b:13); by 1987, some 1,000 maquilas employed a work force of 74,000 (Sklair 1989: table 3.3). By the mid–1980s, the maquila program had become Mexico's second most important source of foreign exchange.

Among the manufacturing sectors most heavily represented in the maquila program are the electronics and apparel industries. In 1985, more than 45 percent of the maquila labor force were involved in electronics assembly, while 14 percent assembled apparel (Clement and Jenner 1987:23).

Although they are similar in that women comprise the majority of their work force, the two types of maquilas differ considerably. The nature of electronics assembly, which requires sophisticated technology, heavy infrastructural outlays, reliable sources of components manufactured to precise specification, and elaborate forward linkages to industrial and commercial consumers, limits participation in the maquila program to transnational companies and their subsidiaries. By contrast, the relatively low level of capital investment and technological sophistication required for apparel assembly makes it possible for small, locally owned shops to operate under subcontract with one or more larger firms (Fernandez-Kelly 1983:102–3; Clement and Jenner 1987:83).

The contrasts in their links to international capital lead to markedly different conditions in electronics and apparel maquilas. Electronics maquilas tend to be large, modern operations that use up-to-date machinery and have amenities such as cafeterias for their workers. Apparel maquilas are more diverse, ranging from clean, modern facilities to poorly ventilated, dingy "sweatshops." Further, assembly jobs in apparel maquilas tend to be less stable, more prone to recruitment abuses, and more strenuous than jobs in the electronics sector (Fernandez-Kelly 1983:111–12).

The disparity in working conditions affords electronics firms an advantage over apparel firms in that the former are better able to recruit the workers they deem most desirable. In Mexico, where the dominant cultural ideology views paid employment as conflicting with women's domestic and child-rearing roles, young, single, childless women have the best employment options. Women who have completed secondary school, involving three years of education beyond the six years of primary school, are also in an advantaged position in the labor market.

Competition for electronics jobs has traditionally been so intense that firms have been able to hire the "most desirable" women workers—secondary school graduates who are single and childless (Fernandez-Kelly 1983:51; Safa 1986:67). Apparel firms, whose position in the international economy is weaker than that of the transnational electronics subsidiaries, are less able to recruit from the "preferred" sector of the labor force; thus apparel assemblers tend to be less educated, are more likely to have children, and are more apt to have partners or to be single heads of households (Fernandez-Kelly 1983:51; Tiano 1987b:83–89)

EXPORT PROCESSING AND UNEMPLOYMENT IN NORTHERN MEXICO

Despite the jobs created by the maquila program, the unemployment problems plaguing northern Mexico continue to persist. Official employment statistics reveal that unemployment more than doubled during the first fifteen years of the program's operation (Fernandez-Kelly 1983:44). In an attempt to make sense of this seeming paradox, a number of scholars have advanced an explanation centering on the gender composition of the maquiladora work force.

This thesis holds that a "structural imbalance" exists between the composition of the maquila work force and the nature of Mexico's unemployment problems. According to this argument, the "traditional" work force in the area is composed of working-age males (Fernandez-Kelly 1983:45), the sector hardest hit by the failure of northern labor markets to absorb the expanding population. One version of this argument has it that unemployment in the border region is essentially a "male" problem (Martinez 1978:132; Fernandez 1977:141; Woog 1980:51, 101), yet, because more than 80 percent of the maquiladora work force is female (Fernandez-Kelly 1983:209), the program has not provided jobs for those who need them most. As Leslie Sklair (1989:chap. 8) says in his thoughtful discussion of the sexual division of labor along the border:

> The current orthodoxy is that unemployment along the frontera norte is a problem mainly of male workers and that the maquila industry has exacerbated the problem by recruiting mainly young women who would otherwise not be in the labor force at all. The imputed blow to male employment prospects is therefore twofold. First, the maquilas tend not to offer many jobs to men, and second, the women who get most of the maquila jobs do not generally vacate other jobs in the process.

This situation is particularly perplexing in light of the original intent of the BIP, which was to supply employment for men left jobless as a result of the termination of the *bracero* program in 1964. Thus, according to this view, the preference for female labor has prevented the maquiladora program from alleviating unemployment in northern Mexico.

The claim, which will hereafter be referred to as the "conventional thesis,"[3] that unemployment in northern Mexico is basically a "male" problem implies a stereotypical image of women's "proper" roles as those of wife and mother, rather than waged worker. It assumes that women typically do not work outside the home because they are adequately supported by male breadwinners and thus have no economic need to work. The only other logical justification for this claim would be that women who need to earn an income are consistently able to secure employment to support themselves. As I have

---

3. The notion that paid employment is antithetical to Mexican women's "proper" roles as wives and mothers finds frequent expression on both sides of the border. It underlies the common criticism of the maquila program for disrupting the Mexican family (see Fernandez-Kelly 1983:134–35) and is used to explain the high turnover rates among female operatives, who presumably "intend to work for only a few months before...beginning a family" (cited in Ruiz nd:21 from a Department of Commerce publication, *Business America*). I label the thesis "conventional" because of its underlying subscription to traditional female gender roles, as well as its widespread acceptance throughout many sectors of northern Mexican society.

argued elsewhere (Tiano 1984) on the basis of aggregate data on women's labor force participation in northern Mexico, neither of these assumptions appears to be warranted. Ellwyn Stoddard (1987:62–63) reaches a similar conclusion in his analysis of the maquila program. The present study subjects this claim to further empirical evaluation using individual-level data from a survey of maquila and service workers in Mexicali.

An intriguing variation on the conventional thesis is that the maquiladora program has contributed to unemployment by introducing a new, previously economically inactive category of workers into the labor market (Martinez 1978:132; Safa 1980:13; Fernandez-Kelly 1983:45; Fuentes and Ehrenreich 1983:28). According to this argument, the maquilas have led to the large-scale mobilization into the labor force of young women who otherwise would not have been in waged employment. Some have argued that multinational companies have consciously targeted and incorporated young women, "a new source of cheap factory labor," into the maquiladora work force (Fuentes and Ehrenreich 1983:28). This thesis holds that without the BIP, most women currently in the maquiladora work force would have been full-time homemakers or students, presumably supported by husbands or fathers. Once these newcomers are drawn into the labor market, they compete with long-time members for scarce jobs and put added strain on the economy's capacity to absorb them (Fernandez-Kelly 1983:101). As Maria Patricia Fernandez-Kelly puts it:

> Maquiladoras have not reduced unemployment rates because they do not tend to employ the members of the traditional work force, that is, males of working age. Rather, they employ members of the so-called inactive population, that is, daughters and wives whose principal activities took place in the school or in the home prior to the existence of the in-bond plant (maquila) program. In other words, these were the components of a formerly unemployable sector. *Maquiladoras have thus created* a new working contingent, expanding, in fact, the size of the potential labor force while at the same time disfranchising [*sic*] from its rank and file the majority of male workers. (1983:45; emphasis added)

This argument, which might be labeled the new-category-of-workers thesis, seems to have gained widespread acceptance in feminist literature. One reason for its appeal is that it avoids, at least on the surface, the patriarchal notions of women's ideal roles underlying the conventional thesis. Its implications, however, have as yet to be derived logically or subjected to empirical test.

Proponents of the new-category-of-workers thesis do not directly address the issue of why such large numbers of women have entered the maquiladora work force. They claim that before the onset of the BIP, young women were generally confined to the domestic sphere, yet after it was established, they entered the maquila labor force en masse. Although these scholars do not explicitly rule out the role of structural factors such as economic conditions in accounting for women's movement into the labor force, they imply, as the above quotation from Fernandez-Kelly's work makes clear, that the maquiladoras themselves caused this mobilization. If this is the case, then it is important to consider the ways in which the maquila program has stimulated women's entrance into the labor force.

Two possibilities suggest themselves, both of which hinge on two sets of concepts. The first concept, prevalent in Mexican culture, distinguishes between women working *por gusto* (for personal satisfaction) and those working *por necesidad* (for economic need). The second concept reflects a distinction prevalent in labor economics between "pull" factors and "push" factors, two complementary dynamics whose interplay underlies a woman's decision to enter waged work. Push factors are forces such as economic need that impel a woman out of the household to earn an income to contribute to its support. Pull factors include a broad range of conditions that either attract women into the labor force or expand their opportunities for paid employment. They may include the availability of suitable, decent-paying jobs; the weakening of cultural norms that symbolically confine women to the household; or the lure of noneconomic rewards, such as personal autonomy, which might stimulate them to enter paid employment. When a woman works *por necesidad*, she is responding to the force of push factors, although pull factors may also come into play. A woman working *por gusto* is more likely to be responding to pull factors, such as financial independence and personal satisfaction, as well as other conditions that provide opportunities for her in the labor force.

The "pull" variant of the new-category-of-workers thesis would emphasize the mobilizing role of the maquiladoras in providing employment opportunities for women and in helping to relax the cultural expectation that women should not work outside the home. On the one hand, the financial independence and personal satisfaction that could accompany paid employment may have lured women into the maquila work force. In this case, women would be working chiefly *por gusto*. On the other hand, the maquilas may be providing formal-sector employment opportunities for women who have to generate an income *por necesidad*.

The "push" variant of the thesis would emphasize the role of the maquila program in augmenting male unemployment, which makes it necessary for women to earn an income to help support their households. Jorge Bustamante (1983) makes this claim, arguing that the maquila program has stimulated migration to northern Mexico, which has expanded the size of the surplus labor pool. Fernandez-Kelly's above-cited argument, that maquilas have expanded the size of the potential labor force while excluding its male members, is also consistent with this interpretation. In this case maquilas would be viewed as pushing women into the labor force by casting them into the role of key secondary, and in some cases primary, breadwinners for households in which male members are unemployed, severely underemployed, or absent. Maquila workers would thus be working *por necesidad*, or out of a financial need brought about at least in part by the economic changes wrought by the BIP. Consistent with this position are the findings of Fernandez-Kelly's (1983:54–58) Juarez-based study, which revealed that the economic need to support themselves and their families forced many women to work for wages. They typically entered the maquila labor force not as individuals but as constituents of households whose survival depended upon the various members' contributions. The males in their households were frequently either unemployed or underemployed.

A comprehensive evaluation of the assumptions of the new-category-of-workers thesis is beyond the scope of this discussion. Such a task would require data collected before and after the onset of the BIP on demographic, economic, and cultural factors underlying women's labor force participation. Perhaps the most difficult challenge would be to establish the causal role of the maquila program, and governmental and private-sector policies surrounding it, in relaxing the cultural expectation confining women to the wife-mother role, and thereby facilitating their entrance into the labor force (one implication of the "pull" variant of the thesis), or in augmenting the economic crises faced by many working-class households that have forced women to earn a wage to help support their families (one implication of the "push" variant of the thesis).

Yet one might accept some implications of the thesis without being able either to demonstrate or embrace the causal assumptions regarding the maquila program's primary or exclusive role in "creating" the new category of workers. Transnational firms may merely have inserted themselves into a context in which widespread cultural and economic changes have prepared women to enter the labor force en masse and taken advantage of this process to absorb these women into their work force. By providing women with opportunities for paid employment, the maquilas simply may have stimulated a process of social and economic changes well under way before their appearance on the northern Mexican scene. In other words, the new-category-of-workers thesis may be descriptively correct even though it is analytically incomplete or untestable.

The following discussion explores some of the assumptions underlying both the conventional and the new-category-of-workers theses. It is based on a study of women workers in Mexicali, the capital of Baja California. The study was conducted in 1983, the year after the first major currency devaluation and the economic changes that accompanied it. I studied women in three sectors of the Mexicali labor force. I drew comparable subsamples of workers from the electronics and garment industries and from the service sector, which enabled me to compare the two types of maquiladora workers with each other and with domestics, waitresses, clerks, and workers in other low-level service jobs. The sample contains sixty-six workers from electronics firms, fifty-eight from apparel maquiladoras, and seventy from the service sector. Respondents were interviewed, typically for an hour, using both closed- and open-ended questions.

Because there is no way to determine how well this sample represents the universe from which it was drawn, caution must be employed in making generalizations about the population of women workers in Mexicali and other northern Mexican cities. At the same time, there is no reason to assume that the sample is skewed in a way that would systematically bias the analysis. To interpret the resulting information better, I also interviewed personnel directors and other managers of both electronics and garment maquiladoras. In light of these data, I will first consider the conventional thesis that unemployment is a "male" and not a "female" problem and then examine certain assumptions underlying the new-category-of-workers thesis.

THE CONVENTIONAL THESIS

The conventional argument that unemployment is primarily a "male" problem would expect almost all women in this sample to have husbands or fathers to maintain them economically. The maquiladora worker might be especially likely to live with a male breadwinner, although service workers might also fit this description. In fact, these generalizations do not apply to many women in the Mexicali sample. The information summarized in table 9.1 indicates that only 23 percent of the electronics workers, 35 percent of the garment assemblers, and 31 percent of the service workers were married or in a free union. Between two-thirds and three-fourths of the respondents in each subsample did not have partners who could contribute to their financial support.

Nor did all the unpartnered women live in households with fathers or other menfolk present. As the data in table 9.2 indicate, the only women in the sample for whom father-headed households were the most common living arrangement were the electronics workers, 50 percent of whom lived in such households. Slightly less than a third of the garment assemblers (32 percent) and the service workers (29 percent) occupied father-centered households. More than a third of the sample belonged to households with no adult male member. Service workers were especially likely to live in female-headed households; 41 percent fit this description. Over a fourth (26 percent) of the garment workers and a fifth (21 percent) of the electronics assemblers also lived in households composed only of women and children. The finding that a third of the sample dwelt in female-headed households is consistent with patterns reported for many

TABLE 9.1. Marital Status, by Employment Category

Marital Status	Electronics Maquila	Clothing Maquila	Service Sector	Total
Single	43 65.2%	30 51.7%	32 45.7%	105 54.1%
Divorced, separated	8 12.1%	8 13.8%	16 22.9%	32 16.5%
Married, free union	15 22.7%	20 34.5%	22 31.4%	57 29.4%
Total	66	58	70	194[a]

[a]Missing cases = 0

Third World nations (International Center for Research on Women 1980a, b).

It is important to distinguish between the demographic composition of women's households and the income-earning role of the various members present. A woman may live in a household nominally headed by a father or husband, but if the man is unemployed or severely underemployed, his economic contribution to the household will be minimal or nonexistent. The notion that male unemployment is a factor that precipitates a woman's entrance into the maquila labor force underlies the work of Fernandez-Kelly and is implied by the "push" variant of the new-category-of-workers thesis.

To shed light on this issue, I asked the women to list the relationship and employment status of each regular contributor to their household's income. The amounts of the contributions were impossible to determine because many respondents did not know how much their fathers, husbands, or other male contributors earned, much less how much they contributed to meeting household expenses. Nevertheless, the findings are informative: of the fifty-six women who lived with a husband or male partner, fifty-three, or 95 percent, stated that he was currently employed and regularly provided income to the household; of the seventy-one women who had fathers present in their households, sixty, or 86 percent, reported a

TABLE 9.2. Presence of Adult Male in Household, by
Employment Category

Male Present	Electronics Maquila	Clothing Maquila	Service Sector	Total
None	14	15	29	58
	21.2%	26.3%	41.4%	30.1%
Husband	16	21	19	56
	24.2%	36.8%	27.1%	29.0%
Father	33	18	20	71
	50.0%	31.6%	28.6%	36.8%
Other	3	3	2	8
	4.5%	5.3%	2.9%	4.1%
Total	66	57	70	193[a]

[a]Missing cases = 1

pattern of regular economic support, either through a job or retirement income; moreover, all of the eight women who had other
adult males in their households reported that these men had jobs
and made steady economic contributions. The theoretical implications of these findings for the new-category-of workers thesis will be
considered in a later section of this chapter. At this point it is sufficient to suggest that for most of the households represented in the
sample, the presence of an adult male suggests some male account-
ability for household support.

Yet, even if the women did share financial responsibilities with
men, this does not imply, as the conventional argument would have
it, that the women's wages were not important to their families' well-
being. On the contrary, they may have made valuable, if not essential,
contributions to the household economy. This possibility can be explored in an approximate way by considering the average size of,
and the mean number of economic contributors to, respondents'
households (tables 9.3 and 9.4). These data evidence slight variations
in household size among the three subgroups. On the average, the
electronics assemblers' households were slightly larger (6.3 persons)
than those of the garment assemblers (5.7) or the service workers

TABLE 9.3. Number of Persons in Household, by Employment Category

Employment Category	Mean	Standard Deviation	Cases[a]
Electronics maquila	6.2769	3.0286	65
Clothing maquila	5.5614	2.5844	57
Service sector	5.1143	2.7691	70
Total	5.6406	2.8360	192

[a]Missing cases = 2

(5.1). This difference probably reflects the fact that electronics workers were more likely than other women in the sample to live with one or both parents or siblings. (Sixty-four percent of the electronics workers lived in this type of arrangement, compared with 48 percent of the garment assemblers and 47 percent of the service workers.)

The average number of wage earners per household varied little among the three subgroups, although it was slightly larger among electronics assemblers (2.7) than among workers in apparel firms (2.3) or service jobs (2.4). The weight of the economic burden borne by wage earners in respondents' households can be evaluated by comparing these two sets of averages. The resulting ratios were almost identical, ranging from a mean of 2.3 for service workers to 2.5 and 2.6 for workers in electronics and garment firms. Although electronics assemblers typically pooled their wages with those of more income earners than did garment or service workers, this potential advantage was overridden by the larger average size of their households. It is clear from these data that the typical maquiladora worker in the sample shared the responsibility for maintaining her fairly large household with one or at most two other family members. There is no indication that maquiladora or service workers were peripheral to the family wage economy, as the conventional argument suggests.

To summarize, whether women in the sample lived in households with no adult males—and almost a third fit this description—or pooled their wages with others, there is no evidence to suggest that their wages were irrelevant to their families' financial well-being.

The alternative explanation for the notion that unemployment is not a problem for northern Mexican women is that all women who want or need a job are able to find one. This claim can be evaluated

TABLE 9.4.   Mean Number of Contributors to Household

Employment Category	Mean	Standard Deviation	Cases[a]
Electronics maquila	2.6970	1.3005	66
Clothing maquila	2.2807	.9591	57
Service sector	2.3714	1.1186	70
Total	2.4560	1.1499	193

[a]Missing cases = 1

by considering the unemployment experiences reported by women in the Mexicali sample. Respondents were questioned about the longest period of time, at any point in their lives, that they were jobless and actively seeking employment. Their answers are summarized in table 9.5. About a third of the sample (30 percent) reported that they were unemployed for longer than a month; electronics assemblers were the most likely (38 percent) and garment workers the least likely (22 percent) to have had this experience.

The higher rates of unemployment among electronics workers are interesting in light of the fact, not shown in the tables, that their mean length of time in the labor force (5.7 years) was shorter than that of the garment workers (9.8 years) and the service workers (8.9 years). Although the duration of economic activity for the average electronics worker was shorter than that of her typical counterpart in the apparel industry, she was more likely to have experienced joblessness at some point in her employment career. This finding is also unexpected given the preference of employers for young, unmarried women. On the whole, the electronics workers in the sample were younger than the women in the garment and service sectors: their average age was 22.2 years, compared to a mean age of 27.9 and 27.2 for the garment and service workers respectively. And, as shown in table 9.1, electronics workers were more likely than women from the other employment sectors to be single, a status that similarly might be expected to spare them from bouts of joblessness.

This finding must be interpreted with caution, for these data tell us little about the type of jobs the women were seeking or their economic circumstances while they were unemployed. Moreover, although unemployment might typically represent vulnerability in

TABLE 9.5. Longest Time Unemployed, by Employment Category

Time Unemployed	Electronics Maquila	Clothing Maquila	Service Sector	Total
No time	31	30	34	95
	47.0%	54.5%	50.0%	50.3%
Few days–4 weeks	10	13	14	37
	15.2%	23.6%	20.6%	19.6%
1–6 months	21	9	13	43
	31.8%	16.4%	19.1%	22.8%
Longer than 6 months	4	3	7	14
	6.1%	5.5%	10.3%	7.4%
Total	66	55	68	189[a]

[a]Missing cases = 5

the labor market, it could also reflect a high degree of selectivity in a worker's job choices. If any women in the sample could afford to be discriminating in their job selection, they would most likely have been in the electronics worker subcategory. Electronics workers were less apt than other workers in the sample to be single heads of households supporting dependent children; thus they might have been better able to weather a period of joblessness while holding out for a position in the more desirable electronics industry.

A more plausible interpretation is that garment workers were less likely than electronics assemblers to be plagued by unemployment because the sewing skills gained through apparel assembly were in more general demand than the skills gained in the electronics industry. The "human capital"—the skills and training—acquired through participation in the garment industry may thus outweigh the disadvantages of older age or marital involvement for experienced seamstresses seeking employment in the garment industry. Conversely, the average electronics worker's youthful, unmarried status may not counteract the negative effect of working in an industry ill suited for imparting transferable skills that might increase one's chances in the job market. Regardless of how these results are interpreted, however, the finding that 30 percent of the sample experienced a period of unemployment ranging from one to six months or longer is not consistent with the conventional argument that unemployment in northern Mexico is confined to the male sector of the population.

In sum, these findings suggest that neither rationale underlying the conventional thesis accurately portrays the situation of maquila or service workers in the Mexicali sample. The notion that unemployment primarily affects males, either because women do not need an income or are consistently able to secure jobs when they want or need them, appears questionable in light of these data.

THE NEW-CATEGORY-OF-WORKERS THESIS

The assumption that the maquiladoras have mobilized a new category of workers who would not otherwise work for wages requires further clarification and exploration. This notion can be explored indirectly by considering workers' employment histories, their perceptions of their economic need to work, and their attitudes toward their own and other women's waged employment.

Table 9.6 presents the number of previous jobs reported by the three sample subgroups. Most notable is the difference between electronics workers and other women in the sample. Almost half (44 percent) of the electronics workers were in their first job, compared to 25 percent of the garment assemblers and 31 percent of the service workers. Whereas 30 percent of those in apparel firms and 26 percent in service occupations had held three or more jobs, only 5 percent of the electronics workers had a similarly lengthy employment career. This finding is consistent with other empirical studies of export-processing workers (Fernandez-Kelly 1983; Fuentes and Ehrenreich 1983; Grossman 1979) and could be interpreted as supporting the thesis that assembly workers constitute a new category of workers in that many were new recruits to the labor force.

Such an inference would not, however, be justified without considerable qualification. First, the differences between electronics and garment assemblers indicate that wholesale generalizations

TABLE 9.6. Number of Previous Jobs, by Employment Category

Jobs Held	Electronics Maquila	Clothing Maquila	Service Sector	Total
0	29	14	22	65
	43.9%	25.0%	31.4%	33.9%
1	21	15	10	46
	31.8%	26.8%	14.3%	24.0%
2	13	10	12	35
	19.7%	17.9%	17.1%	18.2%
3	0	5	12	17
	.0%	8.9%	17.1%	8.9%
4	0	2	4	6
	.0%	3.6%	5.7%	3.1%
5	3	10	10	23
	4.5%	17.9%	14.3%	12.0%
Total	66	56	70	192[a]

[a]Missing cases = 2

about maquiladora workers are likely to be unfounded. In contrast to electronics assemblers, apparel workers were apt to have had fairly lengthy labor histories, as might be expected considering their relatively older ages. To the extent that this subsample adequately represents the population of garment workers in Mexicali, there is little evidence that apparel maquiladoras have incorporated a new contingent of workers into the Mexicali labor force. Second, almost a third of the service workers in the sample were in their first job, demonstrating that limited labor force experience is not confined to maquila workers. Instead, it may be rather common among women in northern Mexico, given the relative youth of the economically active female population (see Tiano 1984). Third, although a considerable percentage of the electronics workers were in their first job at the time of the study, an even larger proportion (56 percent) had lengthier employment histories. Almost a third had held one previous job, and almost a fifth reported two previous positions.

Proponents of the new-category-of-workers thesis might argue that the number of previous jobs is not as important as the type of prior employment. If it could be shown that maquila workers' first jobs were typically in export-processing firms, this would indicate that assembly workers in the sample were originally new recruits to the maquilas who might well have moved from firm to firm within the electronics or garment industries. The data in table 9.7 suggest that this possibility fits only a portion of the sample. One-third of the workers in the electronics firms and half of those in the apparel industry entered the Mexicali labor market through the service sector. These women apparently joined the work force for reasons other than the existence of the maquilas. On the other hand, a majority (66 percent) of the electronics workers and half of the garment workers did have their first employment experience in export processing. These workers were new to the labor market at the time they entered the maquila work force.

Resolving this issue hinges on the meaning of the word *new*. It is not surprising that many electronics workers in the sample have limited labor histories, in that employers in Mexicali firms repeatedly told us they preferred young, inexperienced workers. Not only are these women more likely than others to be single and childless (and hence supposedly better able to devote themselves wholeheartedly to their jobs), but they are also less likely to have had prior experiences with workers' unions (and thus to be less politicized and more docile). Fernandez-Kelly (1983) reports a similar attitude among maquiladora managers in Juarez. Furthermore, it is not unusual for workers to remain in one type of occupation or industry. Some people prefer jobs and tasks with which they are familiar; others make contacts in one firm that help them gain employment in another. Such consistency may be especially common among workers in apparel firms, who through their jobs acquire sewing skills that can be readily transferred from one firm to another. In sum, any worker may be or at one time has been new to the maquila work force or to the labor market generally. Every worker fits the description of "new" at some point.

This individual-level meaning of *new* does not, however, effectively

TABLE 9.7.   First Job, by Present Employment Category

First Job	Electronics Maquila	Clothing Maquila	Service Sector	Total
No prior job	29 43.9%	14 24.1%	22 31.4%	65 33.5%
Electronics firm	8 12.1%	1 1.7%	4 5.7%	13 6.7%
Garment firm	1 1.5%	10 17.2%	5 7.1%	16 8.2%
Maquila—unspecified	6 9.1%	4 6.9%	4 5.7%	14 7.2%
Service sector	22 33.3%	29 50.0%	35 50.0%	86 44.3%
Total	66	58	70	194[a]

[a] Missing cases = 0

encompass the concept of novelty implied by the new-category-of-workers thesis. The thesis refers to aggregates, not individuals, and assumes that labor force participation is a novel and unusual experience for certain types of workers. Young women in northern Mexico are assumed ordinarily to be students, full-time homemakers, or both, but not waged workers. Their presumed "newness" implies that before the BIP young Mexican women generally were not involved in waged labor but that after almost two decades of operation, substantial numbers have entered the maquila labor force. It may be that the maquiladora program and the publicity surrounding it have helped to override the economic, social, and cultural forces that traditionally confined women to the private sphere. These forces are rooted in a gender-based division of labor allocating men to the provider role and women to domestic responsibilities which underlies hiring practices favoring men, normative injunctions against men and women working together, and women's lack of aspirations for waged labor.

The preferential hiring of women for maquila jobs may be helping to undermine this rigid division of labor, creating opportunities for women not just in manufacturing but in other economic sectors as well. The ideology about women's roles and the gender-based division of labor it supports may also be being overridden by economic conditions such as rampant inflation, currency devaluations, and related forces that bring financial hardship to working-class households whose survival strategies involve female members' entrance into the labor force. For traditional norms surrounding women's roles to be widely practiced, most women must be able to form stable partnerships with men who have the economic wherewithal to support them and their children. Men must have access to jobs that pay a sufficient family wage, making it unnecessary for partnered women to earn an income. When, on the contrary, many women live in households headed by females and economic conditions are such that the income of a single male wage earner is insufficient to support the household, the women are propelled by economic need into the labor force.

A key implication of the new-category-of-workers thesis is that were it not for the existence of the maquila program, northern Mexican women would not be in the labor force but in school or the home. This implication could be taken to mean that women would be economically inactive because they would not need to earn a wage. Such a notion is logically inconsistent, however, with the "push" variant of the thesis. If women were forced to enter the labor force because of economic necessity, then they clearly could not afford to be full-time houseworkers or students whether the maquila program existed or not.

Moreover, like the assumption underlying the conventional thesis, this notion is suspect in that the forgoing analysis suggests that most women in the sample would need to earn a wage whether or not the maquiladora program existed. The data on marital status, the presence of male income earners, and household size presented in tables 9.1, 9.2, and 9.3 suggest that many or most women were working out of financial need. The women's own subjective evaluations of their financial situations corroborate these objective data. Table 9.8 summarizes their responses to the question "If for some reason you were unable to work here, would you need, for economic reasons, to find another job?" The overwhelming majority of the

TABLE 9.8. Perception of Economic Need, by Employment Category

Economic Need	Electronics Maquila	Clothing Maquila	Service Sector	Total
No	7	8	11	26
	11.9%	17.4%	17.5%	15.5%
Yes	52	38	52	142
	88.1%	82.6%	82.5%	84.5%
Total	59	46	63	168[a]

[a]Missing cases = 26

sample, 85 percent, answered that they would. The percentages varied little among the three categories of workers, although the electronics assemblers were somewhat more likely to answer affirmatively (88 percent) than the garment workers or service workers (83 percent).

The data in table 9.9 also indicate the women's financial need to work. Respondents were asked whether or not they agreed that "today, women must work to help their families keep up with inflation." Only thirteen, or 7 percent, of the respondents disagreed with this statement. Thus the vast majority felt not only that waged employment was essential for themselves but that women generally are bound by this economic imperative. These data are inconsistent with the notion that maquila workers typically do not need to earn an income, or that they are different in this respect from their counterparts in the service sector. Like other women workers, most would need to earn an income whether or not the maquiladora program existed.

The "push" variant of the new-category-of-workers thesis ascribes a central role to male unemployment in contributing to the economic need that pushes women out of the household and into the labor force. This notion can be partially explored by considering the data presented earlier on the financial contributions and employment status of male household members. The finding that most of these men were employed (or retired) at the time the survey was conducted suggests that open unemployment was not a critical impetus to the

TABLE 9.9.   Percentage Who Agreed That Women Must Work to Help
Their Families Keep Abreast of Inflation

Response	Electronics Maquila	Clothing Maquila	Service Sector	Total
Strongly disagree	4	0	1	5
	6.1%	.0%	1.4%	2.6%
Disagree	2	4	2	8
	3.0%	6.9%	2.9%	4.1%
Agree	8	13	12	33
	12.1%	22.4%	17.1%	17.0%
Strongly agree	52	41	55	148
	78.8%	70.7%	78.6%	76.3%
Total	66	58	70	194[a]

[a] Missing cases = 0

women's economic need for work. Most of the husbands, fathers,
or other male members did have some source of employment that
enabled them to contribute regularly to household finances. This
does not mean, however, that their incomes were sufficient to support the fairly large households in which they lived. It is more likely
that their wives' and daughters' wages made valuable, if not essential,
contributions to the family wage economy.

Such an inference is impossible to evaluate with certainty without
data on the level of men's economic contributions, which the respondents were unable to supply. It is consistent, however, with
previous research on the subject. In the words of Lopez-Garcia, a
sociologist who has studied household survival strategies in northern
Mexico, "Just about everyone who is physically able works" (cited by
Ruiz nd:23). Moreover, in light of the data presented in table 9.9,
this interpretation seems highly plausible. The economic need that
has led many women to enter the labor force does not seem to be
rooted in male unemployment per se but rather in the general economic crisis that has plagued Mexico throughout the 1980s. Although the maquilas have taken advantage of this crisis to use
women's labor power, they are but a small part of the complex

structural conditions that have precipitated it. Amending the "push" variant of the new-category-of-workers thesis to encompass this interpretation might increase its utility.

One way in which maquilas pull women into the formal labor force is by providing job opportunities for women who must work to help their families survive Mexico's economic troubles. Without the jobs the maquilas provide, the women would have to earn incomes other ways. For many, particularly older, partnered women who occupy the most vulnerable sector of the female labor force (Fernandez-Kelly 1983:51), jobs in the formal service sector are difficult to obtain, as are positions as live-in domestic servants. Thus their main employment alternatives involve income-generating activities in the informal sector.[4] The mobilizing role of the maquilas may, to an important extent, be in drawing women into the formal labor force from the informal sector. Another possibility is that they provide manufacturing jobs that women hold in addition to doing informal tasks. Since informal-sector activities often take place in the home, a woman's movement from this sector into the maquila labor force would often involve a change in her locus of activity from the home to the factory. This might be a useful way to interpret the assumption of the new-category-of-workers thesis that without the existence of the maquila program, the female work force would have instead confined its activities to the home. But rather than engaging in unpaid domestic work, the women would have been involved in informal income-generating activities.

A second thrust of the "pull" variant of the new-category-of-workers thesis stresses the role of maquiladoras in overcoming the normative constraints that symbolically assign women to the domestic sphere. This view implies that the maquila program, the vehicle through

---

4. The informal sector of the urban economy involves occupations that are unstable, poorly remunerated, and not covered by worker-protection legislation, such as minimum wage laws. Examples of such activities that employ predominantly women are washing and ironing clothes, preparing and selling food, and other tasks that are often extensions of their domestic roles. Others involve the assembly of garments, toys, electronics components, or other products under subcontracting arrangements (see Beneria and Roldan 1987). Women often perform these activities in their own or other women's homes. While some social scientists view these activities as peripheral to the modern capitalist economy, others hold that they provide low-cost goods and services to workers or firms in the formal sector, thereby increasing the amount of capital accumulated by transnational and locally owned firms (see Portes and Walton 1981:86).

which transnational companies have entered northern Mexico, may have stimulated the spread of norms that hold manufacturing jobs to be appropriate for Mexican women. Part of what Ruiz (nd:13) calls the "packaging" of the maquila program has involved disseminating through trade publications and the mass media the notion that characteristics traditionally ascribed to women, such as patience, manual dexterity, and docility, make them ideally suited for the painstaking tasks involved in assembly work. Whether or not women in fact possess such attributes to a greater degree than men is beside the point; what matters is that these characteristics become the focus of an ideology that considers assembly work to be consistent with female gender roles and thereby serves to legitimate the employment of women. Sklair (1989:chap. 8) notes that this "litany of docile, undemanding, 'nimble-fingered' women workers" is repeated in export zones throughout the world, presumably perpetuated by transnational firms in order to break down resistance to female employment. He argues that "as an ideological rationale for the employment of women workers there is no question that it is accepted by friends and foes of the maquila industry alike." The diffusion of this ideology throughout northern Mexican society would help dissolve the traditional division of labor allocating women to the household, thereby facilitating their entrance into the labor force. Whether women worked *por gusto* or *por necesidad*, the maquilas would indirectly facilitate their entrance into the labor force by helping transform cultural norms about feminine roles.

This possibility can be considered indirectly by considering women's commitment to remaining in the labor force and their attitudes toward female employment generally. Is economic need the only reason women enter the maquila labor force, or do they work for other reasons as well? To explore this question, I asked respondents whether or not they agreed that "I would continue working even if I did not need the money." Their answers are tabulated in table 9.10. The majority, 64 percent, stated they would remain in the labor force. Workers in garment firms were somewhat less likely to agree with the statement (57 percent) than were electronics workers (68 percent) or service workers (67 percent), but the difference is not pronounced. This finding suggests that in addition to financial rewards, many women derive nonmaterial benefits from paid em-

TABLE 9.10.   Percentage Who Agree They Would Keep Working Even If They Did Not Need the Money

Response	Electronics Maquila	Clothing Maquila	Service Sector	Total
Strongly disagree	10 15.2%	21 36.2%	21 30.0%	52 26.8%
Disagree	11 16.7%	4 6.9%	2 2.9%	17 8.8%
Agree	18 27.3%	10 17.2%	11 15.7%	39 20.1%
Strongly agree	27 40.9%	23 39.7%	36 51.4%	86 44.3%
Total	66	58	70	194[a]

[a]Missing cases = 0

ployment which increase their commitment to their roles as waged workers. The *por gusto–por necesidad* dichotomy may be a false one: women may work out of economic necessity and for the intrinsic satisfaction their job provides. In this regard, maquiladora workers are no different from workers in the service sector.

From their responses to this item, it might appear that many women in the sample have overcome—or never experienced—the tendency to perceive themselves and other women primarily or exclusively in domestic terms. If the ideology perpetuated by the maquilas has played a role in diminishing this cultural expectation, then maquila workers might be especially likely to perceive women's work in nontraditional terms. The data in table 9.11 show little evidence that such a supposition is warranted. When asked whether or not they agreed that "it would be better if women did not work outside the home," 71 percent of the sample answered affirmatively. Garment workers were especially likely to hold this opinion: 87 percent, compared with 64 percent of the electronics and service workers, agreed with the statement. These opinions appear incompatible with those summarized in the preceding table. The majority intended to

TABLE 9.11.   Percentage Who Agree That Women Should Not Work
Outside the Home

Response	Electronics Maquila	Clothing Maquila	Service Sector	Total
Strongly disagree	8 12.1%	2 3.5%	13 18.6%	23 11.9%
Disagree	16 24.2%	5 8.8%	12 17.1%	33 17.1%
Agree	15 22.7%	15 26.3%	12 17.1%	42 21.8%
Strongly agree	27 40.9%	35 61.4%	33 47.1%	95 49.2%
Total	66	57	70	193

ᵃMissing cases = 1

remain in the labor force yet felt that women generally should not
work outside the home. They approved of waged labor for themselves but not for other women. Apparently, they subscribed to traditional sex roles for women generally but made an exception for
themselves. This paradox may reflect the fact that most women are
only slowly rejecting conventional norms surrounding women's
roles.

CONCLUSION

These data offer no support for the notion that unemployment is
not a problem for Mexicali women, either because they are adequately supported by men or because those wanting jobs have consistently been able to secure them. More than a third of the sample
lived in households headed by females. Even the women with fathers
or male partners in their households contributed their incomes to
family upkeep. These women shared financial responsibility for
maintaining their typically large families with one or at most two
other members. It is extremely unlikely that maquiladora workers

or service workers are marginal to the family wage economy, as the conventional thesis suggests. Nor do these data indicate that all women in the sample had reliable access to waged employment. About a third reported being unemployed for longer than a month at some point in their lives.

Almost half of the electronics workers were in their first job at the time of the study, and another 15 percent reported their first position as being in some other assembly-processing firm. About half the apparel workers had their first job in export processing. Thus most assembly workers in the sample were novices to the labor market when they entered the maquiladora work force. This finding could be seen as supporting the new-category-of-workers thesis and may account for its popularity among feminist authors such as Fernandez-Kelly (1983), who would probably eschew the more conventional view of Mexican women's ideal roles. The more profound implication of the thesis, however—that young Mexican women in the aggregate would not be in the labor force were it not for the maquiladoras—is not consistent with these data. The overwhelming majority of assembly workers claimed that their wages were necessary for their own and their families' well-being. If they were not working in the maquiladoras, they would have needed to work in another sector of the Mexicali economy. Most believed that their economic situation was not unique but that Mexican women generally must earn a wage to help their families keep abreast of inflation. The maquila program appears to have drawn women into the formal labor force by creating employment opportunities in manufacturing for women who otherwise would have been relegated to the informal sector. Yet there is little indication, as the "pull" variant of the thesis might also predict, that these women have abandoned the normative expectation that women should be devoting themselves to full-time domestic responsibilities. Rather, most women in this study would probably consider it unfortunate that so many Mexican women must earn a wage.

Although most women in the sample subscribe to traditional sex roles for Mexican women generally, many make an exception in their own cases. About two-thirds of the respondents maintained that they would remain in the labor force even if they did not need the money. Apparently they have come to enjoy whatever personal gratification and financial independence waged labor provides. They work *por gusto* as well as *por necesidad.* Although it is common in Mexico to view these motives as mutually exclusive, the work-related attitudes of many women in this study suggest that for many women the conceptual dichotomy is a false one.

At the same time, their attitudes suggest some ambivalence about their roles as wage earners. One might argue, as does Heleith I. B. Saffiotti (1978), that it is this ambivalence that allows women to function as an industrial labor reserve, being coaxed into and out of the labor force according to the labor needs of the capitalist system. This ambivalence might also help explain why maquiladoras prefer female labor, in that it makes women more likely than men to serve as a transitory and flexible labor source. The contradictions that permeate women's attitudes toward their work roles, of which they may be only dimly aware, may make them ideal workers from the point of view of maquiladora management. To understand more fully why women enter the maquiladoras, we must go beyond questioning whether women do or do not need to work for wages and learn more about how the contradictions in their roles and attitudes affect the conditions under which they can be mobilized into the work force.

The link between male unemployment and women's participation in the maquila work force is more complex than the "push" variant of the new-category-of-workers thesis would have it. The households from which maquila workers in the sample were recruited were not typically headed by unemployed males, suggesting that the economic needs that impelled these women into the labor force were rooted in causes other than open male joblessness. Even though male unemployment levels may have risen at the same time that increasing numbers of women were entering the maquila labor force, this does not mean that the two processes are causally linked. Rather, both may be the results of the same underlying complex of factors, and their apparent association may be spurious. The inflation, spiraling debt, and other economic problems that have plagued Mexico's economy for two decades may have both exacerbated male (and female) unemployment and caused economic hardship for working-class households whose female members have had to earn a wage as part of the household's survival strategy. This conclusion need not imply, however, that male unemployment underlies women's entrance into assembly-processing jobs or, conversely, that the maquilas' absorption of women has directly contributed to male unemployment. Indeed, when considered at the household level of analysis, these phenomena appear unrelated. The findings of this study suggest that women need to generate household income not because their menfolk are unemployed but because these men's wages are insufficient to cover family expenses or because there are no men in their households.

Moreover, to the extent that this sample represents the populations in Mexicali and other cities in northern Mexico, these findings indicate that the households from which maquila workers are recruited represent a different segment of the population from that which is troubled by chronic male unemployment. It is likely that the relatively well-educated women preferred for maquila employment represent a different socioeconomic stratum of Mexican society from that encompassing the ranks of the chronically unemployed. Such an interpretation could clarify why the jobs resulting from the maquila program have done little to assuage the problems resulting from male unemployment in the region. Not only do the maquilas not hire structurally unemployed men, but they are unlikely to assist them and their households indirectly through employing their wives and daughters. This hypothesis might be a fruitful focus for further research. As long as the BIP continues to attract foreign export-processing firms whose work force worldwide has been constituted by young, single, relatively educated women, it is unlikely to alleviate male unemployment, regardless of its intent. If policy makers are to develop effective programs to respond to the needs of unemployed males, they will have to look to other solutions than investing in export-led industrialization.

REFERENCES

Acker, Joan. 1988. "Class, Gender, and the Relations of Production." *Signs* 13:473–97.

Afshar, Haleh. 1987. *Women, State, and Ideology*. Albany, N.Y.: SUNY Press.

Agianoglou, Pandelis. 1982. *The Transition from Feudalism to Capitalism in Greece*. Athens: Kentriki Diathesi.

Agora Japan. n.d. *The Low Status of Women in Japan: A Paradox*. Tokyo: Agora Japan.

―――. 1985. *Haruko: A Japanese Working Woman*. Tokyo: Agora Japan.

Aguiar, Neuma. 1986. "Research Guidelines: How to Study Work in Latin America." In *Women and Change in Latin America*, ed. June Nash and Helen I. Safa, 22–34. South Hadley, Mass.: Bergin & Garvey.

"American Business Finds Ireland." 1983. *New York Times*, August 21, F–8.

Amin, Samir. 1976. *Unequal Development: An Essay on the Social Formation of Peripheral Capitalism*. New York: Monthly Review Press.

Andreas, Carol. 1985. *When Women Rebel*. Westport, Conn.: Lawrence Hill.

Annual Planning Information: San Jose Standard Metropolitan Statistical Area, 1983–1984. 1983. Sacramento: California Department of Employment Development.

Annual Report on the Labour Force Survey. 1987. Tokyo: Statistics Bureau, Management and Coordination Agency.

Aptheker, Bettina. 1989. *Tapestries of Life: Women's Work, Women's Consciousness, and the Meaning of Daily Experience*. Amherst: University of Massachusetts Press.

Arizipe, Lourdes. 1977. "Women in the Informal Labor Sector: The Case of Mexico City." *Signs* 3:25–37.

Arnason, Johann. 1987. "The Modern Constellation and the Japanese Enigma: Part 1." *Thesis Eleven* 18/19:56–84.

―――. 1988. "The Modern Constellation and the Japanese Enigma: Part 2." *Thesis Eleven* 18/19:56–84.

Arrigo, Linda Gail. 1980. "The Industrial Work Force of Young Women in Taiwan." *Bulletin of Concerned Asian Scholars* 12(2):25–30.

Asian Women United of California. 1989. *Making Waves*. Boston: Beacon Press.

Atsumi, Reiko. 1988. "Dilemmas and Accommodations of Married Japanese Women in White-Collar Employment." *Bulletin of Concerned Asian Scholars* 20(3):54–62.

Barry, Kathleen. 1979. *Female Sexual Slavery*. New York: New York University Press.

Beauchamp, Marc. 1985. "Problems of a Part-Time Work Force." *PHP Intersect* 1(2):34–37.

Beneria, Lourdes. 1979. "Reproduction, Production and the Sexual Division of Labour." *Cambridge Journal of Economics* 3:203–25.

———. 1982. "Accounting for Women's Work." In *Women and Development: The Sexual Division of Labor in Rural Societies*, ed. Lourdes Beneria, 119–48. New York: Praeger.

Beneria, Lourdes, and Marta Roldan. 1987. *The Crossroads of Class and Gender*. Chicago: University of Chicago Press.

Beneria, Lourdes, and Gita Sen. 1981. "Accumulation, Reproduction, and Women's Role in Economic Development: Boserup Revisited." *Signs* 7:279–98.

———. 1982. "Class and Gender Inequalities and Women's Role in Economic Development." *Feminist Studies* 8:157–76.

———. 1985. "Gender, Skill, and the Dynamics of Women's Employment." Paper presented at Gender in the Workplace Conference, Brookings Institution, Washington, D.C.

Bernard, Jessie. 1987. *The Female World from a Global Perspective*. Bloomington: Indiana University Press.

Blackwell, John. 1982. *Digest of Statistics on Women in the Labour Force and Related Subjects*. Dublin: Employment Equality Agency.

———. 1983. "Statistics on Women in the Labour Force and Related Topics: What Do We Need to Know?" Paper presented at Employment Equality Agency Seminar, February 23, Dublin.

Blake, Myrna L. 1984. "Constraints on the Organization of Women Industrial Workers." In *Women in the Urban and Industrial Labor Force: Southeast and East Asia*, ed. Gavin W. Jones, 149–62. Canberra: Development Studies Center, Australian National University.

Bolles, Lynn. 1983. "Kitchens Hit by Priorities: Employed Working-Class Jamaican Women Confront the IMS." In *Women, Men, and the International Division of Labor*, ed. June Nash and Maria Patricia Fernandez-Kelly, 138–60. Albany, N.Y.: SUNY Press.

Bookman, Ann. 1988. "Unionization in an Electronics Factory: The Interplay of Gender, Ethnicity, and Class." In *Women and the Politics of Empowerment*, ed. Ann Bookman and Sandra Morgen, 159–79. Philadelphia: Temple University Press.

Bookman, Ann, and Sandra Morgen. 1988. *Women and the Politics of Empowerment.* Philadelphia: Temple University Press.

Bornschier, Victor, and Christopher Chase-Dunn. 1985. *Transnational Corporations and Underdevelopment.* New York: Praeger.

Boserup, Esther. 1970. *Woman's Role in Economic Development.* New York: St. Martin's Press.

Broadbridge, Seymour. 1966. *Industrial Dualism in Japan.* Chicago: Aldine.

Bromley, Ray. 1978. "Introduction—The Informal Sector: Why Is It Worth Discussing?" *World Development* 6:1033–39.

Brownmiller, Susan. 1984. *Femininity.* New York: Simon and Schuster.

Bunch, Charlotte. 1974. "The Reform Tool Kit." *Quest* 1:37–51.

Bunster, Ximena, Elsa Chaney, and Ellan Young. 1985. *Sellers and Servants: Working Women in Lima, Peru.* New York: Praeger.

Bustamante, Jorge. 1983. "Maquiladoras: A New Face of International Capitalism on Mexico's Northern Frontier." In *Women, Men, and the International Division of Labor,* ed. June Nash and Maria Patricia Fernandez-Kelly, 224–56. Albany, N.Y.: SUNY Press.

Buvinic, Mayra, Nadia Youssef, and Barbara Von Elm. 1978. *Women-Headed Households: The Ignored Factor in Development Planning.* Washington, D.C.: International Center for Research on Women.

Byerly, Victoria. 1986. *Hard Times Cotton Mill Girls.* Ithaca, N.Y.: ILR Press.

Carey, Pete. 1984. "Tomorrow's Robots: A Revolution at Work." *San Jose Mercury News,* February 8–11.

Carney, Larry S., and Charlotte G. O'Kelly. 1987. "Barriers and Constraints to the Recruitment and Mobility of Female Managers in the Japanese Labor Force." *Human Resource Management* 26:193–216.

CENCOA. 1978. *Investigación socio-económica del grupo precooperativa.* Cali, Colombia: CENCOA.

———. 1983. *Informe sobre los talleres del punto de vista socio-económica de los socias.* Cali, Colombia: CENCOA.

Central Statistics Office. 1981. *Labour Force Survey, 1979 Results.* Dublin: Stationery Office.

Centre for Asian Women Workers' Fellowship. 1987a. "Women Workers' Status Further Lowered in Modern Japan—The Meaning of Recent Labour Legislation." *Resource Materials on Women's Labor in Japan* 1:2–5.

———. 1987b. "New Labour Control System in Japan." *Resource Materials on Women's Labor in Japan* 1:5–9.

Chafetz, Janet Saltzman, and Gary Dworkin. 1986. *Female Revolt.* Totowa, N.J.: Rowman and Allanheld.

Chaney, Elsa, and Marianne Schmink. 1980. "Women and Modernization: Access to Tools." In *Sex and Class in Latin America,* ed. June Nash and Helen I. Safa, 160–82. New York: Bergin & Garvey.

Chapkis, Wendy, and Cynthia Enloe. 1983. *Of Common Cloth: Women in the Global Textile Industry.* Amsterdam: Transnational Institute.

Chesneaux, Jean. 1968. *The Chinese Labor Movement, 1919–1927.* Palo Alto, Calif.: Stanford University Press.

Chiang, Lan-hung Nora, and Yenlin Ku. 1985. *Past and Current Status of Women in Taiwan.* Women's Research Program Monograph no. 1. Taipei: Population Studies Center, National Taiwan University.

Cho, Uhn, and Hagen Koo. 1983. *Capital Accumulation, Women's Work, and Informal Economies in Korea.* Working Papers on Women in International Development no. 21. East Lansing: Office of Women in International Development, Michigan State University.

Clement, Norris, and Stephen Jenner. 1987. *Location Decisions regarding Maquiladora/In-Bond Plants Operating in Baja California, Mexico.* San Diego, Calif.: Institute for Regional Studies of the Californias.

Collins, Patricia Hill. 1989. "The Social Construction of Black Feminist Thought." *Signs* 14:745–73.

Commission on the Status of Women. 1972. *Report to Minister for Finance.* Dublin: Stationery Office.

Cook, Alice H., and Hiroko Hayashi. 1980. *Working Women in Japan: Discrimination, Resistance, and Reform.* Ithaca, N.Y.: ILR Press.

Coughlan, Anthony. 1980. "Ireland." In *Integration and Unequal Development,* ed. Dudley Seers and Constantine Vaitsos, 121–35. New York: St. Martin's Press.

Crawcour, Sidney. 1978. "The Japanese Employment System." *Journal of Japanese Studies* 4:225–45.

de Janvry, Alain. 1987. "Peasants, Capitalism and the State in Latin American Culture." In *Peasants and Peasant Society,* ed. Teodor Shanin, 391–401. London: Basil Blackwell.

Deere, Carmen Diana. 1979. "Rural Women's Subsistence Production in the Capitalist Periphery." In *Peasants and Proletarians,* ed. R. Cohen, P. C. Gutkind, and P. Brazier, 133–98. London: Monthly Review Press.

———. 1986. "Rural Women and Agrarian Reform in Peru, Chile, and Cuba." In *Women and Change in Latin America,* ed. June Nash and Helen I. Safa, 189–207. South Hadley, Mass.: Bergin & Garvey.

Deere, Carmen Diana, and Alain de Janvry. 1978. *A Theoretical Framework for the Empirical Analysis of Peasants.* Working Paper no. 60. Berkeley: Giannini Foundation, University of California.

Deere, Carmen, Jane Humphries, and Magdalena Leon de Leal. 1982. "Class and Historical Analysis for the Study of Women and Economic Change." In *Women's Roles and Population Trends in the Third World,* ed. Robert Acker, Mayra Buvinic, and Nadia Youssef, 87–116. London: International Labor Organization.

Deere, Carmen, and Magdalena Leon de Leal. 1981. "Peasant Production, Proletarianization, and the Sexual Division of Labor in the Andes." *Signs* 7:338–60.

Department of Education. 1968. *Annual Report, 1967–68.* Dublin: Department of Education.

Desai, Manisha. 1989. "Affiliation and Autonomy: The Origins of the Women's Movement in India." Ph.D. diss., Washington University.

Deyo, Frederic, ed. 1987. *The Political Economy of the New Asian Industrialism.* Ithaca, N.Y.: Cornell University Press.

DGBAS. *See* Directorate-General of Budget, Accounting and Statistics.

Diamond, Norma. 1975. "Women under Kuomintang Rule: Variation on the Feminine Mystique." *Modern China* 1:3–45.

———. 1979. "Women and Industry in Taiwan." *Modern China* 5:317–40.

Dill, Bonnie Thornton. 1986. *Our Mother's Grief: Racial Ethnic Women and the Maintenance of Family.* Research Paper no. 4. Memphis, Tenn.: Center for Research on Women, Memphis State University.

———. 1988. " 'Making Your Job Good Yourself:' Domestic Service and the Construction of Personal Dignity." In *Women and the Politics of Empowerment,* ed. Ann Bookman and Sandra Morgen, 33–52. Philadelphia: Temple University Press.

Directorate-General of Budget, Accounting and Statistics. 1982. *Monthly Bulletin of Labor Statistics, Republic of China, December.* Taipei, Taiwan: Executive Yuan.

———. 1987. *Yearbook of Labor Statistics, Republic of China.* Taipei, Taiwan: Executive Yuan.

Dixon, Ruth. 1978. *Rural Women at Work.* Baltimore: Johns Hopkins University Press.

———. 1982. "Women in Agriculture: Counting the Labor Force in Developing Countries." *Population and Development Review* 8:539–66.

Donaldson, Loraine. 1965. *Development Planning in Ireland.* New York: Praeger.

Dore, Ronald. 1986. *Flexible Rigidities: Industrial Policy and Structural Adjustment in the Japanese Economy, 1970–1980.* Palo Alto, Calif.: Stanford University Press.

Downs, Anthony. 1957. *An Economic Theory of Democracy.* New York: Harper and Brothers.

Economic Development. 1958. Dublin: Stationery Office.

Ehrenreich, Barbara, and Annette Fuentes. 1981. "Life on the Global Assembly Line." *Ms.* (January):53–59.

Eisenscher, Mike. 1987. "Organizing the Shop in Electronics." Paper presented at the West Coast Marxist Scholars Conference, November 14, Berkeley, California.

Elson, Diane, and Ruth Pearson. 1981a. "Nimble Fingers Make Cheap Workers: An Analysis of Women's Employment in Third World Export Manufacturing." *Feminist Review* (Spring):87–107.

———. 1981b. "The Subordination of Women and the Internationalisation of Factory Production." In *Of Marriage and the Market: Women's Subordination in International Perspective,* ed. Kate Young, Carol Wolkowitz, and Roslyn McCullagh, 144–66. London: CSE.

Employment Equality Agency. 1978. *Review of the Ban on Industrial Nightwork for Women.* Report to the Minister for Labour. Dublin: Employment Equality Agency.

Enloe, Cynthia. 1983. "Women Textile Workers in the Militarization of Southeast Asia." In *Women, Men, and the International Division of Labor*, ed. June Nash and Maria Patricia Fernandez-Kelly, 407–25. Albany, N.Y.: SUNY Press.

————. 1984. "Third World Women in Factories." *Cultural Survival Quarterly* 8(2):54–56.

Evans, Peter. 1979. *Dependent Development.* Princeton, N.J.: Princeton University Press.

Farley, Noel J. J. 1972. "Explanatory Hypotheses for Irish Trade in Manufactured Goods in the Mid-Nineteen Sixties." *Economic and Social Review* 4(1):5–33.

Fernandez, Raul. 1977. *The United States–Mexican Border: A Politico-Economic Profile.* Notre Dame, Ind.: University of Notre Dame Press.

Fernandez-Kelly, Maria Patricia. 1983. *For We Are Sold: I and My People: Women and Industry in Mexico's Frontier.* Albany, N.Y.: SUNY Press.

————. 1985. "Technology and Employment along the U.S.–Mexican Border." Paper prepared for the Project on the Impact of Global Technological Change on U.S.-ADC Relations. Washington, D.C.: Overseas Development Council.

Fernandez-Kelly, Maria Patricia, and Anna Garcia. 1988. "Economic Restructuring in the United States." In *Women and Work #3*, ed. Barbara Gutek, Ann Stromberg, and Laurie Larwood, 49–65. Beverly Hills, Calif.: Sage.

Filias, Vassilis. 1975. "Some Aspects of the Greek Migration Problems." In *Workshop on the Comparative Study of Reintegration Policy*, ed. Ayse Kudat and Ozkan Kudat, 120–69. Berlin: IICSS.

Fitzgerald, Garret. 1968. *Planning in Ireland.* Dublin: Institute of Public Administration.

Flora, Cornelia Butler. 1987. "Income Generation Projects for Rural Women." In *Rural Women and State Policy*, ed. Carmen Diana Deere and Magdalena Leon de Leal, 212–38. Boulder, Colo.: Westview.

Focus Japan. 1978. "Japan's Subcontractors: The Buck Stops Here." September 10–11.

Frobel, Folker, Jurgan Heinrichs, and Otto Kreye. 1980. *The New International Division of Labour.* Cambridge, Eng.: Cambridge University Press.

Fuentes, Annette, and Barbara Ehrenreich. 1983. *Women in the Global Factory.* INC Pamphlet no. 2. New York: Institute for New Communications.

Fujita, Kuniko. 1987. "Gender, State, and Industrial Policy in Japan." *Women's Studies International Forum* 10:589–97.

————. 1988. "Women Workers, State Policy, and the International Division of Labor: The Case of Silicon Island in Japan." *Bulletin of Concerned Asian Scholars* 20:42–53.

Fujitani, Takashi. 1986. "Japan's Modern National Ceremonies: A Historical Ethnography, 1868–1912." Ph.D. diss., University of California, Berkeley.

Galenson, Walter. 1979. "The Labor Force, Wages, and Living Standards." In *Economic Growth and Structural Change in Taiwan*, ed. Walter Galenson, 384–447. Ithaca, N.Y.: Cornell University Press.

Gallin, Rita S. 1984a. "The Entry of Chinese Women into the Rural Labor Force: A Case Study from Taiwan." *Signs* 9:383–98.

———. 1984b. "Women, Family, and the Political Economy of Taiwan." *Journal of Peasant Studies* 12:76–92.

———. 1986. *Women and Work in Rural Taiwan: Building a Contextual Model Linking Employment and Health.* Working Papers on Women in International Development no. 127. East Lansing:. Office of Women in International Development, Michigan State University.

Garvey, Donal. 1983. "A Profile of the Demographic and Labour Force Characteristics of the Population—Sample Analysis of the 1981 Census of Population." Paper presented to the Statistical and Social Inquiry Society of Ireland, April 28, Dublin.

Gates, Hill. 1979. "Dependency and the Part-Time Proletariat in Taiwan." *Modern China* 5:381–408.

Gayn, Mark. 1948. *Japan Diary.* New York: W. Sloane Associates.

Giddens, Anthony. 1984. *The Constitution of Society.* Berkeley: University of California Press.

Giddings, Paula. 1984. *When and Where I Enter.* New York: Bantam.

Gloster, Margherita, Martha McDevitt, and Amrita Chhachhi. 1983. "Restructuring: The Cutting Edge." In *Of Common Cloth: Women in the Global Textile Industry*, ed. Wendy Chapkis and Cynthia Enloe, 15–37. Amsterdam: Transnational Institute.

Gluck, Carol. 1985. *Japan's Modern Myths: Ideology in the Late Meiji Period.* Princeton, N.J.: Princeton University Press.

Gold, Thomas. 1986. *State and Society in the Taiwan Miracle.* New York: M. E. Sharpe.

Goldstein, Carl. 1987. "A Shift in Power." *Far Eastern Economic Review* (February 26):56–57.

Gordon, Andrew. 1985. *The Evolution of Labor Relations in Japan: Heavy Industry, 1853–1955.* Cambridge, Mass.: Council on East Asia Studies, Harvard University.

Gordon, Matthew. 1986. "Japanese Women in Finance." *Tokyo Business Today* (May):19–23.

Greenhalgh, Susan. 1985. "Sexual Stratification: The Other Side of 'Growth with Equity' in East Asia." *Population and Development Review* 11:265–314.

Grossman, Rachel. 1979. "Women's Place in the Integrated Circuit." *Southeast Asia Chronicle 66—Pacific Research* 9:2–17.

———. 1980. "Bitter Wages: Women in East Asia's Semiconductor Plants." *Multinational Monitor* 1 (March):8–11.

Grunwald, Joseph, and Kenneth Flamm. 1985. *Global Factory: Foreign Assembly in International Trade.* Washington, D.C.: Brookings Institution.

Hadjicostandi, Joanna. 1983. "The Informal Economy in Egypt: Causes and Effects." Master's thesis, Northeastern University.

———. 1987. "International Division of Labour, Export Processing Zones: The Case of Kavala, Greece." Ph.D. diss., Northeastern University.

Halim, Fatimah. 1983. "Workers' Resistance and Management Control: A Comparative Case Study of Male and Female Workers in West Malaysia." *Journal of Contemporary Asia* 13:131–50.

Halliday, Jon. 1975. *A Political History of Japanese Capitalism.* New York: Pantheon.

Hane, Mikiso. 1982. *Peasants, Rebels and Outcastes: The Underside of Modern Japan.* New York: Pantheon.

Hane, Mikiso, ed. 1988. *Reflections on the Way to the Gallows: Rebel Women in Pre-war Japan.* Berkeley: University of California Press.

Hani, Setsuko. 1948. *The Japanese Family System: As Seen from the Standpoint of Japanese Women.* Tokyo: Japan Institute of Pacific Studies/International Publishing Co.

Hareven, Tamara K. 1982. *Family Time and Industrial Time.* New York: Cambridge University Press.

Hart, Gillian. 1986. *Power, Labor and Livelihood: Processes of Change in Rural Java.* Berkeley: University of California Press.

———. 1988. "Disaggregating 'The Household': Gender, Kinship, and the Dynamics of Agrarian Change." Paper presented at Social Science Research Council workshop, Socioeconomic Transformations, Demographic Change and the Family in Southeast Asia, East-West Population Institute, Honolulu.

Hartmann, Heidi. 1976. "Capitalism, Patriarchy, and Job Segregation by Sex." In *Women in the Workplace*, ed. Martha Blaxall and Barbara Reagan, 137–70. Chicago: University of Chicago Press.

Havens, Thomas R. H. 1975. "Women and War in Japan, 1937–45." *American Historical Review* 80:913–34.

Hayashi, Yoko. 1986. "Myth and Reality: Institutional Reform for Women." *Ampo* 18(2–3):18–23.

Hen, Jeanne. 1988. "The Material Basis of Sexism: A Mode of Production Analysis." In *Patriarchy and Class*, ed. Sharon Stichter and Jane Parpart. Boulder, Colo.: Westview.

Hirai, Atsuko. 1987. "The State and Ideology in Meiji Japan—A Review Article." *Journal of Asian Studies* 46:89–103.

Hiroki, Michiko. 1986. *In the Shadow of Affluence: Stories of Japanese Women Workers.* Hong Kong: Committee for Asian Women.

Ho, Samuel P. S. 1976. *The Rural Non-farm Sector in Taiwan.* Studies in Employment and Rural Development no. 32. Washington, D.C.: International Bank for Reconstruction and Development.

————. 1978. *Economic Development of Taiwan, 1860–1970.* New Haven, Conn.: Yale University Press.

Holden, Karen C. 1983. "Changing Employment Patterns of Women." In *Work and Lifecourse in Japan,* ed. David Plath, 34–46. Albany, N.Y.: SUNY Press.

Honig, Emily. 1985. "Burning Incense, Pledging Sisterhood: Communities of Women Workers in the Shanghai Cotton Mills, 1919–1949." *Signs* 10:700–14.

Hossfeld, Karen. 1988a. "Divisions of Labor, Divisions of Lives: Immigrant Women Workers in Silicon Valley." Ph.D. diss., University of California, Santa Cruz.

————. 1988b. "The Triple Shift: Immigrant Women Workers and the Household Division of Labor in Silicon Valley." Paper presented at the annual meetings of the American Sociological Association, Atlanta.

Howenstine, Ned G. 1982. "Growth of U.S. Multinational Companies, 1966–77." *Survey of Current Business* 62(4):34–46.

Hymer, Stephen. 1978. "The Multinational Corporate Capitalist Economy." In *The Capitalist System,* ed. Richard Edwards, Michael Reich, and Thomas Weisskopf, 492–98. Englewood Cliffs, N.J.: Prentice Hall.

IDA. *See* Industrial Development Authority of Ireland.

Imada, Takatoshi, and Sachiko Imada. 1982. "Strata Differentiation, Labor Market Structures and Career Mobility." Paper presented at the Tenth Congress of the International Sociological Association, Mexico City.

Inagami, Takeshi. 1988. *Japanese Workplace Industrial Relations.* Japanese Industrial Relations Series no. 14. Tokyo: Japan Institute of Labor.

INDOC. 1981. "Indonesian Workers and Their Right to Organize." Leiden, The Hague: Indonesian Documentation Center.

Industrial Development Authority of Ireland. 1972. *Regional Industrial Plans 1973–1977, Part 1.* Dublin: IDA.

————. 1982. *Ireland—Consistently the Most Profitable Industrial Location in Europe.* Dublin: IDA.

Inkeles, Alex. 1983. *Exploring Individual Modernity.* New York: Columbia University Press.

Inkeles, Alex, and David Smith. 1974. *Becoming Modern.* Cambridge, Mass.: Harvard University Press.

Inoue, Shozo. 1985. "An Empirical Study of an Internal Labor Market: The Case of a Japanese Iron and Steel Firm." Ph.D. diss., University of Illinois, Urbana-Champaign.

International Center for Research on Women. 1980a. *The Productivity of Women in Developing Countries: Measurement Issues and Recommendations.* Washington, D.C.: Agency for International Development.

————. 1980b. *Keeping Women Out: A Structural Analysis of Women's Employment in Developing Countries.* Washington, D.C.: Agency for International Development.

Isono, Fujiko. 1964. "Family and Women in Japan." *Sociological Review* 12:39–54.

Jackson, Pauline. 1983. "The Republic of Ireland—Europe's South East Asia?" Unpublished manuscript.

Jacobsen, Kurt. 1978. "Changing Utterly?—Irish Development and the Problem of Dependence." *Studies: An Irish Quarterly Review* (Winter): 276–91.

———. 1980. "The Republic of Ireland: Perils of Pragmatism." *Dissent* 27:73–80.

Jacoby, Neil H. 1966. *U.S. Aid to Taiwan.* New York: Praeger.

Japan Institute of Labor. 1981. *Problems of Working Women.* Tokyo: Japan Institute of Labor.

Japan Ministry of Labor. 1988. *The Labor Conditions of Women 1988.* Tokyo: Foreign Press Center.

Japan Prime Minister's Office. 1983. *Comparison of Results of Surveys on Women's Problems in Selected Nations (Summarized). March, 1983.* Tokyo: Foreign Press Center.

———. 1984. *Public Opinion Survey on Women's Employment, March 1984.* Tokyo: Foreign Press Center.

Japan Statistical Yearbook, 1986. 1987. Tokyo: Statistics Bureau, Management and Coordination Agency.

Japan Times. 1986. "Securities Firms Applying Equality System; Women Getting Higher Positions." *Japan Times,* October 5, 9.

Jelin, Elisabeth. 1977. "Migration and Labor Force Participation of Latin American Women: The Domestic Servants in the Cities." *Signs* 3:129–41.

———. 1980. "The Bahiana in the Labor Force in Salvador, Brazil." In *Sex and Class in Latin America,* ed. June Nash and Helen I. Safa, 129–46. New York: Bergin & Garvey.

Jones, H. J. 1976–77. "Japanese Women and the Dual-Track Employment System." *Pacific Affairs* 49:589–606.

Joseph, Gloria. 1980. "Caribbean Women: The Impact of Race, Sex, and Class." In *Comparative Perspectives of Third World Women,* ed. Barbara Lindsey, 143–61. New York: Praeger.

Jules-Rosette, Bennetta. 1982. *Women's Work in the Informal Sector: A Zambian Case Study.* Working Papers on Women in International Development no. 3. East Lansing: Office of Women in International Development, Michigan State University.

Kaji, Etsuko. 1973. "The Invisible Proletariat: Working Women in Japan." *Social Praxis* 1:375–87.

———. 1986. "Herded into the Labor Market." *Ampo* 18(2–3):34–41.

Kaminski, Marguerite, and Judith Paiz. 1984. "Japanese Women in Management: Where Are They?" *Human Resource Management* 23:277–92.

Kandiyoti, Deniz. 1988. "Bargaining with Patriarchy." *Gender & Society* 2:274–91.

Kano, Masanao. 1986. "Changing Perspectives on the Family in Post-war Japan." *Review of Japanese Culture and Society* 1:78–84.

Kassimati, Koula. 1984. *Immigration-Emigration: The Problematic of the Second Generation.* Athens: Social Science Research Centre.

Kawamura, Nozumu. 1983. "The Transition of the Household in Modernizing Japan." *Journal of the Department of Humanities of Tokyo Metropolitan University* 179:1–18.

Kawashima, M. 1985. "Japanese Labor Market in Growing Disarray." *Oriental Economist* 53:24–25.

Kawashima, Yoko. 1987. "The Place and Role of Female Workers in the Japanese Labor Market." *Women's Studies International Forum* 10:599–611.

Kennedy, Kiernan, and Brendan Dowling. 1975. *Economic Growth in Ireland: The Experience since 1947.* Dublin: Gill and Macmillan.

Kidd, Yasue Aoki. 1978. *Women Workers in the Japanese Cotton Mills: 1886–1920.* Cornell East Asia Papers no. 20. Ithaca, N.Y.: Cornell University.

Kitazawa, Yoko. 1986. "An Aging Society: Who Will Bear the Burden?" *Ampo* 18(2–3):55–64.

Kogawa, Tesuo, and Douglas Lummis. 1985. "The Political Economy of Marriage." *Ampo* 17(3):48–53.

Ku, Yenlin. 1988. "The Changing Status of Women in Taiwan: A Conscious and Collective Struggle toward Equality." *Women's Studies International Forum* 11:179–86.

Kudat, Ayse, and Marios Nikolinakos. 1975. *A Comparative Study in Migration Policies: The Case of Turkey and Greece.* Publication 75–18. Berlin: International Institute for Comparative Social Research.

Kuhn, Annette, and AnnMarie Wolpe. 1978. *Feminism and Materialism.* London: Routledge and Kegan Paul.

Kung, Lydia. 1983. *Factory Women in Taiwan.* Ann Arbor: University of Michigan Press.

Kuo, Shirley W. Y., Gustav Ranis, and John C. H. Fei. 1981. *The Taiwan Success Story.* Boulder, Colo.: Westview.

Kusano, Kazuo. 1973. "Industrialization and the Status of Women in Japan." Ph.D. diss., University of Washington.

Lambiri-Dimaki, Joanna. 1965. *Social Change in a Greek Country Town.* Monograph no. 13. Athens: KEPE.

———. 1983. *Social Stratification in Greece: 1962–1982.* Athens: Scoulas.

Lamphere, Louise. 1987. *From Working Daughters to Working Mothers.* Ithaca, N.Y.: Cornell University Press.

Leacock, Eleanor. 1981. "History, Development and the Division of Labor by Sex: Implications for Organizations." *Signs* 7:474–91.

Leghorn, Lisa, and Katherine Parker. 1981. *Woman's Worth.* Boston: Routledge and Kegan Paul.

Leon de Leal, Magdalena. 1980. *Mujer y capitalismo agrario.* Bogota: ACET.

Lianos, Theodore. 1975. "Flows of Greek Out-Migration and Return Migration." *International Migration* 13–14:119–35.

Lim, Linda. 1978. *Workers in Multinational Corporations: The Case of the Electronics Industry in Malaysia and Singapore.* Michigan Occasional Papers in Women's Studies no. 9. Ann Arbor: University of Michigan.

———. 1981. "Women's Work in Multinational Electronics Factories." In *Women and Technological Change in Developing Countries,* ed. Roslyn Dauber and Melinda Cain, 181–90. Boulder, Colo.: Westview.

———. 1983a. "Capitalism, Imperialism, and Patriarchy." In *Women, Men and the International Division of Labor,* ed. June Nash and Maria Patricia Fernandez-Kelly, 70–92. Albany, N.Y.: SUNY Press.

———. 1983b. "Are Multinationals the Problem? A Debate." *Multinational Monitor* 4(8):12–16.

———1985. *Women Workers in Multinational Enterprises in Developing Countries.* Geneva: International Labor Organization.

Lin, Ching-yuan. 1973. *Industrialization in Taiwan, 1946–1972.* New York: Praeger.

Lin, Yin-ting. 1987. "Surplus Spurs ROC to Take New Steps to Offset U.S. Pressure." *Free China Journal* 1 and 4 (November 23).

Livingston, Jon, Joe Moore, and Felicia Oldfather, eds. 1973. *The Japan Reader.* Vol. 1, *Imperial Japan, 1800–1945.* New York: Pantheon.

Long, Frank. 1976. "Foreign Direct Investment in an Underdeveloped European Economy—The Republic of Ireland." *World Development* 4(1): 59–84.

———. 1980. "Foreign Capital and Development Strategy in Irish Industrialization, 1958–70. *American Journal of Economics and Sociology* 39 (April):137–50.

Lu, Min-jen. 1987. "Promotion of Constitutional Democracy Government's Goal." *Free China Journal* 2 (October 5).

Luce, Don, and Roger Rumpf. 1985. *Martial Law in Taiwan.* Washington, D.C.: Asia Resource Center.

MacCurtain, Margaret, and Donncha O'Corrain. 1979. *Women in Irish Society.* Westport, Conn.: Greenwood Press.

MacEwan, Arthur. 1978. "Capitalist Expansion and the Sources of Imperialism." In *The Capitalist System,* ed. Richard Edwards, Michael Reich, and Thomas Weisskopf, 494–98. Englewood Cliffs, N.J.: Prentice Hall.

McAleese, Dermot. 1976. "Industrial Specialisation and Trade: Northern Ireland and the Republic." *Economic and Social Review* 7:143–60.

———. 1977a. "Outward-Looking Policies, Manufactured Exports and Economic Growth: The Irish Experience." In *Contemporary Economic Analysis,* ed. M. J. Artis and A. R. Nobay, 313–51. London: Croom Helm.

———. 1977b. *A Profile of Grant-Aided Industry in Ireland.* Dublin: Industrial Development Authority.

McCrate, Elaine. 1985. "The Growth of Nonmarriage among U.S. Women, 1954–1983." Ph.D. diss., University of Massachusetts.

McGee, Terry. 1983. "Mass Markets, Little Markets: Some Preliminary Thoughts on the Proletarianization Process, Women Workers, and the Creation of Demand." Paper presented at the annual meeting of the Society of Economic Anthropology, University of California, Davis.

McLendon, James. 1983. "The Office: A Way Station or Blind Alley?" In *Work and Lifecourse in Japan*, ed. David Plath, 156–81. Albany, N.Y.: SUNY Press.

McLernon, Douglas. 1980. *High-Level Conference on the Employment of Women. National Report, Ireland.* Dublin.

Mackie, Vera. 1988. "Feminist Politics in Japan." *New Left Review* 167: 53–76.

Marshal, F. Ray. 1978. "Economic Factors Influencing the International Migration of Workers." In *Views across the Border: The United States and Mexico*, ed. Stanley Ross. Albuquerque: University of New Mexico Press.

Marshall, Byron K. 1967. *Capitalism and Modernization in Prewar Japan: The Ideology of the Business Elite, 1868–1941.* Palo Alto, Calif.: Stanford University Press.

Martin, Linda, ed. 1987. *The ASEAN Success Story.* Honolulu: University of Hawaii Press.

Martinez, Oscar. 1978. *Border Boom Town: Ciudad Juarez since 1948.* Austin: University of Texas Press.

Maruyama, Masao. 1963. *Thought and Behavior in Modern Japanese Politics.* London: Oxford University Press.

Mather, Celia. 1982. *Industrialization in the Tangerang Regency of West Java: Women Workers and the Islamic Patriarchy.* Working Paper no. 17. Amsterdam: Center for Sociology and Anthropology, University of Amsterdam.

Mears, Eliot. 1928. *Greece Today: The Aftermath of the Refugee Impact.* Palo Alto, Calif.: Stanford University Press.

Merrick, Thomas, and Douglas Graham. 1979. *Population and Economic Development in Brazil.* Baltimore: Johns Hopkins University Press.

Mies, Maria. 1986. *Patriarchy and Accumulation on a World-Scale.* London: Zed.

———. 1988a. "Introduction." In *Women: The Last Colony*, ed. Maria Mies, Veronika Bennholdt-Thomsen, and Claudia von Werlhof, 1–10. London: Zed.

———. 1988b. "Class Struggles and Women's Struggles in Rural India." In *Women: The Last Colony*, ed. Maria Mies, Veronika Bennholdt-Thomsen, and Claudia von Werlhof, 133–58. London: Zed.

Mies, Maria, Veronika Bennholdt-Thomsen, and Claudia von Werlhof, eds. 1988. *Women: The Last Colony.* London: Zed.

Milkman, Ruth, ed. 1985. *Women, Work and Protest.* Boston: Routledge and Kegan Paul.

Mingione, Enzo. 1985. "The Social Reproduction of the Surplus Labour Force: The Case of Southern Italy." In *Beyond Employment: Household,*

Gender, and Subsistence, ed. Nanneke Redclift and Enzo Mingione, 14–54. Oxford: Basil Blackwell.

Mintz, Sidney. 1971. "Men, Women, and Trade." *Comparative Studies in Society and History* 13:247–69.

Moore, Joe. 1983. *Japanese Workers and the Struggle for Power: 1945–1947.* Madison: University of Wisconsin Press.

Moser, Carol. 1978. "Informal Sector or Petty Commodity Production: Dualism or Dependence in Urban Development." *World Development* 6: 1041–64.

Mousourou, Loukia. 1985. *Women's Work and Family in Greece and Elsewhere.* Athens: Hestia.

Mouzelis, Nicos. 1978. *Modern Greece: Facets of Underdevelopment.* London: Macmillan.

Nash, June. 1983. "The Impact of the Changing International Division of Labor on Different Sectors of the Labor Force." In *Women, Men, and the International Division of Labor*, ed. June Nash and Maria Patricia Fernandez-Kelly, 3–38. Albany, N.Y.: SUNY Press.

———. 1988. "The Mobilization of Women in the Bolivian Debt Crisis." In *Women and Work #3*, ed. Barbara Gutek, Ann Stromberg, and Laurie Larwood, 67–86. Beverly Hills, Calif.: Sage.

Nash, June, and Maria Patricia Fernandez-Kelly, eds. 1983. *Women, Men, and the International Division of Labor.* Albany, N.Y.: SUNY Press.

National Economic and Social Council. 1980. *Industrial Policy and Development.* NESC no. 64. Dublin: National Economic and Social Council.

Neumann, Lin. 1979–80. "Hospitality Girls in the Philippines." *Southeast Asia Chronicle 66—Pacific Research* 9:18–23.

NESC. *See* National Economic and Social Council.

Nikolaidou, Magda. 1975. "The Working Greek Woman." *Greek Review of Social Research* 25:470–506.

Nikolinakos, Marios. 1974. *Economic Development and Migration in Greece.* Athens: Kalvos Publications.

———. 1983. *The Production of Technology and the Transnationalization of the Production Process.* Working Paper. Athens: Institute for the Study of the Greek Economy.

Nolan, Sean. 1981. "Economic Growth." In *The Economy of Ireland*, 3d ed., ed. John W. O'Hagan, 151–96. Dublin: Irish Management Institute.

Nolte, Sharon. 1983a. "Women in a Prewar Japanese Village: Suye Mura Revisited." *Peasant Studies* 10:175–90.

———. 1983b. *Women, the State, and Repression in Imperial Japan.* Working Papers on Women in International Development no. 33. East Lansing: Office of Women in International Development, Michigan State University.

Nomura, Gail. 1978. "The Allied Occupation of Japan: Reform of Japanese Labor Policy on Women." Ph.D. diss., University of Hawaii.

References   239

Nordhaus, William D. 1973. "The Political Business Cycle." *Review of Economic Studies* 40:169–90.

North-South Institute. 1985. *Women in Industry: North-South Connections.* Ottawa, Canada: North-South Institute.

O'Connor, David. 1987. "Women Workers and the Changing International Division of Labor in Microelectronics." In *Women, Households, and the Economy,* ed. Lourdes Beneria and Catherine Stimpson, 243–68. New Brunswick, N.J.: Rutgers University Press.

O'Kelly, Charlotte G., and Larry S. Carney. 1986. "Barriers to Role Sharing in the Dual Career Family in Japan." Paper presented at the Eleventh World Congress of the International Sociological Association, New Delhi.

Ong, Aihwa. 1983. "Global Industries and Malay Peasants in West Malaysia." In *Women, Men, and the International Division of Labor,* ed. June Nash and Maria Patricia Fernandez-Kelly, 426–38. Albany, N.Y.: SUNY Press.

———. 1985. "Industrialization and Prostitution in Southeast Asia." *Southeast Asia Chronicle* 96:2–6.

———. 1987. *Spirits of Resistance and Capitalist Discipline: Factory Women in Malaysia.* Albany, N.Y.: SUNY Press.

Ooms, Hermann. 1987. "Japan: Feudal Values and Work Ideology." *Thesis Eleven* 17:59–75.

Organisation for Economic Co-operation and Development, Ireland. 1962–82. *OECD Economic Surveys.* Paris: OECD.

———. 1979. *Demographic Trends, 1950–1990.* Paris: OECD.

Overseas Education Fund. 1984. *The Maquila Industry in Costa Rica: A Fact-Finding Mission.* Washington, D.C.: OEF.

Palacios, Marcos. 1980. *Coffee in Colombia, 1950–1970.* Cambridge Eng.: Cambridge University Press.

Papandreou, Vasso. 1981. *Multinational Corporations and Developing Countries: The Case of Greece.* Athens: Gutemberg.

Papanek, Hanna. 1979. "Development Planning for Women: The Implications of Women's Work." In *Women and Development,* ed. Rounaq Jahan and Hanna Papanek, 170–201. Dacca: Bangladesh Institute of Law and International Affairs.

Pascale, Richard, and Thomas P. Rohlen. 1983. "The Mazda Turnaround." *Journal of Japanese Studies* 9:219–63.

Patrick, Hugh T., and Thomas P. Rohlen. 1987. "Small-Scale Family Enterprises." In *The Political Economy of Japan.* Vol. 1, *The Domestic Transformation,* ed. Kozo Yamamura and Yasukichi Yasuba, 331–84. Palo Alto, Calif.: Stanford University Press.

Paulson, Joy Larsen. 1983. "Family Law Reform in Postwar Japan: Succession and Adoption." Ph.D. diss., University of Colorado.

Pena, Devon. 1980a. "Female Workers and Trade Unionism in the Mexican Border Industrialization Program." Paper presented at the eighth annual meeting of the National Association for Chicano Studies, Houston.

————. 1980b. "Las Maquiladoras: Mexican Women and Class Struggle in the Border Industries." *Atzlan* 11 (Fall):159–229.

————. 1982. "Emerging Organizational Strategies of Maquila Workers on the Mexico-U.S. Border." Paper presented at the tenth annual meeting of the National Association for Chicano Studies, Tempe, Arizona.

————. 1983. "Class Politics of Abstract Labor: Organizational Forms and Industrial Relations in the Mexican Maquiladoras." Ph.D. diss., University of Texas, Austin.

————. 1985. "The Division of Labor in Electronics: A Comparative Analysis of France, Mexico, and the United States." Paper presented at the meetings of the International Studies Association, Washington, D.C.

Perry, Linda L. 1976. "Mothers, Wives and Daughters in Osaka: Autonomy, Alliance and Professionalism." Ph.D. diss., University of Pittsburgh.

Portes, Alejandro. 1985. "The Informal Sector and the World-Economy: Notes on the Structure of Subsidized Labor." In *Urbanization and the World-System*, ed. Michael Timberlake, 53–62. New York: Academic Press.

————. 1986. *Latin American Class Structure*. Occasional Paper Series. Baltimore: Caribbean and Central American Studies Program, School for Advanced International Studies, Johns Hopkins University.

Portes, Alejandro, and Lauren Benton. 1984. "Industrial Development and Labor Absorption: A Reinterpretation." *Population and Development Review* 10:589–612.

Portes, Alejandro, Silvia Blitzer, and John Curtis. 1985. "The Urban Informal Sector in Uruguay: Its Internal Structure, Characteristics, and Effects." Paper presented at the meetings of the Latin American Studies Association, April, Albuquerque.

Portes, Alejandro, Manuel Castells, and Lauren Benton, eds. 1989. *The Informal Economy: Studies in Advanced and Less Developed Countries*. Baltimore: Johns Hopkins University Press.

Portes, Alejandro, and Saskia Sassen-Koob. 1987. "Making It Underground." *American Journal of Sociology* 93:30–61.

Portes, Alejandro, and John Walton. 1981. *Labor, Class and the International System*. New York: Academic Press.

Programme for Economic Expansion. 1958. Dublin: Stationery Office.

Pyle, Jean Larson. 1990. *The State and Women in the Economy: Lessons from Sex Discrimination in the Republic of Ireland*. Albany, N.Y.: SUNY Press.

Ramzi, Anis Sabirin. 1983. "The Multinational Corporations and Employment Opportunities for Women in Malaysia." In *Women and Work in the Third World: The Impact of Industrialization and Global Economic Interdependence*, ed. Nagat M. El Sanabary. Berkeley: Center for the Study, Education and Advancement of Women, University of California.

Redclift, Nanneke. 1985. "The Contested Domain: Gender, Accumulation and the Labour Process." In *Beyond Employment: Household, Gender, and Subsistence*, ed. Nanneke Redclift and Enzo Mingione, 92–125. Oxford: Basil Blackwell.

Redclift, Nanneke, and Enzo Mingione, eds. 1985. *Beyond Employment: Household, Gender, and Subsistence.* Oxford: Basil Blackwell.

Robinson, Mary. 1979. "Women and the New Irish State." In *Women in Irish Society,* ed. Margaret MacCurtain and Donncha O'Corrain, 58–70. Westport, Conn.; Greenwood Press.

Rohlen, Thomas P. 1974. *For Harmony and Strength: Japanese White Collar Organizations in Anthropological Perspective.* Berkeley: University of California Press.

Roldan, Marta. 1985. "Industrial Outworking, Struggles for Reproduction of Working-Class Families and Gender Subordination." In *Beyond Employment: Household, Gender, and Subsistence,* ed. Nanneke Redclift and Enzo Mingione, 248–85. Oxford: Basil Blackwell.

Rollins, Judith. 1986. *Between Women.* Philadelphia: Temple University Press.

Ruane, Frances. 1980. "Optimal Labour Subsidies and Industrial Development in Ireland." *Economic and Social Review* 2 (January):77–98.

Ruiz, Vickie. n.d. "Mexican Women and the Multinationals: The Packaging of the Border Industrialization Program." Unpublished manuscript.

———. 1988. "By the Day or the Week: Mexicana Domestic Workers in El Paso." In *Women on the U.S.-Mexico Border,* ed. Vickie Ruiz and Susan Tiano, 41–60. Boston: Allen & Unwin.

Safa, Helen I. 1976. "Class Consciousness among Working-Class Women in Latin America: Puerto Rico." In *Sex and Class in Latin America,* ed. June Nash and Helen I. Safa, 69–85. New York: Praeger.

———. 1980. "Export Processing and Female Employment: The Search for Cheap Labor." Paper presented at the Burg Waurtenstein Symposium, no. 85.

———. 1981. "Runaway Shops and Female Employment: The Search for Cheap Labor." *Signs* 7:418–33.

———. 1983. "Women, Production and Reproduction in Industrial Capitalism: A Comparison of Brazilian and U.S. Factory Workers." In *Women, Men, and the International Division of Labor,* ed. June Nash and Maria Patricia Fernandez-Kelly, 95–116. Albany, N.Y.: SUNY Press.

———. 1984. "Female Employment and the Social Reproduction of the Puerto Rican Working Class." *International Migration Review* 18:1168–87.

———. 1986. "Runaway Shops and Female Employment: The Search for Cheap Labor." In *Women's Work,* ed. Eleanor Leacock and Helen I. Safa, 58–71. South Hadley, Mass.: Bergin & Garvey.

Saffiotti, Heleith I.B. 1978. *Women in Class Society.* New York: Monthly Review Press.

Salaff, Janet W. 1981. *Working Daughters of Hong Kong.* New York: Cambridge University Press.

Sanday, Peggy. 1974. "Female Status in the Public Domain." In *Women, Culture, and Society,* ed. Michelle Rosaldo and Louise Lamphere, 189–206. Palo Alto, Calif.: Stanford University Press.

―――. 1981. *Female Power and Male Dominance*. Cambridge, Eng.: Cambridge University Press.

Sassen-Koob, Saskia. 1983. "Labor Migration and the New Industrial Division of Labor." In *Women, Men, and the International Division of Labor*, ed. June Nash and Maria Patricia Fernandez-Kelly, 175–204. Albany, N.Y.: SUNY Press.

―――. 1984. "Notes on the Incorporation of Third World Women into Wage-Labor through Immigration and Off-Shore Production." *International Migration Review* 18:1144–67.

―――. 1985. "Capital Mobility and Labor Migration: Their Expression in Core Cities." In *Urbanization in the World-Economy*, ed. Michael Timberlake, 231–65. New York: Academic Press.

Saxenian, Annalee. 1981. *Silicon Chips and Spatial Structure: The Industrial Basis of Urbanization in Santa Clara County, California*. Working Paper no. 345. Berkeley: Institute of Urban and Regional Planning, University of California.

Saxonhouse, Gary R. 1973. "Country Girls and Communication among Competitors in the Japanese Spinning Industry." In *Japanese Industrialization and Its Social Consequences*, ed. Hugh Patrick, 97–125. Berkeley: University of California Press.

Schaller, Michael. 1985. *The American Occupation of Japan: The Origins of the Cold War in Asia*. New York: Oxford University Press.

Schmink, Marianne. 1977. "Dependent Development and the Division of Labor by Sex: Venezuela." *Latin American Perspectives* 4:153–79.

―――. 1986. "Women and Urban Industrial Development in Brazil." In *Women and Change in Latin America*, ed. June Nash and Helen I. Safa, 136–64. South Hadley, Mass.: Bergin & Garvey.

Scott, Joan. 1986. "Gender: A Useful Category of Historical Analysis." *American Historical Review* 91:1053–75.

Sen, Gita. 1981. "Capitalist Transition and Women Workers—A Comparative Analysis." Paper presented at the Fifth Berkshire Conference on Women's History, Vassar College, Poughkeepsie, New York.

Sen, Gita, and Caren Grown. 1987. *Development, Crises, and Alternative Visions*. New York: New Feminist Library.

Serrin, William. 1984. "Textile Law Orders: A U.S. Label." *New York Times*, Dec. 29, 1.

Sharma, Ursula. 1986. *Women's Work, Class, and the Urban Household*. New York: Random House.

Sheridan, Kyoko. 1984. "Softnomisation—The Growth of the Service Sector in Japan." *Journal of Contemporary Asia* 14:430–41.

Shibukawa, Hisako. 1971. "An Education for Making Good Wives and Wise Mothers (*Ryosai Kenbo no Kyoiku*)." *Education in Japan* 6:47–57.

Shioji, Hiroki. 1980. "The Japanese Family: Economic Pressures Affecting Cultural Values within the Home." Ph.D. diss., University of Arizona.

Shiozawa, Myoko. 1977. "View from the Bottom: Problems of Japan's Women Factory Workers." *Japan Christian Century Quarterly* 43:31–37.

Siegel, Lenny. 1979. "Orchestrating Dependency." *Southeast Asia Chronicle* 66—*Pacific Research* 9:24–27.

———. 1980. "Delicate Bonds: The Global Semiconductor Industry." *Pacific Research* 11(1).

Siegel, Lenny, and Herb Borock. 1982. *Background Report on Silicon Valley.* Prepared for the U.S. Commission on Civil Rights. Mountain View, Calif.: Pacific Studies Center.

Sievers, Sharon L. 1983. *Flowers in Salt: The Beginnings of Feminist Consciousness in Modern Japan.* Palo Alto, Calif.: Stanford University Press.

Silberman, Bernard S. 1982. "The Bureaucratic State in Japan: The Problem of Authority and Legitimacy." In *Conflict in Modern Japanese History: The Neglected Tradition,* ed. Tetsuo Najita and J. Victor Koschmann, 226–57. Princeton, N.J.: Princeton University Press.

Simms, Richard, and Eleanor Dumor. 1976–77. "Women in the Urban Economy of Ghana: Associational Activity and the Enclave Economy." *African Urban Notes* 2(3):43–64.

Sklair, Leslie. 1989. *The Reformation of Capitalism: The Maquila Industry in Mexico and the U.S.A.* Boston: Allen and Unwin.

Smith, Joan. 1984. "Non-Wage Labor and Subsistence." In *Households and the World-Economy,* ed. Joan Smith, Immanuel Wallerstein, and Hans Evers, 64–89. Beverly Hills, Calif.: Sage.

———. 1987. "Transforming Households: Working-Class Women and Economic Crisis." *Social Problems* 34:416–36.

Smith, Joan, Immanuel Wallerstein, and Hans Evers, eds. 1984. *Households and the World-Economy.* Beverly Hills, Calif.: Sage.

Smith, Robert J. 1983. "Making Village Women into 'Good Wives and Wise Mothers' in Prewar Japan." *Journal of Family History* 8:70–84.

Snow, Robert. 1983. "The New International Division of Labor and the U.S. Work Force: The Case of the Electronics Industry." In *Women, Men, and the International Division of Labor,* ed. June Nash and Maria Patricia Fernandez-Kelly, 39–69. Albany, N.Y.: SUNY Press.

Sokoloff, Natalie. 1980. *Between Money and Love.* New York: Praeger.

Spalter-Roth, Roberta. 1988. "Vending on the Streets." In *Women and the Politics of Empowerment,* ed. Ann Bookman and Sandra Morgen, 272–96. Philadelphia: Temple University Press.

Spalter-Roth, Roberta, and Eileen Zeitz. 1981. "Production and Reproduction of Everyday Life." In *Dynamics of World Development,* ed. Richard Rubinson, 193–210. Beverly Hills, Calif.: Sage.

Standing, Guy. 1981. *Labour Force Participation and Development.* 2d ed. Geneva: ILO.

Stanton, Richard. 1979. "Foreign Investment and Host-Country Politics: The Irish Case." In *Underdeveloped Europe: Studies in Core-Periphery Rela-*

tions, ed. Dudley Seers, Bernard Schaeffer, and Marja Liisa Kiljunen, 103–24. Atlantic Highlands, N.J.: Humanities Press.

———. 1981. *The European Periphery as Export Platform: Metropolitan Firms and Local Class Relations in Ireland.* Brighton, Eng.: Institute of Development Studies.

Steinhoff, Patricia G., and Kazuko Tanaka. 1986–87. "Women Managers in Japan." *International Studies of Management and Organization* 26:108–32.

Stites, Richard. 1982. "Small-Scale Industry in Yingge, Taiwan." *Modern China* 8:247–79.

Stoddard, Ellwyn. 1987. *Maquila: Assembly Plants in Northern Mexico.* El Paso: Texas Western Press.

Survey of Grant-Aided Industry. 1967. Dublin: Stationery Office.

Sutoro, Ann. n.d. "The Effects of Industrialization on Women Workers in Indonesia." Jakarta: Ford Foundation. Mimeo.

Taira, Koji. 1970. *Economic Development and the Labor Market in Japan.* New York: Columbia University Press.

Tayama, Taro. 1984. "Equal Rights Will Destroy Japan." *Oriental Economist* 52:883.

Tiano, Susan. 1984. *Maquiladoras, Women's Work, and Underemployment in Northern Mexico.* Women in International Development Working Papers no. 43. East Lansing: Office of Women in International Development, Michigan State University.

———. 1985. "Women Workers in a Northern Mexican City: Constraints and Opportunities." Paper presented at the annual meeting of the Latin American Studies Association, Albuquerque, New Mexico.

———. 1987a. "Gender, Work, and World Capitalism." In *Analyzing Gender*, ed. Beth Hess and Myra Marx Ferree, 216–43. Beverly Hills, Calif.: Sage.

———. 1987b. "Maquiladoras in Mexicali: Integration or Exploitation?" In *Women on the U.S.-Mexico Border*, ed. Vickie Ruiz and Susan Tiano, 77–104, Boston: Allen & Unwin.

Tilly, Louise. 1986. "Paths of Proletarianization: Organization of Production, Sexual Division of Labor, and Women's Collective Action." In *Women's Work #3*, ed. Barbara Gutek, Ann Stromg, and Laurie Larwood, 25–40. South Hadley, Mass.: Bergin & Garvey.

Tilly, Louise A., and Joan W. Scott. 1978. *Women, Work and Family.* New York: Holt, Reinhart and Winston.

Tinker, Irene. 1976. "The Adverse Impact of Development on Women." In *Women and World Development*, ed. Irene Tinker and Michele Bo Bramsen, 22–34. Washington, D.C.: Overseas Development Council.

Truelove, Cynthia. 1987. "The Informal Sector Revisited: The Case of the Colombian Mini-Maquilas." In *Crises in the Caribbean Basin: Past and Present*, ed. Richard Tardanico, 95–110. Beverly Hills, Calif.: Sage.

———. 1988. "Factories in the Fields of Plenty: Gender, Agrarian Transformation, and Industrial Restructuring in Colombia." Ph.D. diss., Johns Hopkins University.

Tsurumi, E. Patricia. 1984. "Female Textile Workers and the Failure of Early Trade Unionism in Japan." *History Workshop* 18:3–17.

———. 1986. "Problem Consciousness and Modern Japanese History: Female Textile Workers of Meiji and Taisho." *Bulletin of Concerned Asian Scholars* 18:41–48.

Ueno, Chizuko. 1987. "The Politics of Japanese Women Reconsidered." *Current Anthropology* 28:575–84.

UNIDO. 1980. *Women in the Redeployment of Manufacturing Industry to Developing Countries*. Working Papers on Structural Change no. 18. New York: UNIDO.

United Nations. 1980. *Equality, Development, and Peace*. Report of the World Conference on the United Nations Decade for Women, Copenhagen, July 14–30, 1980. New York: United Nations.

van Allen, Judith. 1976. "African Women, 'Modernization,' and National Liberation." In *Women in the World*, ed. Lynne Iglitzin and Ruth Ross, 25–54. Santa Barbara, Calif.: Clio.

von Werlhof, Claudia. 1980. "Notes on the Relation between Sexuality and Economy." *Review* 4:33–44.

———. 1984. "The Proletarian Is Dead: Long Live the Housewives?" In *Households and the World-Economy*, ed. Joan Smith, Immanuel Wallerstein, and Hans Evers, 131–47. Beverly Hills, Calif.: Sage.

———. 1985. *Why Peasants and Housewives Do Not Disappear in the Capitalist World-System*. Working Paper no. 68. Bielefeld, Germany: Sociology of Development Research Centre, University of Bielefeld.

———. 1988. "Women's Work: The Blind Spot in the Critique of Political Economy." In *Women: The Last Colony*, ed. Maria Mies, Veronika Bennholdt-Thomsen, and Claudia von Werlhof, 13–26. London: Zed.

Walby, Sylvia. 1986. *Patriarchy at Work*. Oxford: Polity Press.

Wallerstein, Immanuel. 1974. *The Modern World System I*. New York: Academic Press.

———. 1984. *Historical Capitalism*. London: Verso.

Walsh, Brendan M. 1982. *The Impact of EEC Membership on Women in the Labour Force*. Policy Paper no. 1. Dublin: Center for Economic Research, University College.

Ward, Kathryn. 1984. *Women in the World-System: Its Impact on Status and Fertility*. New York: Praeger.

———. 1985a. "The Social Consequences of the World-Economic System: The Economic Status of Women and Fertility." *Review* 8:561–94.

———. 1985b. "Women and Urbanization in the World-System." In *Urbanization in the World-Economy*, ed. Michael Timberlake, 305–24. New York: Academic Press.

———. 1986. *Women and Transnational Corporation Employment: A World-System and Feminist Analysis*. Women in Development Working Paper no. 120. East Lansing: Office of Women in International Development, Michigan State University.

————. 1987. "The Impoverishment of U.S. Women and the Decline of U.S. Hegemony." In *America's Changing Role in the World System*, ed. Terry Boswell and Albert Bergesen, 275–90. New York: Praeger.

————. 1988a. "Are Women in the World-System?" Paper presented at the annual meetings of the American Sociological Association, Atlanta.

————. 1988b. "Women in the Global Economy." In *Women and Work #3*, ed. Barbara Gutek, Ann Stromberg, and Laurie Larwood, 17–48. Beverly Hills, Calif.: Sage.

————. 1988c. "Female Resistance to Marginalization." In *Racism and Sexism in the World-System*, ed. Joan Smith, Jane Collins, Terence Hopkins, and Akbar Muhammad, 121–36. Westport, Conn.: Greenwood Press.

Watanabe, Ben. 1985. "New Labor Dispatch Law—More Insecurity for Japanese Workers." *Ampo* 17(4):12–14.

Watanuki, Joji. 1986. "Is There a 'Japanese Type Welfare Society?' " *International Sociology* 1:259–69.

Watts, Michael. 1988. "Putting Humpty Dumpty Back Together Again: Some Comments on Studies of Households, Gender and Work in Rural Africa." Paper presented to Social Science Research Council workshop, Structural Transformations, Demographic Change and the Family in Southeast Asia, East-West Population Institute, Honolulu.

Westwood, Sallie. 1985. *All Day, Every Day: Factory and Family in the Making of Women's Lives*. Champaign: University of Illinois Press.

Westwood, Sallie, and Parminder Bhachu. 1988. *Enterprising Women: Ethnicity, Economy, and Gender Relations*. London: Routledge and Kegan Paul.

White, Benjamin. 1976. "Production and Reproduction in a Javanese Village." Ph.D. diss., Columbia University.

White, Padraica. 1981. "Ireland's Employment Needs in the Eighties: The Nature of the Challenge and the Response." Paper presented before the IDA, Dublin, Sept. 30.

Wickham, Ann. 1982. "Women, Industrial Transition and Training Policy in the Republic of Ireland." In *Power, Conflict and Inequality*, ed. Mary Kelly, Liam O'Dowd, and James Wickham, 147–58. Dublin: Turoe Press.

Wickham, James. 1980. "The Politics of Dependent Capitalism: International Capital and the Nation State." In *Ireland: Divided Nation, Divided Class*, ed. Austen Morgan and Bob Purdie, 53–73. London: Ink Links.

Wickham, James, and Peter Murray. 1983. "Women Workers and Bureaucratic Control in Irish Electronic Factories." Paper presented at the meetings of the British Sociological Association.

Willner, Anne Ruth. 1961. "From Rice Field to Factory: The Industrialization of a Rural Labour Force in Java." Ph.D. diss., University of Chicago.

Wolf, Diane. 1984. "Making the Bread and Bringing It Home: Female Factory Workers and the Family Economy in Rural Java." In *Women in the Urban and Industrial Workforce*, ed. Gavin W. Jones, 215–31. Development Studies Centre Monograph no. 33. Canberra: Australian National University.

———. 1986. "Factory Daughters, Their Families, and Rural Industrialization in Central Java." Ph.D. diss., Cornell University.

———. 1988a. "Factory Daughters, the Family, and Nuptiality in Java." Paper presented at IUSSP conference, Women's Position and Demographic Change in the Course of Development, June, Oslo.

———. 1988b. "Father Knows Best about All in the Family: A Feminist Critique of Household Strategies." Paper presented at the annual meetings of the American Sociological Association, Atlanta.

———. 1988c. "Female Autonomy, the Family, and Industrialization in Java." *Journal of Family Issues* 9:85–107.

Wolpe, Harold. 1972. "Capitalism and Cheap Labour Power in South Africa." *Economy and Society* 1:425–54.

Wong, Aline K. 1981. "Planned Development, Social Stratification, and the Sexual Division of Labor in Singapore." *Signs* 7:434–52.

Wong, Diana. 1984. "The Limits of Using the Household as an Unit of Analysis." In *Households in the World-Economy*, ed. Joan Smith, Immanuel Wallerstein, and Hans Evers, 56–63. Beverly Hills, Calif.: Sage.

Woog, Mario. 1980. *El Programa Mexicano de Maquiladoras.* Guadalajara: Instituto de Estudios Sociales, Universidad de Guadalajara.

Worsley, Peter. 1984. *The Three Worlds.* Chicago: University of Chicago Press.

Yoshino, M. Y. 1968. *Japan's Managerial System: Tradition and Innovation.* Cambridge, Mass.: MIT Press.

Young, Gay. 1984. "Women, Development, and Human Rights." *Journal of Applied Behavioral Science* 4:383–401.

———. 1988. "Gender Identification and Working-Class Solidarity among Maquila Workers in Ciudad Juarez." In *Women on the U.S.-Mexico Border*, ed. Vickie Ruiz and Susan Tiano, 105–28. Boston: Allen & Unwin.

Young, Kate, Carol Wolkowitz, and Roslyn McCullagh, eds. 1981. *Of Marriage and Market.* London: CSE.

Zavella, Patricia. 1987. *Women's Work and Chicano Families.* Ithaca, N.Y.: Cornell University Press.

———. 1988. "The Politics of Race and Gender: Organizing Chicana Cannery Workers." In *Women and the Politics of Empowerment*, ed. Ann Bookman and Sandra Morgen, 202–26. Philadelphia: Temple University Press.

Zinn, Maxine Baca. 1987. "Structural Transformation and Minority Families." In *Women, Households, and the Economy*, ed. Lourdes Beneria and Catherine Stimpson, 155–71. New Brunswick, N.J.: Rutgers University Press.

CONTRIBUTORS

Larry S. Carney teaches in the COPACE division of Clark University, and **Charlotte O'Kelly** is a professor of sociology at Providence College. They are co-authors of *Women and Men in Society: Cross-cultural Perspectives on Gender Stratification.* They are working on a new book, *Captives of Affluence: Women and Work in Japan.*

Rita Gallin is director of the Office of Women in International Development and a visiting associate professor in the Department of Sociology at Michigan State University. She is the editor of the Women in International Development Working Paper Series and head editor of the *Women and International Development Annual*, published by Westview Press. She has published numerous articles on women, development, and Taiwan.

Joanna Hadjicostandi is an assistant professor of sociology at Clark University. She was brought up in Egypt and Greece and was educated in England and the United States. Her current research is on the international division of labor, especially the influence of informal and formal employment on women's status and empowerment, with a focus on social class, gender, and race.

Karen J. Hossfeld is an assistant professor of sociology at San Francisco State University. Her chapter in this volume draws from her book *Small, Foreign, and Female: Immigrant Women Workers in Silicon Valley*, forthcoming from the University of California Press.

Jean L. Pyle is an assistant professor of economics at the University of Lowell in Massachusetts. Her current research includes a study of the extension of export-led development strategies into successive tiers of Pacific Asian countries (with particular emphasis on its impact on women) and an examination of the socioeconomic aspects of the recent and substantial influx of Southeast Asian refugees into Lowell.

Susan Tiano is an associate professor of sociology at the University of New Mexico. She has also directed the Office of Women in International Development at Michigan State University and served as associate director of the Latin American Institute at the University of New Mexico. She has edited, with Vickie Ruiz, *Women on the U.S.–Mexico Border: Responses to Change*, and has published articles on women in development, the new international division of labor, and the maquiladora labor force.

Cynthia Truelove is an assistant professor of rural sociology at the University of Wisconsin at Madison. She is completing a manuscript on industrial restructuring and rural women's work, entitled "Factories in the Fields of Plenty: Gender, Agrarian Transformation, and Industrial Restructuring in Colombia," and is continuing her comparative international research on industrial and agrarian restructuring in Colombia, Costa Rica, southern Europe, and the midwestern United States.

Kathryn Ward is coordinator of women's studies and an associate professor of sociology at Southern Illinois University at Carbondale. She is the author of the book *Women in the World-System: Its Impact on Status and Fertility* and of articles on women in development and the feminist critique of sociology. She is currently researching the effects of the international debt crisis and austerity programs on economic development, inequality, and the status of women.

Diane L. Wolf is an assistant professor of sociology at the University of California at Davis. Her book on Javanese factory daughters, their families, and industrialization in rural Java is forthcoming from the University of California Press. She plans to return to Java in 1990 to continue her research on the life courses of the women she studied in the 1980s.

INDEX

Library of Congress Cataloging-in-Publication Data

Women workers and global restructuring / Kathryn Ward, editor.
    p.   cm. — (Cornell international Industrial and labor
relations report ; no. 17)
    Includes bibliographical references.
    ISBN 0-87546-161-1 (alk. paper). — ISBN 0-87546-162-X (pbk. :
alk. paper)
    1. Women offshore assembly industry workers. 2. Work and family.
I. Ward, Kathryn B.   II. Series.
HD6073.033W66   1990
331.4'87'091724–dc20   89-71699
                                           CIP